DAVID & CHARLES SOURCES FOR SOCIAL & ECONOMIC HISTORY

Money and Banking in England

The Development of the Banking System
1694–1914

DAVID & CHARLES SOURCES FOR SOCIAL & ECONOMIC HISTORY

GENERAL EDITOR: *Professor E. R. R. Green*
Director of the Institute of Irish Studies
The Queen's University of Belfast

published

BRITISH AND IRISH ELECTIONS 1784–1831   *Peter Jupp*

EDUCATION: ELEMENTARY EDUCATION   *J. M. Goldstrom*
   1780–1900

THE ENGLISH POOR LAW 1780–1930   *Michael E. Rose*

THE FACTORY SYSTEM   *J. T. Ward*
   VOLUME I   BIRTH AND GROWTH
   VOLUME II   THE FACTORY SYSTEM AND SOCIETY

FREE TRADE   *Norman McCord*

NINETEENTH-CENTURY CRIME   *J. J. Tobias*
   PREVENTION AND PUNISHMENT

READINGS IN THE DEVELOPMENT OF   *R. D. Collison Black*
   ECONOMIC ANALYSIS

in preparation

EARLY SOCIOLOGICAL WRITINGS   *G. Duncan Mitchell*

ENCLOSURES   *Margaret Roake*

THE GREAT DEPRESSION 1928–33   *A. J. Robertson*

VICTORIAN HOUSING   *David Rubinstein*

DAVID & CHARLES SOURCES FOR SOCIAL & ECONOMIC HISTORY

B. L. ANDERSON
Lecturer in Economic History
University of Liverpool

and

P. L. COTTRELL
Lecturer in Economic History
University of Leicester

Money and Banking in England

The Development of the Banking System
1694–1914

DAVID & CHARLES
NEWTON ABBOT   LONDON   VANCOUVER

0 7153 6366 2

For M's and J's

Set in 11 on 13pt Baskerville
and printed in Great Britain
by Latimer Trend & Company Ltd Plymouth
for David & Charles (Holdings) Limited
South Devon House Newton Abbot Devon

Published in Canada
by Douglas David & Charles Limited
3645 McKechnie Drive West Vancouver BC

Contents

INTRODUCTION   *page* 9

PART ONE: MONETARY EXPERIMENTS
AND THE FOUNDATION OF THE
BANK OF ENGLAND   13

1 Sir William Killigrew. *State Credit*   19
2 Sir Thomas Neale. *Raising a Million*   27
3 Dr Hugh Chamberlen. *Land Banks*   33
4 *The Charter of the Bank of England*   40
5 William Paterson. *The Bank and its Critics*   53
6 Michael Godfrey. *The Business of the Bank*   60
7 Sir S. T. Janssen. *The Future of the Bank – A Director's
    View*   68
8 Daniel Defoe. *The Future of the Bank – A Projector's
    View*   74
9 Charles Montagu. *The Origin of Exchequer Bills*   85

PART TWO: THE MERCANTILISTS ON
MONEY   88

10 Sir William Hodges. *A Glimpse of the Multiplier*   96
    THE ORTHODOX METALLIST TRADITION:
11 Sir William Petty. *Money and Coin*   101
12 John Locke. *Defence of the Standard*   110
13 David Hume. *Money and the Trade Balance*   116

ANTI-METALLISTS AND INFLATIONISTS:

14   Nicholas Barbon. *Money, Credit and Interest*   129
15   John Law. *The Benefits of Paper Money*   134
16   Sir James Steuart. *Money and Economic Growth*   139

PART THREE: PRIVATE BANKING AND THE MONEY MARKET TO 1825   150

17   Anonymous. *The Goldsmith Bankers*   159
18   William Forbes. *Credit Instruments*   165
19   The State of Commercial Credit 1793. *Report*   173
20   Henry Thornton. *The Money Supply – Its Definition and Increase*   185
21   Sir Francis Baring. *The Bank of England in Crisis*   194
22   M. Dorrien Magens. *Attack on Country Note Issues*   199
23   Thomas Richardson. *The Rise of the Bill Broker*   205
24   Vincent Stuckey. *Country Banking in the Suspension Period*   214
25   Thomas Joplin. *Reform of the Banking System*   223
26   George Carr Glyn. *Defence of the London Private Bankers*   237

PART FOUR: THE DEVELOPMENT OF JOINT STOCK DEPOSIT BANKING   241

27   *The Banking Co-partnerships Act, 1826*   250
28   R. Conway. *Hostility to Corporate Banking*   267
29   T. Joplin. *Banking and Limited Liability*   270
30   J. W. Gilbert. *Joint Stock Banks*   271
31   T. Joplin. *London as the Centre of the Banking System*   276
32   *The Bank Charter Act, 1833*   279
33   D. Salomons. *The London and Westminster Bank*   281
34   J. W. Gilbart. *The Bank of England and the Joint Stock Banks*   285
35   *The London Clearing House and the Joint Stock Banks*   286
36   Daniel Robertson. *The National Provincial Bank of England*   287

CONTENTS 7

37 *The Circular to Bankers. New Banks in 1836*   294
38 *Rediscounting by Joint Stock Banks*   297
39 *The Regulation of Joint Stock Banks*   298
40 *The Economist. The Failure of the Royal British Bank, 1856*   299
41 D. Salomons. *London Deposit Rates and Bank Rate*   301
42 R. B. Wade. *Provincial Deposit Rates*   303
43 *Joint Stock Banks and the Companies Act of 1862*   304
44 *The Bankers' Magazine. New Banks in the 1860s*   307
45 *The Bankers' Magazine. The Failure of the City of Glasgow Bank*   308
46 *The Companies Act, 1879. Reserved Liability*   312
47 Treasury Committee. *Bank Amalgamations*   316
48 J. W. Birch and B. W. Currie. *The Extension of Banking in the 1880s*   325
49 *The Economist. London Joint Stock Banks and International Acceptances*   330

SUGGESTIONS FOR FURTHER READING   335

ACKNOWLEDGEMENTS   341

INDEX   343

Introduction

THE object of this book is to bring together some of the more important documentary sources, from the vast bulk in existence, in order to illustrate the main strands in the evolution of the English domestic banking system over two centuries or more. The lack of accessible original material can be a serious handicap to those working in a field where the secondary literature, much of it of a technical nature, is particularly thick on the ground. We have attempted to fill this gap by concentrating on the main themes and landmarks in the history of money and banking, sometimes at the expense of continuity and comprehensiveness, in the hope that most of the basic sources of relevance to students of the subject have been included. This approach also permits us to incorporate seminal readings in the development of monetary thought, so as to enable the reader to follow the interplay between theory and practice and enhance an understanding of both. There are few subjects where the realm of ideas impinges on the framework of policy to the same degree as in monetary history and Part Two is designed to take account of that. The aim has been to provide as balanced a selection as possible, by drawing on pamphlets, and periodicals as well as government inquiries and legislation; where appropriate, important documents have been reproduced in entirety and a number are reprinted here for the first time.

Part One deals with the background to the foundation of the Bank of England in 1694, and emphasises how much a part of the first great boom in company promotion were the financial institutions of the early 1690s. Against the background of the

government's financial difficulties and the failure of many of
the other projects at this time, the Bank was assured of a close
and continuing relationship with the government and a growing
dominance in the financial world of London. The subsequent
confirmations of its special position and the gradual expansion
of discount and note-issuing operations by the Bank require
relatively little illustration. Accordingly, Part Two looks at the
development of some of the key ideas about the role of money
and credit in the working of the economy. From the coinage
controversy of the 1690s, which is merely alluded to and not
given detailed attention, to the onset of economic growth and
financial crisis in the last quarter of the eighteenth century,
there was growing discussion of the money economy and its
problems. The great achievement of those who wrote in this
period was to rescue the subject of money from a preoccupation
with the weights and values of coins, and to look, increasingly,
at the nature of the relationship between money and economic
activity.

The following two Parts chart the main lines of development
leading to the emergence of the commercial banking system.
For the sake of a true perspective it needs to be emphasised
how relatively slight was the progress made before the late
eighteenth century, particularly outside of London. In 1750
there were only about a dozen private banks in the provinces;
rapid growth occurred at the end of the century, as part of a
general credit expansion, and the number of country banks
increased approximately three-fold during the Napoleonic
Wars. Private banking in London was an earlier growth and is
normally dated as beginning with the appearance of goldsmiths
keeping 'running cashes' at the time of the Restoration; Bank
of England notes drove private notes out of circulation in
London at an early stage with the result that a cheque system
was well developed by the middle of the century. From this
time the rise of the correspondent system, bringing country
bankers in touch with London, began to lay down the first
tenuous links of a money market based on the capital. Financial

crises took a rising toll of casualties in a unit banking system that included too many undercapitalised firms with a few partners. A large crop of failures in the crisis of 1825 finally produced the much-needed reform and liberalisation of the law, and the following year banking co-partnerships with any number of proprietors were permitted outside a radius of sixty-five miles from London.

After 1826 the modern joint stock banks began to develop but it was not until after 1857 that their dominance within the banking system was finally assured. The growth of the joint stock banks was encouraged initially by the government in order to strengthen the base of the banking system but the first banks were very similar in nature to their private counterparts, having little capital and being parochial in their outlook. Their development was opposed by both the Bank of England and the London and country private bankers. The joint stock banks, especially the London banks formed in the 1830s, did bring with their foundation a new approach to banking in their concern for the collection and employment of deposits rather than note issuing. The permissive legal environment after the 1826 Act was changed drastically in 1844 when a very restrictive code of regulation was introduced for new joint stock banks and it held back further bank formation for almost two decades. The joint stock banks, formed before 1844, prospered during the 1840s and 1850s and gradually overwhelmed the private banking community which at the same time was being depleted by bankruptcy. The modern banking system did not fully develop until after 1857 when the onerous code of 1844 was repealed, but the following two decades were troubled by mismanagement, bank failures and financial crises. The present organisation of the banking industry began to emerge as amalgamations, a feature of joint stock banking since its inception, during the late 1880s and 1890s resulted in the appearance of a few large banks with branch networks which covered the country.

The theory of money and the practice of banking has been an

area of human affairs in which English influences have been especially strong. In a companion volume, the themes of the development of the London money market in the nineteenth century, the great monetary debate of the first half of the nineteenth century and the relationship between the Bank of England with both the domestic banking system and the international gold standard, have been dealt with, but our regret is that we have not had space or time enough to deal with the equally important international aspects of English banking—the merchant banks and the overseas banks.

PART ONE

Monetary Experiments and the Foundation of the Bank of England

INCREASINGLY from the 1640s English writers had been acclimatising public opinion to the idea of a national bank and lauding the advantages of the joint stock banks already in existence on the continent.* It is important to be clear at the outset, however, that the Bank of England owed its birth in 1694 not to these precedents but to the ferment of monetary ideas that arose in late seventeenth century England, and to the numerous financial schemes which drew a brief life from it. In fact the Bank was only one of a number of schemes that came into being during the hectic years of the 1690s, accompanied by a wide-ranging pamphlet literature. Of the many projects advocated at this period, including a variety of plans to capitalise State revenues, Lombard banks to exploit credit on commodities, and Land banks, only three actually came into existence in the form of the Million lottery, the Bank of England and Exchequer bills.

The notion that an expansion of credit could be achieved by issuing a paper currency that was founded upon the credit of

* The Bank of Geneva was founded in 1345; Bank of Barcelona, 1401; Bank of Genoa, 1407; Bank of Venice, 1457; Bank of Amsterdam, 1607; Bank of Hamburg, 1619; Bank of Rotterdam, 1635; Bank of Stockholm, 1688.

13

the government itself was not new. In 1663 Sir William Killigrew had put forward a proposal for the issue of paper money by the government in anticipation of taxes, and between 1667 and 1672 this idea was put into practice with 'Exchequer Orders' circulating from hand to hand in addition to the traditional tallies (1). The 'Stop of the Exchequer' in 1672 brought the experiment to an end and it was not until the 1690s that confidence was sufficiently restored, by which time Killigrew's device, itself republished, had spawned a host of imitators and variants. Many proposals such as those of Thomas Neale, were for a direct government issue of bills, either by the Treasury or by the Crown itself, with various suggestions as to the amount to be raised and the interest to be paid (2). Others, like that of William Paterson, were more specific and concentrated on promoting a bank, or permanent 'fund of credit' (5). Yet others were for a short-term debt instrument to be issued by the Exchequer, thereby allowing it to create its own obligations (9). In the event all three kinds of proposals came to fruition in the last decade of the century.

The Million Acts of 1693 and 1694 originated the so-called 'Million Adventure' or Lottery Loan of the latter year. It was the first of many lotteries to raise public loans and occupies an important place in the history of the English National Debt. By it 100,000 lottery tickets were to be sold at £10 each; 97,500 were blanks and simply entitled the holders to £1 p.a. interest for sixteen years, but 2,500 were benefit tickets and allowed holders, in addition to normal interest, to draw prizes of up to £1,000. The following year a 'Bank on the Tickets of the Million Adventure' was floated, with lottery tickets being accepted towards subscriptions, and it proceeded to speculate in the life annuities originally granted to the subscribers to the Million loan of 1693. The Million Adventure was the first recognised public loan to the government; the Bank of England was the second such vehicle and outlived all the rest.

There are many reasons to explain why the Bank of England alone achieved lasting success. In common with most of the schemes put forward at the time, it promised to supply the Crown's financial needs, to discourage hoarding and enlarge the supply of currency, as well as to quicken the circulation of a diminished quantity of specie. The Bank would also have a favourable impact on the rate of interest. Unlike its rivals, the Bank did not demand 'legal tender' status for its notes, at least in its final form, and this was an important concession for it meant no challenge to the metallic standard. On the other hand, the gains promised to the subscribers were sufficiently attractive to draw influential support from the City. The question of timing was also significant; in retrospect only one financial institution of any consequence could have emerged intact from the lean years of the coinage crisis. Perhaps for the first time, the government fully understood the implications of waging expensive war on the basis of loans that were far and away larger than the total of its current receipts, and it had to take a positive step. Finally, that Paterson's plan was adopted at all can be attributed in some measure to the determination and influence of two key figures, Charles Montagu, the Chancellor of the Exchequer who pushed the scheme in Court and Parliament, and Michael Godfrey, the financier who rallied support in the City of London. At its inception, and well into the next century, the Bank was primarily a financial venture of the merchant community of the capital and hardly yet a national bank.

Perhaps the most popular foundation for the issue of paper money at this time was the Land bank. There were numerous schemes of this type projected, and a few realised; behind them all was the idea of issuing legal tender paper money up to a certain proportion of the value of land, and of receiving as deposits money that would otherwise have lain idle. In this way it was thought, money would never be too cheap nor too dear. Clearly, the landed classes had a vested interest in sponsoring such schemes, or so they thought, since they promised landowners the facility of borrowing as easily and as cheaply as the trading community; the Tories, especially, tended to support them. The most famous exponent of the land bank idea was Dr Hugh Chamberlen who published with rash energy on the subject before and during the 1690s (3). At the root of his various schemes was the belief that since credit expansion was beneficial to trade, the surest way of raising credit was on the basis of lands, the ultimate security. His plan would have given loans to landowners at 4 per cent and the government, it was contended, would have benefited more from it than from supporting the Bank of England. Four distinct land bank schemes came to fruition, and to grief, in the years following the foundation of the Bank of England. The important names here, apart from Chamberlen, are Nicholas Barbon, a City promoter of considerable ability, John Asgill, a currency visionary and John Briscoe, second only to Chamberlen in his advocacy of land-banking.

Asgill and Barbon's land bank of 1695 set out to attract depositors, intending to advance their savings on mortgages and, to that extent, acted as a building society. Although the capital of the bank was raised repeatedly, subscriptions were slow to come in. In 1696 Asgill and Barbon negotiated with Briscoe to bring about a fusion of their two banks, but still success eluded them. Barbon died in 1698 and the land bank he had founded survived him by only a year. John Briscoe had published his views on land banks in 1694 under the title *A Discourse on the Late Funds* and the following year, without waiting for an act of parliament, he established his National Land Bank. Surprisingly there was a rush of subscribers, chiefly from the south-eastern counties but including names from almost every part of the country. Nevertheless, actual cash payments to the bank were made with great reluctance and the terms for attracting funds had to be repeatedly enhanced before any business was done at all. It would appear that the problem afflicting all land banks, namely a looming cash crisis, drove Briscoe into the welcoming arms of Asgill and Barbon in 1696. The result was the 'Land Bank United' which was established, despite furious opposition from the Bank of

England, by Act of Parliament on 27 April 1696. Its history of a few months—it had to raise over £2½ million by August in order to survive—was a complete fiasco. In the monetary conditions of 1696 it is doubtful if even the Bank of England could have been successfully launched; for a land bank, with its manifold deficiencies already laid bare in a virulent bout of pamphleteering, there was no hope.

Apart from Charles II's experiment with Exchequer Orders already mentioned, the first permanent fiduciary issue of paper money by the government occurred in 1696 with the circulation of Exchequer bills. As with so many monetary experiments of the time, their appearance coincided with the dearth of currency brought about by the calling in of specie for the Recoinage of 1696–9. There is no doubt that much official thought was given to the operation of this expedient, especially by Montagu (9). The original idea has been variously attributed to Thomas Neale in his tract *A Way How to Supply the King's Occasions* . . . (1694), and to Robert Murray in his *The Manner and Method of an Exchequer Credit* . . . (1695) but Montagu must ultimately be credited with their issue. The Bank of England was to help the Treasury to circulate them and they were to be accepted in payment of all taxes, apart from the land tax; they were issued in small denominations, ie less than £20, and were negotiable at the Bank for cash. These conditions, plus the fact that they bore interest, enhanced confidence in them and ensured a reasonable circulation. Subsequently, with co-operation between the Treasury and the Bank, they became an important instrument for the financing of government supplies.

It was no accident that the monetary controversy and banking experiments of the last years of the seventeenth century coincided with a currency crisis; it was a time for ideas, not all of them new, and for expedients, few of which were successful. So far as the operation of a bank was concerned, the lesson was clear, to achieve success a bank did not have to found its activities upon a tangible asset. Confidence, it was now realised, was the vital ingredient; the privilege of legal tender for notes

B

was not something to be granted out of hand, it had to be gained
by the public approval of a prudent administration of the bank
over time. The debates over the metallic standard, the deflation-
ary impact of the recoinage, and the inflationary effects of
paper money issues, taught lessons that were difficult to grasp at
first. But in the following century, as we shall see in Part Two,
the monetary experience of the 1690s helped to crystallise the
issues and produced a continuing polarisation of views on the
nature and role of money in the economy. This experience also
represented, again from the standpoint of the eighteenth century,
a significant shift of emphasis from the narrow discussion of the
standard and the factors influencing the supply of coin to a
concern with the total quantity of purchasing power and the
mechanism of credit.

As for the Bank of England, it was able to move safely into
the next century primarily because it was possessed of a unique
asset—its perpetual loan to the government; and its future
security was to rest in its ability to extract privileges in exchange
for its assistance in financing a rising curve of government
expenditure in the long term. In the first years of its establishment its supporters held widely different prospects of the Bank's
course of development. Defoe's futuristic vision of a much
enlarged national Bank with numerous branches was too
optimistic and looked beyond the eighteenth century (8). In
the same year Janssen, the conservative banker, published his
plea for discretion and restraint (7). Although there seems little
doubt as to which of them was the more influential in shaping
English banking practice generally, the Bank itself did exceed
the latter's expectations in the next half century. It is true that
for all practical purposes the Bank remained the 'Bank of
London' until very late in the eighteenth century, and that its
private business was almost wholly with metropolitan business-
men. The bulk of its business was with the government and
remained so throughout; it contracted for Exchequer bills each
year, it advanced funds on the tax revenues, it paid the dividends on the growing national debt and it assisted with new

loans and lotteries (6). But it was a bank of issue, its first central
banking function, and the circulation of its notes does appear
to have been increasing in the Provinces, at least until the rise
of the country banks from the 1760s. Only from then, as we
shall see in Part Three was there a growing need for it to
function as a bankers' Bank.

1 Sir William Killigrew   State Credit

Sir William Killigrew (1606–95), a Royalist commander
during the Civil War and gentleman-usher to both Charles I
and Charles II, was sometime MP for Newport and Penryn
in Cornwall, and Governor of Pendennis Castle and Fal-
mouth Haven. He was responsible for draining parts of the
Lincolnshire Fens but is best known as a dramatist, notwithstanding the fact that he appears to have been the first
writer of note to have put forward a coherent plan for antici-
pating government revenue and issuing securities that would
be free to circulate. Most subsequent schemes of this type
were simply variants of his original plan of 1663, which was
published in 1690 and reprinted in 1696.

I Put this Design in Writing, at the Request of several
considerable Members of both Houses of Parliament, in the
Reign of King Charles II when a War was voted against
France; but a Peace being concluded, no Money was given;
and since that, I have had no Opportunity to do my Country
the Service I designed by this Proposal.

But the general Approbation this Paper had from all that
saw it, in Three several Parliaments, and very many considerable Members having declar'd, that they could not couch any
one Rational Objection against what I here humbly offer; I
have thought fit, in this juncture of Time, to revive this Design;
and most humbly refer it to the Wisdom of the King, and both
Houses of Parliament.

As I have not the Nomination of the Sums now to be given

to the Crown, so I shall only suppose a Sum of Two Millions; but the Case will hold on all Occasions, of the same Nature . . .

PROPOSALS

1. Suppose, that a Tax be set, that will raise £300,000 per Ann. this Tax to continue till £2m. is paid with the Interest and Charges.

2. Let there be an Office erected in the City of London, near the Royal-Exchange; let the Tax of £300,000 be paid into the said Office, in the same Species, as they receive it; Because most of the Taxes will be paid in Money, in small Sums, which they must not change for Bills; yet they must take Bills, where the Sums amount to so much.

Now this is necessary to create a Cash, to pay Interest, or Foreign Bills; which must be compos'd thus.

7 Commissioners, of which one or more to be Treasurers,	£7,000 per Ann.
1 Secretary,	£500
10 Clerks,	£1,200
2 Door-Keepers,	£200
6 Messengers,	£300
House-Rent, Fire, Candle, Paper, &c.	£800
	£10,000 per Ann.

3. The Tax and Office being fram'd, it must, by Act of Parliament, be order'd, that the Office shall be govern'd thus.

4. The Office must be open, and Commissioners must sit from Eight of the Clock till Twelve every Morning (except Sundays and Holy-Days) and from Two till Four in the Afternoon.

5. The Office must accomodate all Persons, without Fees or Delays.

6. The Office must pay every Creditor, in as many Bonds as the Creditor pleases; and at the Creditor's Choice to have his Name in the Bonds, or Blanks; saying, Payable to A.B. or to the Bearer: This Last is Best, because of transferring them.

7. No Bonds to be above a Hundred Pounds, nor none under Five; for the lesser the Bonds are, the better they will pass in Trade.

8. The Act of Parliament must also make it Treason for the Office to issue out more in Bond, than is order'd by the said Act; else, like too much Allay in Coyn, the Bonds would be imbased: These Bonds must also be Sign'd by Three Commissioners at the least, besides the Secretary.

9. At the Expiration of every Six Months, the Office must pay the Interest of every Bond standing out, and according to their Date; and mark those Bonds they design to pay off, at the Expiration of the next Six Months, by writing on these Bonds, thus, This Bond shall be paid off, Principal and Interest, this day Six Months: This must also be Registered in the Folio of those Bonds, in the Office-Books.

10. The Commissioners must issue out these Bonds or Warrants from the Treasury; by which means, the Crown, nor the Treasury, are not lessen'd, but remain still the Fountain-Head.

11. These Warrants must be brought by some Person or Persons, Authoriz'd for that Purpose, to avoid false Warrants. The Treasury must also send a Letter of Advice, before such Warrants may be accepted.

12. If any Bonds are Lost, Stoln, or Burn'd, the Parties concern'd must give Notice thereof to the Office; to the end that the Office may stop them that bring the Bonds, and give Notice thereof to the Owners: But, if the Bonds are so lost, or burnt, that they come not to the Office, then it must be made publick in the Gazette several times; and if the Bonds appear not in Six Months, the Officers must give the Owners new Bonds, on good Security, that they are the Parties whose Names are last Registred in the Office-Books for the Lost or Burn'd Bonds.

13. The same Act that settles the Office, and the Tax, must declare, That the Crown has Credit at the Office for Two Millions, payable thus; The Parties, concern'd to receive the Money, shall, on Warrants from the Treasury, receive the Office-Bonds, and £6 per Cent. per Ann. Interest. That the

Interest shall be paid every Six Months, and Six Months warning given before the Principal shall be paid off: This, because People shall have time to find out other ways to dispose of their Money, to new Advantages.

14. The Act further declaring, That the Office-Bonds shall not only be transferrable, but Currant, as Money, in all Payments whatsoever, even into the Exchequer: And it must be made Treason for any of the Publick Receivers, to refuse the Office-Bonds, when tender'd in the Payments. Counterfeiting of these Bonds must also be made Capital; altho' I know, 'tis impossible to Counterfeit the Bonds, which must be made on a Marbled, or Flourished Paper, fairly Tallied and Registered in the Office-Books, where the Counterparts must be kept.

On this Paragraph depends the whole Proposals, the Objections, and Sir James Sheene's Questions: This causes the Bills, or Tallies, to be a new specy of Money, superior to Money made of Gold or Silver: This makes the Security a hundred times more than ever was proposed or given; because all the Revenues of the Crown, all our Trade and Consumption, is Security, as well as the Taxes, set to pay the Principal and Interest, and Charges; which Security is far more than I have said, of a hundred times more than was ever given; This unites the King and People, by the strongest Bonds; I mean, their Interest, to support each other: And it was an Argument for the Million-Lottery, That it would oblige so many Families to be Friends to this Government.

I propose the Bonds on Marbled Paper, because less Burthensome, and easiest to Register, and turn'd to their Folio, else a Tally of Wood, or Mettal, is as good.

Now, I ask, if all our late Tallies had been made Currant by a Law, how would our ill-affected, and our Money-Mungers, have imposed on the necessitous; who had been forced to sell at vast Loss, and intollerable Usury of the Buyers?

Consider the vast Loss our Trade has had of late, by This, and the Bank-Bills, and what People have suffer'd for want of their Money: How impudently have Men been refused their own Money, payable on Demand; not that it is impossible, that the Nation wants Money, or Bullion, to Circulate our Trade.

Many cry out, That our Money, and Bullion, is Exported, never to return; I wish our Knavery, Usury, Factions, and Self-Interest, were Exported; and am confident, these Proposals will send away a great part of these Destroyers of the Publick Welfare; a worse People than our Coyners, Clippers, or Robbers.

Pray, Is not a Government oblig'd to make Laws for the Publick Good? And, do we not daily desire the Increase of Trade? Ought not the Government to oblige the People to do what is for their Advantage? Who will not force a Mad Man to be let Blood, and take wholsome Medicines? Is not the Nation in a Distraction about their Money and Credit? Is not this Method a Wholsome, Secure, and Infallible Cure for this National Distemper? Why then should not the Government oblige Men to take this Proposed Currant Credit, grounded on so Solid, and so great a Security, and so generally advantageous?

15. It must also be made Capital for the Office to make any Use, or Private Advantage of the Publick Cash; and they must order it so, as to have a good Cash, because many times the Tax may not be paid in, time enough; it may be, a Month or two later than the Interest is due.

And a considerable Cash may be kept, to answer Foreign Bills, if ready Money be requir'd: This I add, to answer a Noble Lord's Objection: But, suppose these Bonds, or Bills, will not pay Foreign Bills, I shall make Use of a Saying of Dr Chamberlen, viz. That a Stage-Coach is a good Convenience to a Man, to go to York; yet that Coach cannot set another Man down at Exeter. And what is hereafter added, will bring in Cash enough, to answer any Foreign Bills; besides, how will the Bills be paid, without this Proposal, which must, of necessity, make Gold and Silver Coyn free and common in the Nation?

16. These Bonds being thus made Currant, and Grounded on a Law, and the Security of the whole Nation, they will not only be of an Intrinsic Value, equal with Gold and Silver,

but superior to either; and of the same Consequence, as if so much Money were Imported, and given this Nation, to Trade with.

17. I say, these Bonds will be superior to Gold or Silver, because these Bonds cannot be Counterfeited, Lost, Stoln, or Burnt, without Recovery; they will be a new Species of Money, that will grow in our Coffers, every day increasing; which Gold nor Silver does not, but is liable to many Inconveniencies; as Thieves, False and Clipp'd Money, Counterfeiting, Loss of Time in Counting, and Chargeable to carry in large Sums.

18. These Bonds will soon become our best Payments, and Coyn, for every one will covet them; nor will any scruple to fetch their Payments at the Office, more than now they do fetch their Money at the Exchequer, or Lombard-street; and the Bonds must be transferred at the Office, because the Counterparts are kept there; the Office becomes Witness to the Payments, and avoids Disputes at Law.

19. All Mankind must confess, That Credit grounded on a good and solid Security, if it can be made currant, is not only as good, but better than Money itself; for Money does no man good, until he has disposed of it for good Security: And I desire to know, what Security can be offer'd so great, and of so Intrinsic a Value, as these Bonds?

Note, There is no end of Security, as long as there is a Fund to support it; it runs ad infinitum, and we can never be over-burthened with it: for it stops when there is no Occasion for it.

The First Years Accompt stated.

20. In Bonds the Debt is   £2,000,000

For Interest at 5 per Cent.	£120,000 }	£130,000
For the Office Charges	£10,000 }	
The Tax comes to	£300,000	
The Charges	£130,000	
There will rest in Cash	£170,000	

Thus, then at Twelve Months end, the Interest & Charges of the Office will be paid, and there will be £170,000 in Cash; out of which may be paid £150,000 of the Bonds, and keep

£20,000 in Cash; and for the future, Pay off Part of the Debt, proportionable every Six Months, keeping still a Cash of £20,000 or £30,000 more or less, as shall be thought fit.

Thus the Debt of £2m at the Years end is diminish'd to £1,850,000 and will dwindle away in a few Years, by a Rebate of Interest upon Interest, and by a small Tax the Nation will not feel.

21. Now in case greater Sums must be given, or a war carry'd on, which may require large Sums, and yearly, so long as a War lasts, then the Taxes must be made proportionable.

But still there will be no necessity ever to set any Tax above what will pay double or treble the Interest of the Money given to the Crown. And now let us see the Advantages that will arise from this Method of giving Money.

Benefits arising to the Crown, and to the Nation, by this way of giving Money

1. By this means the Crown receives the entire Sums of Money, given by the Parliaments; and the Crown has the Money immediately, without staying till the Taxes come in, or being oblig'd to take up Money, or buy Stores at hard Rates, and paying by uncertain Assignments; so that part by the raising and collecting the Taxes, part by taking up Money, and buying Goods on Credit; This will save very near on Third Part of what is given by the Nation, besides the great Disappointments our Kings have met with by Delays, and the Nation also, who expect from the Crown the same thing, as if the Crown had the whole Sums given, and in due time.

2. The Crown will buy all Stores at least 20 per Cent. cheaper than usually; for Men will prefer these Bonds before any Assignments, or Money itself, because these Bonds will increase in their Coffers, and are not lyable to a Postpone: For the Crown may as easily call back the Money paid out of the Exchequer, as stop what is given out for Money, and made currant by a

Law; besides, these Bonds will be in the Hands and Possession of the People.

3. This Currant Credit will do the duty of Gold and Silver; and is the same thing in all respects, as so much Money, Imported and Distributed, and added to the general Stock of the Nation; which will increase our Trade proportionably, as the Crown will soon find, by the increase of the Revenue; for we have not Seven Millions in Money, to support our Trade, and Consumption; and by adding Two or more Millions of this currant Credit, we add proportionably to our Trade and Consumption.

4. These Bonds will produce a double Gain to the Nation; first, by drawing out the Money, which lies dead for want of Security; secondly, Men will Trade with these Bonds, or draw the Interest, which makes the Bonds daily of more Value, altho' they lie dead in their Coffers.

5. Our poorer sort of People may improve their small Talents, without the Expences of Scriveners, Brokers, and the like, who daily make a prey of them, and often let their Money lye dead, and take not always good Security: But by this Method, Men may put their Money to a secure Interest, and without Charges, and have their Money still in their own keeping, ready to make a new Advantage by it; which they cannot do by our usual ways, nor be secured, that they shall have their Money or Interest, when it is due.

This Paragraph ought to be well consider'd; It shews great Advantages.

6. This undeniable Security will bring Bullion from abroad, as Holland, and other Places, where they draw but 4 per Cent. and it will disperse our own Money, which now lyes dead, for want of security, and makes it more free and common amongst us.

7. Our Retailers, thro' whose Hands passeth the greatest part of our currant Cash, will Change or Buy these Bonds, as soon as they have but £5 or £10 in their Shops; for they let such Sums lye by them, till they have a Stock, either to pay a Debt,

or go to Market, which they may as well do with these Bonds;
by which they will gain more in the Interest, than their share
of the Tax will come to; therefore they'll pay Taxes with Joy.
8. These Bonds (like Money) will pass thro' five or six Hundred
Hands in the Year, every Trade gaining £10 per Cent. as
they must needs do, or they cannot subsist; because most
Traders pay £6 per Cent. for the Money they Trade with.
Now, I will suppose these Bonds, the one with the other, pass
thro' forty Hands only in a Year, every Trader gaining but
5 per Cent. then every £100 in these Bonds produce £200 per
Ann. gain to the Nation, as long as they are standing out. If so,
then the Nation may well dispense with the Charges of the
Office and Interest, since for £2m given, the Nation will gain
£4m the first Year, little less the second and third Years:
Consider, then, the Advantage accrues to the Nation on the
whole, and before all the Bonds are paid off.
9. I could say much more on every Paragraph, in this Paper,
but am loth to be too tedious: besides, this Business requires
to be discoursed; and it does not become me to say more, till
commanded . . . Sir William Killigrew. *A Proposal. Shewing
How This Nation May Be Vast Gainers by All the Sums of Money,
Given to the Crown* (1696)

---

2 Sir Thomas Neale   Raising a Million

Thomas Neale (d 1699), Master of the Royal Mint from
1678, was reputed to have dissipated two fortunes through
gaming and speculation. The Million Lottery Act of 1694
originated from his several proposals on the subject and in
that year he was appointed master of the transfer office in
Lombard Street for conducting the lottery. In addition,
Neale speculated in the East India trade, was a subscriber to
Briscoe's National Land Bank of 1695 and projected many
buildings and mines (he built the Seven Dials). He died
insolvent.

This Hundred Thousand Pounds yearly to be settled on

Trustees, who are at first to bring in Two Hundred Thousand Pounds to Circulate the rest; for which, as aforesaid, 8 per Cent. is to be paid, and 8 per Cent. for the Million: Out of which last 8 per Cent. for the Million, the Trustees to have half per Cent. for their Conduct and Care, and One and a Half per Cent. Procuration; and those that advance the Money, or take the Bills, to have a Currant Interest on them of 6 per Cent. only; and yet taking it altogether, there must by this Proposition be Ninety Six Thousand Pounds yearly Paid, and for it One Hundred Thousand Pounds yearly settled, which brings this Million to be took up at near £10 per Cent. Interest yearly, and that for Eleven Years certain, but at Three Years Warning redeemable after that time.

The Fund spoke of for this Settlement, is the Tax (talkt of) on Salt for Four Years, and then Six Pence out of one Nine Pence Excise on Beer and Ale, engaged for so long, and which after that time may be given and settled for any Use the King and Parliament shall think fit to Enact.

A Proposal for Raising Two Millions on part of the Security must be used for Raising, as aforesaid, One Million: And yet the People in General, who are either to Advance (or be Paid with) this Money, will have the same Yearly Profit and Interest by it, and as much Security and Satisfaction (when well understood) as the other Proposal affords.

The way of doing it thus:

1. Let One Hundred and Forty Thousand Pounds yearly, that is, the Nine Pence a Barrel Excise (agreed on all Hands to be one Hundred and Forty Thousand Pounds yearly) be settled for ever to pay the Interest of Two Millions and Three Hundred Thousand Pounds, at 6 per Cent. yearly, but redeemable by Parliament on repaying the Principal at any time after the War, supposing it cleared from the present Incumbrance, which may be paid off, as herein after express'd.

2. Let Officers on purpose, either in or of the Exchequer, or some other place as fit near the Exchange, be appointed to

give out Bills with a running Interest on them of 6 per Cent. to whoever will take them for such Money as the King is to pay to any Man on any Account whatsoever, and at the same time and place, in Books to be purposely kept. Let Credit be given to the Person receiving such Bills for the Money for which those Bills were then given.

Let such Credit be made easie Assignable.

Let it be Enacted, That the King for his Custom, Excise, or for any other part of his Revenue, shall accept of such Bills and Credit in Payment, which will be no Inconvenience at all to the Crown, because on every occasion (as they were at first) they may be again paid out.

And let it be also Enacted, That Interest at 6 per Cent. shall be Yearly, Half-yearly, or Quarterly paid to whoever has the Possession of the Bills and Credit so given out for this Money.

And thus the whole Two Millions and Three Hundred Thousand Pounds may be disposed by the Crown, as occasion shall require; and when Merchants and others come to see (which they'll presently do) such a safe Credit and Ease, as this way of paying and receiving Money will give them in every Case, answering Ready Money itself, with this further Advantage, That whereas Money kept by them for any occasion (which sometimes happens many Months together) brings them no Profit, Money thus Put out is always Ready Money for every occasion, and yet brings them in 6 per Cent. Interest till the very Hour they use it: And for these Reasons, and the Reasons that follow, both Usurers, Merchants, and others will quickly be so fond of having thus Money in Bank, that in a very short time (as in Holland it is) 'twill come to be One or Two per Cent. better than Ready Money itself: And as aforesaid, the whole Two Millions (and the odd Money going to clear the Anticipation of what is owing now on the Nine Pence) will be ready Money to the King, and cost the Nation less by near 4 per Cent. than 'twill by the other Proposal, and be Honourable and Safe for the King and Kingdom, and to all that shall be in it concerned: And if instead of 6 per Cent. as proposed, it shall be thought reasonable, and be Enacted by Parliament, That a Currant Interest of 7 per Cent. yearly shall be Quarterly paid, for what Money soever there shall Credit be given in the Books to be kept for this Bank, in such case the Credit of this Bank will answer just as much Ready Money, as the Fund to be settled will at 6 or 7 per Cent. pay the Interest of, and to shew this will certainly do.

It cannot be denied, but that the King may at first Pay it all out as ready Money to whoever his Majesty has occasion to pay any Money to, who would be much more glad to take it than Tallies, to be struck upon any Tax or Revenue, not presently to come in, whatsoever: For when any Tallies are struck (if not on a Land Tax) they are Five per Cent. immediately worse than ready Money, because there is no way certain whereby the Person that has them can come to his Money, without hiring some Body to pay it him, at least till the Tally grows due, and must stay longer if the Money by that time be not come in to pay it; whereas the Man that takes this sort of Payment has not only as good Security, and as good Interest for his Money (as the Man that takes the Tally has) but also a way certain of turning it into Money by finding a way how to pay it as such to the King, which for a very small matter at any time may be easily found.

Now the great Objection to this is, A Supposition that the King will be paid his Revenue all in this Credit, and what shall he do with it in case it should happen to be so? Answer, The King may still Pay it out to others (on any occasion) as he did at the first; but 'tis a great mistake to think that that supposed inconvenience can in any great measure happen in this Case. For note,

As Usurers, when they have well placed out their Money at good Interest in the Hands of Persons that can pay it them again in a short time after 'tis called for, they will never call for it, but upon mighty Occasions; so here when the Money for which Credit is given in the Books of this Bank shall come to belong to Rich Men, (which in a very short time it will do) they seeing they have as good a Security, and as good Interest as the Government gives, besides a certain way how to come in to their Money at any time upon Urgent Occasion, they will chuse rather to have Money owing them this way than upon any other Security whatsoever, and will not part with such Credit in the said Bank to any of their Neighbours, without having something more given them than Principal and Interest for so doing, and this will be the Case of this Bank, the Credit of which, as aforesaid, will answer full as much ready Money as the Fund to be given will at Six or Seven per Cent. Pay Interest for, and Three Hundred Thousand Pounds of this Credit will doubtless be chearfully taken as payment by those who are to be paid in Four Years out of the Nine Pence, and so the Nine Pence will be clear to be presently setled (if the King and Parliament shall so please) for this Fund.

Now, as aforesaid, it must be agreed on all hands, That if the King will receive this Credit in Payment for his Revenue, 'twill answer all other ends whatsoever. And

The Objection (and only one more that seems to have weight) against the King's being obliged to receive back in payment of any of his Revenues, this Credit so before by him paid out, raised by some much concerned in great Money Affairs, is this, say they, The King's Revenue is greatly Anticipated, and is (as it comes in) to be paid presently out in specie to those it is Due, who have already Tallies for it: And suppose the Revenue which is to pay them is paid to the King in this Credit; and that those to whom 'tis to be paid, will expect to be paid in hard Money, and will not be content with this Credit, what must be done in that Case?

Note, this is a Supposition only, and it may as well be supposed (for Reasons aforesaid) that by the time those Debts grow due, this Credit will, even in the Opinion of those to whom 'twill be due, come to be esteemed so much better than ready Money, that 'twill be chosen before it, and then the aforesaid Objection will be quite out of Doors; but supposing those to whom such Debts, as aforesaid, are due already by

Tallies, should say, they would not (when their Debt becomes due) be content to be paid in this Credit; it cannot be supposed but that those very Men (unless out of their Wits, or in Crosness to strive to ruin this Bank) who have those Tallies, and must stay for payment till such Tallies are due, will be glad if (instead of such Tallies) they may be presently paid in this Credit; since the Objection they themselves make of the King's Revenue being Anticipated will be this way took off; and if so, they that instead of Tallies shall have this sort of Credit, will have a much easier way of coming in to their Money than when they only had remote Tallies for it; and the King being Capacitated presently to pay off those Anticipations by this sort of Credit, may without inconvenience do it, being instead thereof enabled to receive his Revenue so cleared, as it shall come in by it, or to engage it for ready Money to others again, if he wants it before it comes in, and if the worst comes to the worst that some of those that have Tallies will not take this Credit now, and resolve to refuse it, (as aforesaid out of Crosness) when their Tallies grow due, 'tis much unlikely there should be many such; and for those that are, the Lords of the Treasury may easily contrive to pay them in Money, having such Bills by them to turn into Money, or use to pay others for any other Occasions, who if this Credit were not in being, must be paid in Money, and who instead of Money will always be glad of such pay as this Credit will be.

And if (after all has been said) the Wisdom of Parliament shall fear in the least the thus Present Supplying the Wants of the Publick with Two Millions of Money at Six per Cent. as aforesaid, (it being taken for granted, that the Charge of the War (when ended) must be paid by the Nation) it may be Enacted, (if the King and Parliament please) that at the end of Seven Years a Tax of Two Shillings in the Pound for Two Years, or of Four Shillings in the Pound for one Year shall be laid upon Land to pay off the Principal, and so free the Kingdom from paying the Interest of it by the Nine Pence till that time secured, which done, and all Persons in such Credit concerned being thereby assured of a time certain when they may (if they will) see their Money in specie again, there will be no room left to doubt but that this sort of Credit will most certainly do, and answer Two Millions, if so setled by Parliament as above in this Paper Proposed. Thomas Neale. *A Proposal for Raising a Million on a Fund of Interest* . . . and *A Proposal for Raising Two Millions* (1694)

3 Dr Hugh Chamberlen   Land Banks

Dr Hugh Chamberlen (c 1634–1720), physician to Charles II; his fame as a male midwife arose out of the family secret of the midwifery forceps. He was the most persistent of the land bank promoters and his reasoning may be taken as typical of the species. An expansion of credit was necessary for the promotion of trade; land was the foundation of all credit and should be utilised to float bills of credit, which would be superior to money in many respects. To have even a remote chance of success, Chamberlen would have had to secure the privilege of legal tender for his bills, which was out of the question, and without such a privilege it would have proved impossible to liquidate mortgage assets to meet any short-term necessity for redeeming the bills in cash.

The great Scarcity of Money, together with the danger of receiving so much False, and the uncertain Rates of Guineas, makes the People willing to receive their Debts in Bank-Bills, or Goldsmith's Notes, rather than Money in Specie; by which means Credit, securely Founded, may be the easier brought into use: And this hath encouraged several to propose the Establishing of Banks, the Motion of which, having met with so general Approbation, it is hoped that Dr. Chamberlain's Proposals shall not fail of as good Encouragement; especially since he was the First Promoter of Banks upon Annual Incomes, to his great Expence both of Money, Time and Pains; and also because his Proposals offer Greater Advantages, both

c

to the Nation in general, and Subscribers in particular, than any others whatsoever; and for that the Fund (by him proposed) in all respects is the Best and Safest: And, tho' all the Banks that are now Erecting, should flourish together, yet the Nation may, nay must, thrive the better; and indeed it will be a certain and effectual means to lower the interest of Money, and bring the Usurers and Money'd Men to more conscionable Terms, and yet without damage to themselves, as it may be ordered. Thus may things be managed to the mutual Benefit, both of those whose Fortunes lye in Land, and those who have theirs in Money: Whereas at present, tho' the Landed-Man be never so willing to sell his Estate to pay his Debts, yet because he cannot get the Money, the Merciless Money'd Man takes the Advantage of him, seizeth his Estate, imprisoneth his Person, forecloseth the Equity of Redemption, and leaves the miserable Landed-Man's Family to starve, and many Traders to suffer Loss, to whom he was indebted: And what, except killing the Man, can our Enemies the French do more? This Proposal of Credit on Land, will heal the aforesaid Evils, and fully Answer all our present Necessities; there being now no other way left that is possible to be found out. For the present Royal Bank refuses to supply Mortgagers, tho' they offer'd it in their Advertisements; and yet at the same time endeavour to engross all the Money in the Nation to themselves; which makes the other Money'd Men to put the more extravagant value on what they have; and this looks as if they had all combined together to undermine the Landed-Men, and seiz their Estates; and that this is carrying on, may be proved by there being at this instant near Two hundred Bills for foreclosing the Equity of Redemption. It is the Interest of Landed-Men therefore, and the only Remedy left, nay it is absolutely necessary for the better support of their Families, and the preservation of the Value of their Lands, to agree together with one Consent, and in their Defence to run Counter to the Designs of all unfair Dealers in Money, and to shake off their Slavery by engaging their Lands to make good all Bills and Tickets of

Credit that shall be given out thereupon; and this will make Lands perform the Use of Money, as well as Gold and Silver when Coined. All Shopkeepers, and others whatsoever, may more safely take them in payment, than the present Royal Bank, or Goldsmith's Notes; these having no other Fund to make them good but their bare Reputation, which is nothing at all; for if they Break, it is lost; if Dye, it is an hazard; but the Land is the best and certainest Security the World can give: And by this Means the Interest of Money will be lower'd, the Landed-Man saved from Ruine, and Enabled to pay his Debts, and spend more freely, to the great Encouragement of Trade: For as the Case now stands, all our Land and Staple Commodities dance Attendance on Money, made of a Foreign Commodity, and of which we can therefore have no certainty: for that the Industry, Cunning, or Caprice of Foreign Princes and Merchants may not only debar its Entrance, but draw away what we are already possess'd of, which makes Landed-Men pay £8 or £10 per Cent. for all Moneys and Foreign Commodities, as Silk, Linnen, and Spices; Whereas the Merchant gives but £3 or £4 per Cent. for Land and its Product, as Wool, Corn, &c. So that by degrees the Landed-Men are eaten out of their Estates, for want of having the Ballance kept even between Interest of Money, and Rents of Land. But when once our Land shall be thus by Bills or Tickets of Credit, turn'd into the Nature of Money, it may wait on Commodities, and serve all our Occasions full as well as Money. Land-Banks have this Prerogative over all other Banks, viz. We are sure none but English shall have the immediate benefit of them, without any disobliging Exclusive Clauses. Whereas we can have no Certainty that the Royal Bank of England doth not belong intirely to Foreigners; 'tis sure a good part of it doth. Further, The Fund of Land can never be imbezled, nor transported; but 'tis possible all the Fund of Money'd Banks may be drawn out to Holland, France, or Constantinople, and nothing left to England, but an *Hinc illa Lachryma.*

The Methods and Practices of Banks have fully discovered

the Advantages and Benefits of the use of Credit, so that all that is necessary to be insisted upon, is to recommend This to the Favour of the Nation, by shewing wherein it excells all the rest; that it is more safe, and therefore best, for all Persons to accept the Bills hence issued, tho' upon an hundred years Rent, because there is no difference in the use of those to the Dealers in them, from such as are issued upon ten years.

For these Reasons therefore, and the following, the Doctor's Land-Bank ought to have the Preference. Because,

1. There are more Landed-Men in the Nation than Money'd-Men.
2. There is a greater Value of Land than there is of Money.
3. There is no Money but what is the Product of this Land.
4. The Landed-Men have chiefly contributed to the Support of this War.
5. The Landed-Men are the most that want Money, and the least esteemed and considered.
6. The Land doth yearly yield its increase, for our Support, but Commodities perish in their use.
7. The Land remains a sure Fund, when Money or Commodities are carried away, or worn out.

We will now show wherein This Excells all the rest. As,

1. Because whatever Money you deposit, you may have Bills, or Tickets of Credit, with Interest at – – per Cent. per diem for the same.
2. It furnisheth Landed-Men with double the Value of their Estates in Credit, sufficient not only to pay off all their Debts and Mortgages, and clear their Titles, but likewise to purchase so much more, or to improve the same by building or otherwise: Whereas no other Bank will supply them with the full value of their Estate.
3. It affords you likewise a Stock to manage in Trade, which at Ten per Cent. does not only pay your Annuity, but gives you twice as much clear gain; by which returns you can the better make good the Bills.
4. It will enable the Society to erect, and carry on, the so much

desired Fishing Trade, or any other that the Subscribers shall think fit.

5. It will lower the Interest of Money, more than any other Bank, and more Effectually than by the Restraint of Laws.

The next is, that it's as safe to accept Bills secured by one Hundred Years Rent, as those by Ten, or on demand, and no difference to the Dealers in them for first.

1. No Bank can find Money for all their Credit, if call'd in at once; if there be a Fund to make it good some time or other 'tis sufficient, and more than in any of the present Banks besides the Doctor's; therefore this Bank of Land can no more be disliked for that reason than any other; and 'tis very unreasonable to require, his Bank should discharge all at once, which is not expected from others. And these Bills may as well pass in the mean time as any other; for most of the Credit of the Banks abroad hath passed above one Hundred Years, without drawing out any Money, and most of our Lands has yielded Rent very much longer: These joyned make this Bank; for One Hundred Years Rent paid can fully satisfy One Hundred Years Credit of like value.

2. The sole end of giving out Bills is to supply the Money not now to be had in England: If then an Estate be Mortgaged for One Hundred Years purchase, and Bills given out thereupon, and if all be return'd at Ten Years end, and then the same, or another Estate be Mortgaged for Ten Years more, and so on to One Hundred or One Thousand Years, still the Bills are passing in the Nation as Money, and are the same in Effect. Now in the Doctor's you have above double your Estate in Bills presently, as Estates are now valued, which is the encouragement, and makes you amends for tying your Estate so long as One Hundred Years: In the other Bank you can have but two Thirds of the present value of your Estate, which does but just ease you for the present, by paying off the Mortgages, but still leaves you as much in debt to the Bank, tho' with smaller Interest. And as you pay the Bills away, it answers your ends; for after your wants are

supplyed, what matter is it to you, whether that Bill you have payd away be cancelled Ten Years or one Hundred Years hence? And it is all one to the Dealers, when they know it is well secur'd at last, and can Trade with them the while, and that the Number of these Bills will be limitted to the Fund, being under a severe check by the Directors, and will all be certainly bought up, so that the Nation will not loose. Whereas, the Bills of the other Banks are not limitted, but may abundantly exceed their Fund: And therein lies the secret gain to themselves, but apparent danger of loss hereafter to the Nation.

3. There will be a great Number of Subscribers engaged, whose Lands lye scattered in all parts of England, and these will agree to receive the said Bills in all payments of Rents, and Fines from their Tenants, and all other Persons they Deal with: and likewise will purchase Commodities of all such Tradesmen and Merchants, that will accept them, before any other.

4. There will be a great Number of Traders and Merchants, who will find it their Interest by engaging so many Subscribers to be their Customers, to take these Bills and Tickets for their Goods, so that all may be Supply'd by them, with what Necessarys they shall want, as well as for ready Money; which will save the trouble of telling, as well as fear of taking bad Money.

5. There will be a great Summ of ready Money deposited in the Bank to exchange (if there be occasion) Tickets, or Bills; so that no Person need scruple to take them, when he can turn them into Money at any time: And this will be a means to prevent long Accounts, and all the inconveniences of Law-suits that usually attend them; and a sufficient Encouragement for the Trader to take the Bills or Tickets, and discharge the Gentleman or Debtor: His business being afterwards only with the Bank, which is well secured by the Fund of Land that is tyed to make all good, which it effectually does by the annual payment into the Bank where they

are cancel'd: I hope here is enough said of the following Proposal, to encourage Landed Men to Subscribe, and to promote the general Currency of the Bills, to the perfecting of this great and good Undertaking.

It is Proposed by Dr. Hugh Chamberlain, That every Freeholder, who will, for a General, so well as for his own Private Good, subscribe One hundred and fifty Pound per Annum, for One hundred and fifty Years, (unless sooner Discharged) to secure the Payment of One hundred Pound per Annum, only for One hundred Years (the first Rent not Commencing till two or three Years after the Subscription) and will further Exchange One Thousand Pound in Gold or Silver, current Money of this Kingdom, into this Societies Bills, payable on Demand, at the several Times, and in such Proportions as is hereafter mentioned: That is to say,

£400 down,	£1,000	
		At the same respective
£300 at a years end,	£1,100	
Shall		Times in the said
£200 at two years end,	£1,200	
Receive		Bills, or Current Credit.
£100 at three years end,	£1,300	

And £1,400 more in the same Credit, at Four years end, from the time of the First Payment.

And he shall have also £3,000 viz. The Thousand Pound he paid in Money, and Two Thousand Pound in like current Credit, paid into a Joynt Stock of Trade for his own particular Advantage, to be managed by Persons chosen by the Subscribers; which Stock shall not be Alienable, nor Transferable, but together with his said Estate, and will (if it should yield but Five per Cent. per Annum, tho' much more may reasonably be expected) not only pay the Rent Reserved, but also make good Defective Titles, put Money yearly into his Purse; and, being added to the Five Thousand Pound advanced to him in manner aforesaid, will be a very large clear Gain; and all this for nothing in effect, more than a Collateral Security of One

hundred and fifty Pounds per Annum in Lands. And the like
Manner and Proportion will be observed for any greater or
lesser Yearly Payment subscribed.

And, for preventing all manner of Loss and Hazard to the
Subscribers, both Freeholders and Traders, Trustees shall be
appointed at first, to whom the Estates shall be Convey'd;
and also Directors (with good Salaries, and without Interest in
the Profit) shall be Elected to take Care, that no Credit be
issued without a sufficient Fund first setled, or Money equivalent thereto paid in . . . Dr Hugh Chamberlen. *A Proposal By
Dr Hugh Chamberlain* [sic] *in Essex Street, for a Bank of Secure
Current Credit To Be Founded upon Land* . . . (1695)

4 The Charter of the Bank of England

The Charter of 27 July 1694 has been described as a turgid
document. The abstract reproduced below certainly shows
that those responsible for it were more concerned with the
legal restraint of the new institution than with clearly setting
out the nature of its functions and the extent of its powers.
In this it merely reflected the Tunnage Act from which it
arose, after various articles relating to the imposition of
taxes had been recited. In return for 'engrafting' the tallies
in 1697 the Bank's Charter had been extended for another
five years, to 1711, and the establishment of any more Banks
was prohibited. A loophole in the Act of 1697 allowed the
company of the Mine Adventurers to issue its own notes
between 1704 and 1708, so that the Bank of England's
complete monopoly of joint-stock banking actually dates
from 1709. In 1713, after another loan to the government,
the Charter was continued until 1743, while in 1716 the
Bank was exempted from the Usury Laws. Two further
renewals came in 1764 and 1781.

Whereas by an Act, Intituled, An Act for Granting to Their
Majesties several Rates and Duties upon Tunnage, &c. It is

Enacted, That for four years, from the first of June 1694 there shall be paid upon the Tunnage of all Vessels, wherein any Goods shall be Imported from any the Countries in the Act named, or Coast-wise, from Port to Port in England, the several Rates in the Act mentioned, and certain Additional Duties of Excise, on Beer, Ale, and other Liquors. And that Weekly, on every Wednesday, if not an Holy-Day, and if it be, the next day not an Holy-Day, all the Monies arising by the said Rates shall be paid into the Exchequer.

And that Yearly, beginning from the first of June 1694, the Sum of £140,000 arising out of the said Duties and Rates (in Case the Weekly Payments extend thereunto) shall be the Yearly Fund, (and if they do not extend thereunto) then the said Weekly Payments, so far as they will extend, shall be part of the Yearly Fund: And in Case the said Duties and Rates shall be so low, as that within any one Year the Weekly Payment shall not amount to £140,000 or be sufficient to answer the Annuities by the Act intended; in such Case, the Commissioners of the Treasury are strictly enjoyned, without any Warrant from the King, to make good such Deficiency, out of any Treasure or Revenue of the Crown (not appropriated) Yearly to discharge the said Annuities.

And that it should be Lawful for Their Majesties, to Commissionate any number of Persons to receive such Subscriptions as should be made before the first of August next, by any Natives or Foreigners, or Corporations, towards paying, into the Exchequer, the Sum of £1,200,000 and that the Yearly Sum of £100,000 shall be Appropriated to such Subscribers.

And that the said Weekly Payments, as they come in, shall be divided into 3/7 parts, and 2/7 parts, which 5/7 parts, shall be Appropriated to the paying of the said £100,000 per Annum, and shall be paid as the same comes into the Exchequer, to the use of such Subscribers.

And that the King may appoint how the said £1,200,000 and the said £100,000 per Annum, shall be Assignable; and may Incorporate such Subscribers by the Name of the Governour and Company of the Bank of England, subject to the Condition of Redemption.

And if £1,200,000 or a Moiety, or greater part thereof, be not paid into the Exchequer, by the first of January 1694, then the Subscribers shall have only after the Rate of 8 per Cent. per Ann. And the Commissioners of the Treasury are required without any Warrant from the King to pay the said £100,000 per Annum to the Subscribers.

And that no person or Corporation shall Subscribe more than £20,000 and every Subscriber, at the time of his Subscribing, shall pay down 1/4 of his Subscription, and in Default thereof, such Subscription shall be void; that the Residue of the Subscriptions shall be paid into the Exchequer, before the first of January; and in Default thereof, the first fourth part shall be Forfeit; and that none before the first of July shall write above £10,000.

Provided if £1,200,000 or a Moiety thereof be not subscribed by the first of August then the Powers for Erecting a Corporation shall cease: And in such Case, so much of the £100,000 as shall belong to the Subscribers may be assignable; and that the Monies payable by the Act to any Person, shall not be Chargeable with any Duties or Impositions, as by the said Act may appear.

And whereas, Their Majesties by Commission under the Great Seal, did authorize divers Commissioners therein named to take such Subscriptions as should be made before the first of August pursuant to the said Act; and therein did promise, that in case £1,200,000 or a Moiety were subscribed before the said first of August, that His Majesty immediately after the said Day, or as soon as £1,200,000 should be subscribed, which should first happen, would incorporate the Subscribers by the name aforesaid, and did declare, that the whole Sum subscribed and paid, should be the Capital Stock; and that all the Subscribers should have an Interest therein, and in the said £100,000 per annum which Interest should be assignable, so as such Assignments be Entred and Registered, as in the said

Commission is directed, as by the same may more fully appear.

And Whereas, it appears by Duplicates transmitted into the Exchequer, under the Hands and Seals of Five or more of the Commissioners, that the Sum of – – hath been subscribed, and the first fourth part thereof paid to them on, or before the – – day of – – last by – –.

And Whereas, it also appears by the entries of several Assignments, made in the Auditors office, that – – are by mean Assignments, severally intituled to the Subscriptions, made by the said – – Their Majesties in pursuance of the Powers in the said Act do appoint, that the said – – and all and every other Persons, Natives, and Foreigners, and Bodies Politick, who over and besides the Persons before-named, have subscribed any Sum of Money towards the Sum of – – and paid the fourth part thereof upon their Subscriptions, and who are now living and have not assigned, and all the Heirs and Successors of any the Original Subscribers now dead, who have not assigned in their life, and the Heirs and Successors of the Assigns now dead, who did not in their life assign; and all Persons, Natives, or Foreigners, or Bodies Politick, who either as Original Subscribers, and not having parted with their Interests, or as Heirs, Successors, or Assigns, or by other lawful Title, have or shall have any Interest in the said Capital Stock, or Yearly Fund, so long as they have any Interest therein, shall be, and be called one Body Politick, &c. by the name of The Governour and Company of the Bank of England.

That by the name they shall have perpetual Succession, and a Common Seal, and be capable to purchase and hold Lands and Tenements, and Goods, and Chattels (not restrained by the Act) and to grant or dispose the same.

And shall sue and be sued, and do all other matters and things, that to them appertains, subject nevertheless to the Condition of Redemption in the Act mentioned, and to all other the Conditions and Clauses therein.

That all Persons having any Interest in the said Capital Stock, or Yearly Fund, as Original Subscribers, or by Assignments, or as Heirs, &c. shall be, and be esteemed members of the said Corporation, and be admitted into the same without Charge.

That the aforesaid Sum of – – subscribed as aforesaid, shall be, and be called the Capital Stock of the said Corporation, and that all Persons, their Heirs, Successors, and Assigns, in proportion to the Sums by them respectively subscribed, shall have an Interest in the said Capital Stock, and Yearly Fund of £100,000.

That the Commissioners of the Treasury now, and for the time being, without any Warrant from the King, do direct their Warrants and Orders for Payment of the Yearly Sum of – – to the said Corporation and their Successors for ever, by and out of the 5/7 parts of the Money, arising by the Duties granted by the said Act, (Subject nevertheless to the Payment of the Issues, Fines, and Debts upon Judgment against the Corporation) the first Year to be reckoned from the first of June 1694.

That the Commissioners of the Treasury, and the Officers of the Exchequer, do pay the said 5/7 parts of the Monies arising by the said Duties, or so much of it as shall be sufficient for this purpose to the said Governour and Company, and their Successors, by Weekly Payments or otherwise, as the same shall come into the Exchequer, in satisfaction of the said Yearly sum of – –.

And in case 5/7 parts of the said Weekly Payments intended to be the said Yearly Fund, shall not amount to so much as the said Yearly Sum of – – which is the Annual Fund Established for the said Corporation, then Their Majesties Grant and Agree with the said Corporation, that 5/7 parts of the said Weekly Payments, so far as the same will extend shall be part of the Yearly Sum of – –.

And if the said Duties shall at any time appear to be so deficient, as that within any one Year to be reckoned from the said First of June 5/7 parts of the Weekly Payments on the said Duties shall not amount to so much as – – within the same

Year: Then the Commissioners of the Treasury, without other Warrant from the King, shall make good every such deficiency, by paying so much of any Treasure of the King's (not appropriated by Parliament) toward the Payment of the said Yearly Fund of – – as (together with 5/7 part of the Moneys, paid into the Exchequer for the said Duties) shall compleatly pay off the said Yearly Fund of – – according to the meaning of the said Act.

That for the better ordering the Affairs of the Corporation, and for a succession of Persons to be Governor, Deputy, and Directors thereof, there shall be for ever a Governor, Deputy, and 24 Directors, who, or any 13, or more of them (whereof the Governor or Deputy be one) shall be, and be called a Court of Directors, for the ordering the Affairs of the said Corporation with such Powers as are hereafter mentioned.

That – – (who is chosen for this purpose by a Majority of the Subscribers having each £500 Stock) be the first Governor, and – – who is chosen in like manner, be the first Deputy-Governor, and – – who are chosen in like manner, be the first Directors of the said Corporation.

That the said Governor, Deputy, and Directors, shall continue in their Offices till the 25th of March, 1696, and till others be chosen and sworn, unless any of them shall dye, or be removed, as is after-mentioned.

That all the Members of the Corporation may meet for the Choice of their Governor, Deputy, and Directors, and for the making By-Laws for the Corporation, or other their Affairs (publick Notice being affixed at the Royal Exchange Two days at least before the said Meeting).

That all the Members, or so many as meet, shall be called a General Court, which shall assemble in manner hereafter mentioned.

That all succeeding Governors, Deputies, and Directors, after the 25th of March 1696 shall be Yearly chosen forever between the 25th of March and the 25th of April in each Year, by the Majority of the Members, having each £500 Stock, who shall be personally present, and each have One Vote and no more; which Governor, Deputy, and Directors, shall continue in their Offices for one Year, and till others be chosen and sworn.

And in case of the Death, Avoidance, or Removal of the Governor, Deputy, or Directors, the Survivor of them, or the Majority of those in Office, may Elect other Persons as aforesaid.

That every Deputy in the Absence of the Governor shall have the same power as a Governor.

That no Person shall be an Elector for the Choice of Governor, Deputy, or Directors, or making of By-Laws, or in any other the Affairs of the Corporation, who shall not have in his own Right, and not in Trust, £500 Stock; and also take the Oath hereafter mentioned, if required, viz. I A. B. do swear, That the Sum of £500 or more of the Capital Stock of the Governor and Company of the Bank &c. doth at this time belong to me in my own Right, and not in Trust.

That no Member in any Election, or other Business of the Corporation, shall have more than one Vote.

Provided that any Quaker who shall have £500 Stock, and shall (if required) sign the following Declaration; viz. I A. B. Do solemnly declare in the Presence of God, That the Sum of £500 or more, of the Capital Stock of the Governor and Company of the Bank, &c. at this time belongs to me in my own Right and not in Trust, SHALL HAVE A VOTE AT ANY GENERAL COURT.

That the Governor or Deputy, or any two of the Directors, do administer the said Oath and Declaration.

That no Person shall be Governor, unless he be a Natural-born, or Naturalised Subject, and shall then have in his own Right £4,000 Stock.

That none shall be chosen Deputy, unless at such time he be a Natural-born, or Naturalised Subject, and shall then have in his own Right £3,000 Stock.

That none be chosen a Director, who shall not be a Natural-born, or Naturalised Subject, and shall then have in his own Right £2,000 Stock.

That no Governor, Deputy, or Director, shall continue in their Offices longer than the continuance of their respective Stocks in their own Rights; but upon reducing their Stocks to any lesser Sum than as aforesaid, their respective Offices shall determine, and others be chosen in the Places by a General Court.

Provided that the said – – appointed to be the first Governor, or any hereafter chosen into the said Office, shall not execute the said Office, until he hath taken the Oaths appointed to be taken by the Act, made for Abrogating the Oaths of Supremacy and Allegiance; and, until he hath taken the Oath following, viz. I A. B. do swear, That the Summ of £4,000 of the Capital Stock of the Governor and Company, &c. doth at this time belong to me in my own Right, and not in Trust: And another Oath, viz. I A. B. do swear, That I will to the utmost of my Power, support the Fellowship of the Governor and Company of the Bank, &c. and that in the Execution of the said Office, I will honestly demean myself according to the best of my Skill.

Which Oaths, to the first Governor, may be administered by the Lord Keeper, or the Chief Baron; and to any future Governor, by the Lord Chancellor, or Lord Keeper, or by the Chancellor, or Chief Baron of the Exchequer, or by the last preceeding Governor, or Deputy, or (in case a Deputy be sworn) by such a Deputy, who are empowered to administer the same.

Provided that the said – – appointed the first Deputy, or any hereafter in that Office, shall not execute the same till he hath taken the like Oaths (mutatis mutandis): Which Oaths, to the first Deputy shall be administered by the Lord Keeper, or Chancellor of the Exchequer, or Chief Baron of the Exchequer, or by the first Governor after he is sworn: And to any future Deputy may be administered by the Lord Chancellor or Keeper, or the Chancellor or Chief Baron of the Exchequer, or by the preceding Governor, or Deputy, who are empowered to administer the same.

Provided that none of the said – – hereby appointed the first 24 Directors, or any hereafter, in that Office shall execute the same until they have taken the Oath mentioned in the Act for abrogating the Oaths of Allegiance, &c. and until they have taken the Oath following; viz. I A. B. do swear that the Sum of £2,000 of the Stock of the Governor and Company of &c. doth at this time belong to me in my own Right and not in Trust.

And another Oath, viz. I A. B. do swear, That in the Office of a Director I will be indifferent to all Persons, and give my best advice for the support of the said Corporation, and in the said Office honestly demean myself to the best of my Skill.

Which Oaths to the first Directors shall be administered by the Lord Keeper, Chancellor of the Exchequer, or Chief Baron, or by the First Governor, or Deputy-Governor sworn, as aforesaid: And the said Oaths, to any future Director, shall be administered by the said Chancellor or Lord Keeper, Chancellor, or Chief Baron of the Exchequer, or by a sworn Governor or Deputy.

That all the other Members having each £500 Stock before they shall give any Vote in ary General Court, shall take the said Oaths appointed by the Act for Abrogating the Oaths of Allegiance, &c. before the Governor, or Deputy, for the time being, who are required to administer the same, and also this Oath, viz. I A. B. do swear, That I will be faithful to the Governor and Company of the Bank, &c. and in all General Courts, according to the best of my Skill, give my assistance for support of the said Corporation.

Provided that any Quakers having £500 Stock before they shall Vote in any General Court, shall before the Governor, or Deputy, solemnly promise and declare in the Presence of God, in Words to the same Effect, with the Oath last mentioned, and shall severally Subscribe the same, together with the Declaration appointed by the Act for exempting Their Majesties

Protestant Subjects, Dissenting from the Church of England, from the Penalties of certain Laws: Which Declarations and Subscriptions the Governor and Deputy are empowered to administer.

That the Court of Directors shall have Power to give the following Oath to the Servants of the Corporation for due Execution of their Places; viz. I A. B. being Elected Treasurer of the said Corporation, do swear, That I will be true and faithful to them, and will faithfully Execute the said Office to the utmost of my Skill. And the like Oaths to other Officers.

And in case any Person Elected Governor, Deputy-Governor, or Director, shall neglect or refuse for Ten Days to take the Oaths appointed, the Place of all such Persons shall be void, and others shall be chosen in their Places by a General Court.

That no Dividend shall be made, save out of the Interest, or Produce, arising out of the Capital Stock; or by such dealing, buying or selling, as are allowed by the Act, until Redemption by Parliament of the Yearly Fund: And that no Dividend be made without Consent of a General Court.

And that the Governor, or in his Absence, the Deputy, upon notice to be given, as aforesaid shall summon Four General Courts, at least every Year; One in September, another in December, another in April, and another in July.

And if there be failure of holding a General Court in any of the said Months, by default of the Governor or Deputy, any Three or more of the Directors shall call a General Court, which shall be holden in the Month next after the Month in which the same should have been holden.

And that the Governor, or, in his Absence, the Deputy-Governor upon Demand to be made by any Nine, or more of the Members, having £500 or more Stock, shall within Ten Days, after Demand, summon a General Court to be held.

And in default of the Governor or Deputy-Governor, it shall be lawful for the said Nine or more Members, having each £500 Stock, upon Ten Days Notice in Writing, to be fixed on the Royal Exchange, to summon a General Court, and to do any

D

Business of the Corporation, and to hear and debate any Complaint made against any Governor, Deputy-Governor, or Directors, for Mismanagement: And if such Governor, Deputy-Governor, and Directors, shall not clear him or themselves to Satisfaction of the General Court; then within Ten Days another General Court shall be called finally to determine the same, who may remove the Governor, Deputy-Governor, and Directors for such Misdemeanors, and Elect others in their rooms in the same manner as before directed.

And where any Governor, Deputy, or Director shall die, or be removed, or his Office be void, the Members in a General Court, qualified as aforesaid, may Elect any other Member, qualified as aforesaid into their Places, who shall continue therein to the next usual Election, and until others be chosen and sworn.

That the Governor, Deputy-Governor, and Directors for the time being, or any Thirteen or more of them, (the Governor or Deputy-Governor being always one) from time to time may meet at any convenient Place or Places, for Management of their Affairs, and hold Courts of Directors for the purposes aforesaid, and summon General Courts as often as they see cause.

That the Governor, Deputy-Governor, and Directors, or the Major part, (The Governor or Deputy-Governor being one) shall Act by such Bye-Laws as shall be made by the General Court; and where the same shall be wanting, they shall direct and manage all Affairs of the Corporation in borrowing and receiving Monies, and giving securities under the Common Seal, and in their dealing in Bills of Exchange, Buying or Selling Bullion, Gold or Silver, or selling Goods deposited for Money lent, and in selling Goods, being the produce of Lands purchased, or in lending any Monies, and taking securities for the same; and to chuse Servants, and allow them reasonable Salaries, and to remove them if they see cause, and generally to act and do in all matters, which by the Act may be done, which they shall judge necessary for the well ordering and managing the Corporation, and to enjoy and execute all Powers, &c. as fully as if done by the Governor and Company of the Bank, or by the General Court, subject to the Clauses and Restrictions, &c. in the Act.

And Their Majesties give Power to all and every Members, qualified for Electors at a General Court by Majority of Votes, to make By-Laws for the Corporation, and imposing Mulcts and Fines, (not repugnant to the Laws of the Land) so as they be confirmed according to the Statute, which Fines shall be received and recovered to the Use of the Governor and Company, without any Account to be rendered to Their Majesties, and to allow Salaries to the Governor, Deputy, and Directors.

That the first General Court shall be holden within Twenty eight Days after the Date of this Charter.

And for ascertaining how the Capital Stock and Yearly Fund of £10,000 shall be assignable and assigned, Their Majesties direct there be constantly kept in the Office of the Company, a Book wherein all Assignments shall be entered: And Their Majesties (pursuant to the Powers in the Act) direct that the Method of making all Assignments of the Capital Stock, or any Part, shall be by an Entry in the said Book, Signed by the Party Assigning in the Words following, viz. Memorandum, That I A. B. the − − day of − − in the Year of our Lord − − do Assign − − of my Interest in the Capital Stock of the Governor, and Company, &c. and the benefit arising unto − − his Heirs, &c. Witness my Hand − − Or in case the Person be not personally present, then by an Entry signed by some Persons authorized by Letter of Attorney, or Writing under Seal in the words following, viz. Memorandum, I A. B. this − − day of − − in the Year of − − By Virtue of a Letter of Attorney or Authority, under the Hand and Seal of − − Dated the − − do in the name, and on the behalf of the said − − Assign − − of the Interest and Share of the said − − in the Capital Stock of the Governor and Company, &c. unto − − his Heirs and Assigns, Witness my hand − − under which transfer the Person or Persons, or Bodies Politick, to whom the Assignment is made, or some by them lawfully authorized shall sign his name, attesting his acceptance thereof.

And that the Entry so signed, and no other way shall be the method of transferring the Interest in the Capital Stock, and such transfer shall be good, and convey the Interest of the Party transferring.

Provided, That any Person having Stock may dispose thereof by Will, attested by Three or more Witnesses; however such Devisee shall not transfer, or be entituled to receive any Dividend, till entry of so much of the Will, as relates to the said Stock, be made in the Books of the Corporation.

Their Majesties appoint, that the Governor, or in his absence the Deputy-Governor, shall not have any Vote, but only where there is an Equality of Votes.

Provided, That all Matters, which the Governor, Deputy-Governor, or Directors, shall order as aforesaid to be done by Sub-Committees, or others appointed under them, shall (by Vertue of such Order) be done by such Sub-Committees or others so appointed.

And Their Majesties grant, that this Charter, or the Inrollment thereof, shall in all things be valid in the Law, according to the true intent of the same, and be taken in the most beneficial sense, for the best advantage of the Company in all Courts of Record or elsewhere, notwithstanding any mis-recital, defect, &c.

And that this Charter shall be Made and Sealed without Fine or Fee, Great or Small, to be paid Their Majesties in their Hanaper or elsewhere.

And their Majesties promise to grant such further and other Powers, &c. as shall be reasonably advised by the Counsel learned of the said Governor and Company, to be approved by the Attorney or Sollicitor-General. In Witness &c.

FINIS

An Abstract of the Charter to the Governour and Company of the Bank of England, 27th July 1694

5 William Paterson   The Bank and its Critics

The Scot who founded the Bank of England, William
Paterson (1658–1719) was a merchant of considerable fortune
and influence in the City by the 1690s. After putting forward
the first Bank proposals in 1691, together with Michael
Godfrey and other merchants, he was the principal negotiator
down to its foundation when he was appointed a Director.
Paterson severed his connection with the Bank in 1695 after
differences with his colleagues. Although the Bank was his
great achievement, he spent much of his life perfecting his
ill-fated scheme to plant a colony in Darien. A staunch
supporter of the union of England and Scotland, Paterson
was largely responsible for those articles of the treaty relating
to trade and finance and, as a result of his controversy with
John Law in 1705, he helped prevent the adoption of an
inconvertible paper currency in Scotland.

The want of a Bank, or publick Fund, for the convenience
and security of great Payments, and the better to facilitate the
circulation of Money, in and about this great and oppulent
City, hath in our time, among other Inconveniencies, occasioned
much unnecessary Credit, to the loss of several Millions, by
which Trade hath been exceedingly discourag'd and obstructed:
This, together with the height of Interest or Forbearance of
Money, which for some time past hath born no manner of
proportion to that of our Rival Neighbors, and for which no
tolerable Reason could ever be given either in Notion or Practice,
considering the Riches and Trade of England, unless it were
the want of publick Funds; by which the Effects of the Nation,
in some sort, might be disposed to answer the Use, and do the
Office of Money, and become more useful to the Trade and
Improvements thereof.

These, and such as these, were the Causes that the Nature and
Use of Banks and Publick Funds; have been the Discourse and
Expectation of many Years; but all this while our more refined

Politicians assured us, that we must never think of setling Banks in England without a Commonwealth; And this Notion became so universal, that it was a matter of derision, for any one to seem to be of a contrary opinion. Thus the modish vein, of Farce and Ridicule, so prevalent over the Morality, Virtue, and Reason of our Times, had like to have deprived us of this.

But the notion of Banks and Publick Funds were entertained by some mercurial Heads, who finding the main Objection against them in England to be, the danger of Violence from the Prince, they therefore invented certain imaginary Banks and Funds, which they designed to settle far enough from the Prince's reach, or any bodies else. The first Design of this nature was, to turn a Lumbard into a Bank, and to that end they cried down the use of Gold and Silver, and up that of other Materials in lieu thereof; but when they found the world very unwilling to leave their old way without a better Reason, or something more enticing, they run from their new Mistake to an old one, which was, That the Stamp or Denomination gives or adds to the value of Money. With this they resolved to run counter to all Mankind; yea, they would anticipate Ages, and attract, or rather imagine, inestimable Value from innumerable Years to come; all which was to be crammed down Mens Throats as a Punishment of their Infidelity, who could not believe a Lumbard to be a Bank; and here was occasion for the power of an Act of Parliament at least, to conjure every Man's Imagination into the latitude of theirs. Thus we see the Genius of some of our Countrymen are as vastly above and beyond, as others are below and beside, the practice of extraordinary things.

Thus between the new-acquir'd Maxims of our modern Politicians on the one hand, and the incomprehensible Notions conceived on the other, it became very scandalous to countenance or; espouse any thing of a Proposal relating to a Bank; but when this War begun, the Credit of the Nation was low, and the Wits on both sides, found no better nor honester way to supply the Necessities of the Government, than by enhauncing the Price and Interest of Money; the effect of which was, that the Government was obliged to pay from double to treble, or higher Interest: The Disease growing daily worse, Men were tempted to draw their Effects from Trade and Improvements, and found the best and securest Gain in making Merchandise of the Government and Nation.

For remedy of which it was proposed some years ago, That a publick transferrable Fund of Interest should be established by Parliament and made convenient for the Receipts and Payments, in and about the Cities of London and Westminster, and to constitute a Society of Money'd Men for the government thereof, who should be induced by their Interest, to exchange for Money, the Assignments upon the Fund, at every demand. In this manner it was proposed, that the constitution of this Fund, should in the practise answer, the End of a publick transferable Fund of Interest, of a Bank, and of a publick Lumbard at once, and a good part of the Effects of the Nation, might thereby be rendered useful to the Trade and Business thereof, which would of course, have lower'd the Interest of Money, and prevented the drawing thereof, from the Countries and places remote from Trade. But no sooner was this Proposal stated by a Society of considerable Persons, but the notion of Currency was started, and carried so far before it was well perceived or understood by some, that it then proved of pernicious consequence, to the success of this Undertaking: Some understood it only as a Convenience, others, as it seems, it was at the bottom intended, a downright Force, the effects of which would have been, to turn the Stomachs of Mankind against it, Coertion being of sufficient force, to marr a good thing of this nature, but never to mend a bad one.

All this while the very Name of a Bank or Corporation was avoided, tho' the Nature of both was intended, the Proposers thinking it prudent, that a Design of this nature, should have as easie and insensible a beginning as possible, to prevent, or at least gradually to soften and remove, the Prejudices and bad Impressions, commonly conceived in the Minds of Men against things of this kind, before they are understood: but that sort of People, who ought, and in whose power it was, to encourage this Undertaking, could in no ways understand it, which put the Proposers, upon heightening the Proposal for Interest, and upon particular Undertakings, for the Sum proposed, which at several times, and upon divers occasions, produced certain narrow and sinister Designs, no way becoming so noble and universal a Work as this.

As the Proposers found great discouragement from one sort of Men, who could by no means reconcile this Proposal with their own Apprehensions, and the old Norman way of borrowing Money; so others seem'd to understand it too much, and would only have it proposed at four, or four and an half per Cent. whereof three per Cent. to be allowed to the Fund, and the remainder for those who should furnish Money to circulate the same, for otherwise, say they, it will quite and clean discourage Land, for every body will be for disposing their Money upon so convenient, clear, and secure an Interest, rather than to expect something more with Trouble and Uncertainties; but afterwards it was found convenient to put it to hazard, and expose so much of the nature of the thing, and its constitution, as was needful to have it espoused in Parliament.

But though the gilded name of a Bank, and the popular one of a Corporation, became more formidable to the Senses of a sort of People who wanted the Money; yet what by the instigation of a few, from a Principle of Interest, and of some who are no great Friends to the Government, as from some jealous Apprehensions arising from the newness and strangeness of the thing, divers otherwise well-meaning People, became possest with monstrous and frightful Ideas and Conceptions of the Matter, which begot whole Swarms of Objections, which are hardly ever like to be answered, unless it be with one another, or with the Practice, or at least until the Antagonists have reconciled their Positions.

One pretended Patriot comes and tells us, This Design will make the King Absolute, by becoming Master thereof, nor is there any way to prevent it; For, says he, Rich and Money'd Men, we find by experience, are naturally timerous and fearful, and are easily brought to comply with the Times to save what they have. And the keeping of this Fund being of necessity committed to such, the prospect of their Profit, in conjunction with their natural Easiness, will of course induce them to joyn with the Prince, who is always best able to encourage and support them.

Another comes Cock-a-hoop, and tells ye, That he, or his Grandsire, Uncle, or some of the Race, have been abroad in some Country or other, and in all their Peregrinations they never met with Banks nor Storks any where but only in Republicks. And if we let them set footing in England, we shall certainly be in danger of a Common-wealth. Nay, he goes further, and tells ye, That the very establishing of a Bank in England, will of course alter the Government, for that is to entrust the Fund of the Nation in the Hands of the Subjects, who naturally are, and will always be sure to be of the popular side, and will insensibly influence the Church and State.

Some who pretend to see further into a Milstone than others, will undertake to make it plain, that it will raise and enhance the price of Land, and utterly discourage and ruine Trade; For by this means, say they, all Real Securities will become current, or near as good as current, in or by the Bank; which will very much lessen, if not put an end to the Credit of Personal Securities, for Usurers will be content with such an easie, secure, and convenient Profit, rather than hazard their Principal, and embarase themselves in Trouble for a greater Interest.

Others of the Learned tell us, That this Bank or Fund will be so profitable, easie, and secure for Receipts and Payments, that all the Money of the Nation will naturally run into Trade, and none will be left to purchase Lands, since Men may continue their Money in Bank, on demand, upon the best Security in Europe, and yet have a daily Interest running upon it, and thus have Trade and a Real Estate at once.

But to leave the Objectors to confer Notes, reconcile their

Notions, and to answer one another, it may be to better purpose to give some brief Account of the Nature of this intended Bank, with the good Effects and Consequences which may be expected therefrom; and in the first place it is necessary to premise whatever our Notionists may imagine to the contrary.

1. That all Money or Credit not having an intrinsick value, to answer the Contents or Denomination thereof, is false and counterfeit, and the Loss must fall one where or other.

2. That the Species of Gold and Silver being accepted and chosen by the Commercial World, for the Standard or Measure of other Effects; every thing else is only counted valuable, as compared with these.

3. Wherefore all Credit not founded on the Universal Species of Gold and Silver, is impracticable, and can never subsist neither safely nor long; at least till some other Species of Credit be found out and chosen by the Trading part of Mankind, over and above, or in lieu thereof.

Thus having said what a Bank ought to be, it remains to shew what this is designed, and wherein it will consist. This Bank will consist in a Revenue or Income of Eight per Cent. per Annum, for and upon the Money subscribed; and what Profits and Improvements can be made from the Business or Credit of the Bank, will be also divided among the Proprietors. Thus this Company or Corporation will exceed all others of that kind known in the Commercial World. For here will be Eight per Cent. per Annum certain upon the Capital; and as good and great a probability of other Profits as ever any Company had. And as to the Security of the Bank, for such as may intrust their Effects therein, it will be clear and visible, and every way equal to, if not exceeding the best in Christendom; for the other Funds or Banks in the Christian World, at best have only Effects to answer, without pretending to have any thing over: Nor are they Corroborated by the Interests, Property and Estates of Private Men, that of Genua only excepted; but this Bank will always have Twelve Hundred Thousand Pounds, or One Hundred Thousand Pounds per Annum, over and above Effects to answer, whatsoever Credit they may have. For the Company will be obliged never to make any Dividend, but out of the yearly Profits arising from their capital Stock or Fund; nor will they ever make any Dividend out of their Profits, until after some Months notice, that such as apprehend the Security will be weakened thereby, may have opportunity to withdraw their Effects, before the same be made. Thus a Society of Private Men will be obliged by their Estates and Interests, to strengthen and corroborate the publick Security of this Bank.

As to the common Objection of the danger from Alteration or Changes of Government, This Foundation is grounded upon a Revenue that cannot fail, but with the Nation, setled by Parliament for the uses thereby limited and appointed, it will, for many Reasons both of Right and Interest, become the best and highest Property, grounded upon so just and valuable a Consideration, as the Value paid to Their Majesties, for the use and service of the Government: and there being no Country in Christendom where Property hath been more sacred and secure for some Ages past, notwithstanding all our Revolutions, than in England, it must needs follow, that nothing less than a Conquest, wherein all Property, Justice, and Right must fail, can any way affect this Foundation: And in such case this would be but in common with every thing else.

Being to shew how this Design may redound to the Benefit of the Trade and Improvements of England, we find our Politicians have split the Connexion, the better to understand the Text, and distinguish between the Interest of Land and Trade, as they have lately done between that of a King and his People. The Truth on't is, they are possest with a sort of factious Reason, which runs extreamly upon Divisions and Separations; for when any Principle or Position proves too heavy for their Heads; they are presently for dividing it, and as it were of spite, because they cannot apprehend themselves: they employ their Faculty to reduce every thing to such Confusion, as not to be understood by anybody else: but until our Politicians are

pleased to shew some better Reasons than they have hitherto
done, for their splitting the Interest of Land and Trade, we will
leave it as it is, concluding that they are, and were, and of
right ought to be, in and of one and the same Interest; and
as such we shall consider how this Bank may be beneficial
to both.

It is an infallible sign that Money abounds and is plentiful,
when the Interest thereof is low; for Interest or Forbearance is
the Price of Money, as it is such; and if Money be plentiful,
People will thereby be enabled and induced to Trade and
Purchase, and by the plenty of Money other things must in
proportion bear the better Price. And if the Proprietors of
the Bank can circulate their Fundation of Twelve hundred
Thousand Pounds, without having more than Two or Three
Hundred Thousand Pounds lying dead at one time with another,
this Bank will be in effect as Nine Hundred Thousand Pounds,
or a Million of fresh Money brought into the Nation; and Nine
Hundred Thousand Pounds, or a Million, that must have been
employed in doing what the Bank will supply, may be employed
to other purposes. And as the Effects in this Bank will be a
growing and encreasing Money, and bring great Advantage to
Trade, by the secure, easie, and convenient way of Receipts
and Payments therein: It's Safety from Fire, Thieves, and other
Disasters, which Gold and Silver are subject unto: it's giving
a Profit upon a great part of the running Cash of the Nation,
the practice of which will naturally and gradually lower the
Interest of Money, as it has done in Holland, Genoua, and all
other places where Banks and Publick Funds are used: all
which will render it the highest Interest of the Government
and People, to preserve, maintain, and improve it in all time
to come . . . William Paterson. *A Brief Account of the intended
Bank of England* (1694)

6 Michael Godfrey   The Business of the Bank

Michael Godfrey (d 1695) was the London financier who
supported Paterson in founding the Bank and became its

first deputy-Governor. He was killed at the Siege of Namur in 1695; he had been visiting the King in connection with the Bank's intention to open a branch at Antwerp for coining money to pay the troops.

. . . The Bank is a Society consisting of about 1300 Persons, who having Subscribed £1,200,000 pursuant to an Act of Parliament, are Incorporated by the Name of the Governour and Company of the Bank of England, and have a Fund of £100,000 per an. granted them, redeemable after 11 Years, upon One Years Notice; which £1,200,000 they have paid into the Exchequer, by such Payments as the Publick Occasions required, and most of it long before the Money could have been demanded.

The Subscriptions to the Bank were made by vertue of a Commission under the great Seal of England, grounded upon the said Act of Parliament, of which Publick Notice was given, and the Commissioners were appointed to take all such voluntary Subscriptions as should be made on or before the first day of August last, by any Person or Persons, Natives or Foreigners, Bodies Politick or Corporate, towards the raising the said £1,200,000 and there was a Proviso in the said Act, that if £600,000 or more of the said £1,200,000 should not be subscribed on or before the first day of August then next coming, that the Power of making a Corporation should cease, and the Mony be paid into the Exchequer by the respective Subscribers and Contributors. And notwithstanding all the Endeavours of its Adversaries, the whole £1,200,000 was Subscribed in 10 days time, though if the Subscriptions had not amounted to £600,000 the Subscribers would have had but a bad Bargain, and such as no Body would have taken off their hands for 20 per cent. loss of their Principal, and yet they would have received £8 per cent. per annum for their Mony, nor would the £1,200,000 have been any thing near Subscribed; but upon the Prospect of their being Incorporated to be the Bank of England.

It's observable, That the Promoters of the Bank have proposed no Advantage thereby to themselves above any of the other Subscribers, all the Profit being only pro Rata, according to their Stock; and though it cannot be imagined but that they intended to be largely concerned, yet it is so setled, that those who have but £500 have One Vote, and those who have never so much can have no more; and the Directors have no Salary fixt, for their Pains and Attendance, but submit themselves wholly to what a General Court will think fit to allow them; and any 9 Members having each £500 Stock, may call a General Court, and turn out the Governour, Deputy-Governour, and all, or any of the Directors, and choose others in their places. Which are Provisions so wise, and effectual to prevent Fraud in some, to the prejudice of the rest, that it hardly leaves room for any doubt of that nature.

I shall not attempt to enumerate all the Advantages which the Nation will receive by the Bank, however I will mention some few, which alone are sufficient to recommend it, viz.

The Bank, besides the raising £1,200,000 towards the Charge of the War, cheaper than it could otherwise have been done, (and like the other Publick Funds, tying the People faster to the Government) will infallibly lower the Interest of Money; as well on Publick as Private Securities, which all other Funds have advanced, and which hath been raised to an Exorbitant Rate, as to the Publick, by those who have made use of its Necessities, and are now angry at the Bank, because that will reduce it. And the lowering of Interest, besides the Encouragement it will be to Industry and Improvements, will by a natural consequence raise the Value of Land, and encrease Trade, both which depend upon it; but it cannot be expected that Land should rise much whilst such high Taxes continue upon it, and whilst there are so great advantages to be made by lending Money to the Publick.

The Bank gives Money for Tallies on Funds, having a Credit of Loan by Act of Parliament, and which are payable in 2 years time, for the growing Interest only, without any other

Allowance, on which there was used to be paid for the Change, as much or more than the Publick Interest: For even on the Land Tax, which is counted the best of all the Funds, there has been frequently given on Tallies payable in 3 or 4 Months time 1, $1\frac{1}{2}$, $1\frac{3}{4}$, and 2 per cent. premio, over and above the Publick Interest; and Tallys on some Funds, on which but 12 or 18 Months past there was £25 and £30 per cent. given over and above the Publick Interest, are now taken by the Bank for nothing, and instead of allowing Mony to change them, there is now Mony given to procure them; so that Tallys are become better than Mony, because there is 7 or 8 per cent. per annum benefit whilst they are kept; and they are paid by the Bank upon demand, to all those who desire to have Money for them, which is in effect so much Quick Stock which the Bank has already increased to the Nation, besides what it will farther add by its own Credit.

Thus by a regular course, and without any violence, the Bank has made Tallys currant in Payment, which is what has been so long wisht for, but could not have been effected without the Bank, (although there had been a Law to compel it), and this has given such a Reputation to all Tallys, even those which are the most remote, that they are now currantly taken by private persons at 6, 8, 10, 15, and 20 per cent. less allowance than what was given but some few Months before the Bank was Establisht, all which Losses on Tallys was paid by the Publick, for it cannot be suppos'd but those who are to allow 15 or 20 per cent. for discount of their Tallys, make provision accordingly in the Price they are to have for their Commodities.

The Bank will likewise facilitate the future Supplies, by making the Funds which are to be given, more useful and ready to answer the Publick Occasions, and upon easier terms than what has been done during the War: for its said, they will Lend Money on the Land Tax at 6 per cent. per annum, nay some say at 5 per cent. per annum; which will save the Nation a great Sum of Money in Interest, as well as what was usually paid for Gratuities and other Charges to procure Loans, a Method that some of the Opposers of the Bank have been well acquainted with.

But now the Bank is Establisht, and that all who want Mony, and have Securities, know where to be Supplied, and the Terms, there cannot be such Advantages made on the Publick or Private Mens Necessities for the future.

The more Credit the Bank has, and the more Money is lodged in it, the more it will lessen Interest, for want of Occasions to improve it; and those who lodge their Money in the Bank have it as much at their disposal as if it were in the hands of the Goldsmiths, or in their own Cash-Chest, and there is a greater Value than the Money which is deposited in the Bank that circulates by their Credit as much as if it were stirring in Specie: And the Bank-Bills serve already for Returns and Exchange to and from the remotest parts of the Kingdom, and will in a little time do the like in Foreign Parts, which will lessen the exporting of Bullion for the paying and maintaining our Armies abroad during this War; and if the Bulk of the Money of the Nation which has been Lodged with the Goldsmiths, had been deposited in the Bank 4 or 5 years past, it had prevented its being so Scandalously Clipt, which one day or other must cost the Nation a Million and half, or Two Millions to Repair.

Those who are concerned in the Bank cannot fail to lessen the Interest of Mony, for its their own Interest to do it, else they cannot employ it; and their Fund being setled at £8 per cent. per annum, the lower they bring all other Interest, they make the Stock of the Bank the more Valuable; and it must be allowed, That it is the only Fund that ever was setled in England which has lessened the Interest of Mony. And its very observable, That any resolution that those Concerned in the Bank have taken to be more serviceable in accommodating the Publick or private mens Occasions, has always given it a farther Reputation, and increased its Value; and the more they serve the Interest of the Nation, so much the more they serve their own, they being under this happy circumstance, That they cannot do good to themselves but by doing good to others.

The Nation pays for the Million on Annuities £14 per cent. per an. for 16 years, besides about one tenth part which was expended in Charges, and reckoning Interest upon Interest at 5 per cent. per an. as some have computed it, the Lottery amounts to above three Millions, and the Annuities amount to above 260 Millions.

The Funds of Wine, Vinegar and Tobacco, East-India Goods, Joint-Stocks, Paper and Parchment, and New Impositions, are all at £8 per cent. per an. as well as the Bank; and yet there has been 20 to 30 per cent. Loss on Tallys upon several of these Funds, besides the Publick Interest; the like has been on the remote parts of the 2/3 Excise and 3/4 Customs before the Bank was Establisht, and thereby the Nation has Paid 12, 14, 16, 18, and 20 per cent. per an. Interest for Mony, which if it had continued must have Ruined the Kingdom; but now that they who have made these Advantages by the Publick are prevented of the like for the future, they will be more ready to Lend Money on Private Securities, or to Purchase Lands, for want of Occasions to Improve their Mony to so much better Advantage.

It's a matter which is very surprizing and without any example, that after the Nation has been Six Years ingag'd in such a Chargeable War, and has been at near Thirty Millions Expence, and such quantities of Bullion have been Exported, besides the Loss of several Millions which the Enemy has taken; that after all this, instead of the Interest of Mony rising, (as has been usual in all Wars) there should now be such a fall of Interest, which must be acknowledged to be wholly owing to the Bank, and that it could not have been effected without it; for till the Bank exerted itself, the Interest of Mony was rising apace, and would have continued so, and have come to a strange Exorbitancy e'er this, if the Bank had not been Establisht.

The Bank being thus useful to the Publick, extends itself

E

likewise to accomodate all Private Mens Occasions; for they lend Mony on Mortgages, and real Securities at 5 per cent. per annum, and their very Publishing they would do it, has given a Check to the raising the Interest on them from 5 to 6 per cent. per an. as was attempted; and if the Titles of Land were made more secure, Money would be Lent thereon at 4 per cent. per an. and in time of Peace at 3 per cent. per an. Foreign Bills of Exchange are discounted at $4\frac{1}{2}$ per cent. per an., and Inland Bills and Notes for Debts at 6 per cent. per an. and those who keep their Cash in the Bank, have the one discounted at 3 per cent. per an. and the other at $4\frac{1}{2}$ per cent. per an. for which most Goldsmiths used to take 9 or 10 per cent. per an. And Mony is lent on Pawns of Commodities which are not perishable, at 5 per cent. per annum, for which some in their necessities have paid more than double as much, to the Ruine of many great Traders.

Money is likewise Lent on the Fund of the Orphans of the City of London, at 5 per cent. per an. which will hinder several, who are necessitous, from being forced to Sell their Interest at Under-rates. And its said they have agreed to set up a Lumbard to lend Mony on small Pawns, for the Relief of the Poor, at One Penny per Month for 20 shillings for which they now pay Six Pence or Twelve Pence every Week: and its probable, if the Bank was not restrained by Act of Parliament, they might take into Consideration the Exchanging Seamens Tickets for Money, for a very small Allowance, for which they have often times paid 7 or 8 shillings in the Pound.

The Bank will reduce the Interest of Mony in England to 3 per cent. per an. in a few years, without any Law to enforce it, in like manner as it is in all other Countreys where Banks are Establisht, whereby the Trade of the Nation may be driven upon more equal Terms with the rest of our Neighbours, where Mony is to be had at so much lower Rates than what we in England have hitherto paid: And as the lessening the Interest of Mony will Infallibly raise the Value of Land, it had been worth while for the Nobility and Gentry who are the Proprietors of the Real Estates in England, to have given a Land Tax for the Bank, of double the Sum which was raised by it, if they could not otherwise have obtained it; for the falling the Interest of Mony to 3 per cent. per annum, to which Rates the Bank will reduce it, will unavoidably advance the Price of Land to above 30 Years Purchase, which will raise the Value of Lands in England at least 100 Millions, and thereby abundantly reimburse the Nation all the Charges of the War, and will not only enable the Gentry to make better Provision for their Younger Children, but those who now owe Money on their Lands, to pay off their Debts, by the Increase of the Value of their Estates.

The Ease and Security of the great Receipts and Payments of Mony which are made by the Bank, (where Peoples Cash is kept as it is at the Goldsmiths) together with the safe depositing of it, are such advantages to recommend it, that they ought not to be past over without some Observation; especially considering how much Mony has been lost in England by the Goldsmiths and Scriveners Breaking, which in about 30 Years past, cannot amount to so little as betwixt Two and Three Millions, all which might have been prevented, had a Bank been sooner Establisht, For none can lose by the Bank, they having a Fund of £100,000 per an. and Money, or good Securities besides, for as much as they owe, wherewith to pay all that trust them.

These are such Services to the Nation in General, which have been (and will be) done by the Bank, as could not have been done without it, and such Arguments as these arising from Fact, are better Demonstrations and more Convincing of the Usefulness of it, than meer Speculative Notions urged by its Opposers, can be to prejudice others against it; and therefore it would be an unaccountable sort of Policy, to endeavour to deprive the Nation of those vast Advantages, which it now does and will receive by it . . . Michael Godfrey. *A Short Account of the Bank of England* (1695)

7 Sir Stephen Theodore Janssen The Future of the Bank – A Director's View

Born in France, Janssen (1658–1748) came to London in 1680, created a large fortune, and was naturalised in 1685. For his services to the Crown he was knighted by William and created a baronet by Anne. He was a director of the Bank of England and later of the South Sea Company. In the Bubble and its aftermath he lost around £300,000 in all, together with his reputation for prudence. He was expelled from the House of Commons when Walpole made scapegoats of the South Sea Company's directors.

At this present time, when so much is thought to depend upon the well-modelling of a Bank in England, a short Account of Banks settled in other Parts, 'tis hoped, will not be unacceptable to the Publick. I am the more induced to give this Account, by the reading of a Paper lately come abroad, debating *the Reasons for and against Ingrafting*, full of Notions so directly opposite to what I ever heard or understood of Banks, that there is good Ground to believe, the Author having had a Share in the Management of the B. of E. and his Opinions having prevailed, hath been in a great measure the Cause of all the false Steps that have brought so excellent a Constitution under this present Dispute. The great Mistake of this Gentleman, which leads him into all his other Errors, is; That a Bank ought to get; and therefore to admit of new Sharers in that imaginary Profit, is a manifest Self-denial. The best way to confute his Opinion, will be, to shew the Practice of other Banks, and thereby make it appear, that they have been very useful to the Publick, and wonderfully beneficial to themselves, without ever aiming at any other Advantage than that of circulating the Whole upon part of the Capital.

There are, in several Parts of Europe, about 30 Banks; they vary more or less in some part of their Constitution or Management; but they are chiefly of three sorts. Some are only for

Safety and Conveniency; others are for the Benefit of the Income only; and others both for Safety and Conveniency, and
likewise for Benefit and Advantage.

Of the first kind are the Banks of Amsterdam, Rotterdam,
Hamburgh and Stockholm: These Banks have no Income, no
Adventurers or Sharers in their Profits: They are only great
Chests, for the Conveniency of transferring from one Account
to another; and where Merchants deposite their Money, if they
think it safer there than in their own Houses. In Places of great
Traffick, such as Amsterdam and Hamburgh, all foreign Bills
of Exchange and other great Paiments, are, by Law, to be paid
in Bank, unless both Parties agree it otherwise; but if one of
the Parties insists, the Paiment must be made in Bank; else it
would be very difficult for great Traders to deal for such vast
Sums as they do in both those Places. These Banks are under
the Care and Conduct of the Magistracy of the Places where
they are erected: and as they never trade or meddle with any
Business, there is very little Trouble in their Management;
two or three of the Magistrates having an Eye upon the Servants
and Books of Transfer, direct the whole Matter. The Banks of
Amsterdam and Hamburgh lend some small Sums upon Pawns,
but the Sum they have liberty to lend is limited, and the Profit
thereof accrues to the Benefit of the Town, which defrayeth the
Charge of the Bank, and is answerable for all the Money lodg'd
therein: So that these Banks are safe and secure, and serve only
to avoid the Trouble of Telling: which Conveniency is found
of so great Importance for carrying on a great Trade, that no
considerable Trading-Town can well be without it.

The Banks of the second kind, that are for the Benefit of the
Income only, are, the Banks of Rome, the Banks of Bolonia and
Milan, and the Bank of Paris; (the Rents constituted on the
Town-house of Paris being of the same nature as the Rents of
the Banks of Rome, and some others in Italy). These Banks are
made up of a certain number of Men, who in time of War or
other Exigencies of the State, advanced Sums of Money upon
Funds, granted *in perpetuum*, but redeemable: Those concern'd

therein content themselves with the Interest, else they sell their Stock, or part thereof, when they have occasion for the Principal. But these Banks keep no Cash, or ever have any Stock of Money: They are under the Management of some few Overseers, all equal in Dignity, that take care to divide the Revenue to the Proprietors; only the Bank of Paris hath the King for a Governour, who sometimes disposes of the Incomes at his pleasure, or stops part thereof for his own Use. These Banks are properly Funds of perpetual Interest, transferable and redeemable, and sute best with Places of little Traffick, where the gathering into one Place a great Mass of Treasure might endanger the Loss of it.

The third kind of Banks, that are both for the Conveniency of the Publick, and for the Advantage of the Undertakers, are, the several Banks of Naples, one of the Banks of Bolonia, and the Bank of St. George at Genoa: These Banks did not only advance Sums of Money upon Funds of perpetual Interest, at the time of their Establishment, but by their being a safe Depository of Money, obtaining a Credit, they have been able to lend great Sums upon good Securities: Some of these Banks have been prosperous to that degree, as to enjoy their Revenue, upon their having in Stock only one fourth, one third, or one half of the Capital: And if I am rightly inform'd, one of them is so happy, that the Proprietors have the Benefit of the full Income, without having a Penny of their own in Stock; so great and so solid a Credit hath acquired to this Bank, the prudent and regular Conduct of its Directors. But none of all these Banks ever attempted to trade, much less concern'd themselves in Exchanges, which of all Trades is the most ticklish and dangerous: They arrived at that vast Credit, by keeping within Bounds, by lending upon undoubted Securities, for a short time, and at a very low Interest. The Bank that hath the Benefit of its full Income without any Capital of their own, never exceeded the Rate of 4 per cent. their constant Practice is to take but 3 per cent. and sometimes upon a Security to their liking and entire Satisfaction, they have lent at 1 per cent. per annum. By such

Methods, they are not only look'd upon as wise and judicious
Managers, that do not venture too far upon Uncertainties; but
by lending at these low Rates, they gain the Love of the People,
and no body grudges them their Cash, when they see it us'd more
for the Advantage of the Publick, than for the private Lucre of
the Undertakers.

The Bank of England is of this mixt kind: It is squared both
for Conveniency and Safety, and also for Benefit and Advantage: No Bank in the World ever was so happily constituted,
no Bank hath so great a Revenue, settled upon so good a Fund,
and so little paid for it. Had not its Managers aim'd at greater
Gains than their Income, there had been no occasion to have
call'd in more than the Subscription-Money, which was 25 per
cent. Their first Deputy Governour Mr. M. G. often us'd to
say, that he would never have called in for more, had he not
design'd some further great Undertaking: I cannot tell whether
those that have had the governing part since have acted by the
same Spirit; but 'tis certain, that through a mistaken Notion
of Banks, *which are design'd to help others to trade, but not to trade
themselves*, they endeavour'd to get over and above their hundred
thousand Pounds a Year. Had they been contented with their
Revenue, never incroach'd upon other Mens Imployments, by
dealing in Exchanges, and importing and exporting Silver;
nor coveted great Profits, by lending vast Sums, without a
Prospect of being in a short time repaid; but made use of the
Money that was trusted in their Hands, for the Relief of such
as had occasion for it, upon very good Securities, and at a very
low Interest; they had given more Satisfaction, and had the
Cash of the whole Town; by which means, without adventuring
at Sea, or running the hazard of bad Bills and of bad Correspondents, they might by a well-settled Credit, upon the first
25 per Cent. or upon 50 per Cent. at most, have circulated the
whole; and so without any other Gain, might constantly have
injoyed a Benefit of 16 if not of 32 per Cent. per annum; which
is Profit enough to satisfy any moderate or reasonable Man.
But if a Bank grounds its Advantages upon getting beyond its

Income, such a Design will create Envy and Enemies, and the Hazards run in the Attempt of such Gains, render it less safe and secure, and consequently lessen its Credit.

The Case being thus, viz. That a Bank ought not by aiming at vast exorbitant Gains, to spoil its Credit; but on the contrary, ought by a judicious and cautious Conduct, to endeavour to maintain it so, as to circulate the whole on part of the Stock, and thereby instead of 8 per Cent. make 16 per cent. or more per annum: what Reason can any Member of the present B. of E. have (except such a desire to be perpetual Directors) to be against an Ingraftment? They ought rather to wish for an Addition of new Adventurers; for 'tis evident, the greater Income it hath, and the more Members there are, the better will it be able to support itself, and to circulate one hundred with fifty or less: which in my opinion is a surer way of Gain, and turns to better account, than to add 2 or 3 per Cent. to the 8 per Cent. for £20 or 30,000 per annum is as much, as those that are so fond of the Trade of a Bank are in hopes to get by their Management; and for the doing of which, they must run great Hazards, and disoblige an infinite number of People. But such is the natural Temper of some Men, that they had rather get less, and have no Sharers in their Profits, than to get more, if others are also to reap a Benefit by it: whereas the principal Care of good Directors should be, how to get the good will of Mankind, as being the best, if not the only way to make a Bank great and flourishing. Therefore 'tis a question with me, whether a Bank ought to lend at any higher Interest than after the rate of 3 per Cent. per annum: This Limitation, and its being restrained from all Trade without exception, would secure to the B. of E. a firm and lasting Credit, and in time perhaps make it as successful as that Bank of Bolonia, which injoys its Revenue intirely upon its Credit: for what cannot one expect from a Constitution so happily framed, which hath no means left to procure its own Good, but by procuring the good of others, that is supported by so many Thousands, as it will be after its Ingraftment; and which sets to itself a Rule, to Study nothing so much, as the promoting the Ease, Conveniency, and Accomodation of all People?

I shall conclude with some few Remarks, viz. *First*; That no other Bank gives out Notes payable to the Bearer, they all keep to a Transfer, excepting the Bills payable to Order allow'd by their Settlement. Such as have a mind to place their Money in the Bank, must bring it thither, and there they have Credit given them for the Sums they bring: This preserves the Majesty of the Bank, prevents Cheats and Counterfeits, hinders inconsiderable Dealers from having to do with the Bank; which by this means keeps within a certain Compass of great Business, avoids Confusion and a great deal of unnecessary Trouble: Banks being indeed only for the Conveniency of great Payments, and not to keep the Cash of every petty Retailer; to do both is inconsistent, and not practicable where there is much Trade. In Amsterdam, there are a great many Cashiers who keep the small Cash of Merchants and others, no Body being allow'd to transfer a lesser Sum than 300 Gilders or £30 in the Bank-Books, without a Penalty.

Secondly; That no Bank, unless on some emergent occasion, ever paid Interest, except the B. of E. the Managers whereof drew upon themselves the great Inconveniency they lay under of paying so much Interest, by their Ambition of grasping at all; therefore if nothing be undertaken for the future, but what is regular and according to the true Nature of a Bank, it needs not pay Interest, when 'tis once a float.

Thirdly; A Bank must never presume upon its own Merit, or pretend to have done Services; it becomes a Bank of all other Constitutions, to keep within the Bounds of Modesty; it hath nothing of its own; when it lends Money, 'tis other Peoples Money; the Government is not oblig'd to the B. of E. for having lent it great Sums; the Government is oblig'd to those Persons whose Money it was, and who now suffer for it: (altho' some, who had the chief hand in lending the last £200,000 when the E. of P. came over, claim a great Merit to their F – –, whose Health for that Service was drunk as often, as the Health of

John King of Poland, after his Raising the Siege of Vienna, if what they have exprest themselves may be believ'd). If a Bank boasts of its Loans, it gives offence to those who enabled it to lend, and consequently they will withdraw their Cash . . . Sir Stephen Theodore Janssen. *A Discourse Concerning Banks* (1697)

8 Daniel Defoe   The Future of the Bank – A Projector's View

Best known journalist and novelist of his age, Defoe (1661–1731) led an extremely adventurous life which provided the experience for his acute social comments on almost every conceivable subject.

Banks, without question, if rightly managed are, or may be, of great advantage, especially to a trading people as the English are and among many others, this is one particular case in which that benefit appears, that they bring down the interest of money and take from the goldsmiths, scriveners and others who have command of running cash, their most delicious trade of taking advantage of the necessities of the merchant in extravagant discounts and premiums for advance of money when either large customs or foreign remittances call for disbursements beyond his common ability; for by the easiness of terms on which the merchant may have money, he is encouraged to venture farther in trade than otherwise he would do. Not but that there are other great advantages a Royal Bank might procure in this kingdom, as has been seen in part by this, as advancing money to the Exchequer upon Parliamentary funds and securities, by which in time of a war our preparation for any expedition need not be in any danger of miscarriage for want of money, though the taxes raised be not speedily paid, nor the Exchequer burdened with the excessive interest paid in former reigns upon anticipations of revenue. Landed men might be supplied with moneys upon securities on easier terms which would prevent the loss of multitudes of estates now ruined and devoured by insolent and merciless mortgagees and the like. But now we unhappily see a Royal Bank established by Act of Parliament and another with a large fund upon the Orphan Stock and yet these advantages, or others which we expected, not answered, though the pretensions in both have not been wanting at such times as they find it needful to introduce themselves into public esteem, by giving out prints of what they were rather able to do than really intended to practise. So that our having two banks at this time settled, and more erecting, has not yet been able to reduce the interest of money not because the nature and foundation of their constitution does not tend towards it, but because, finding their hands full of better business, they are wiser than, by being slaves to old obsolete proposals, to lose the advantage of the great improvement they can make of their stock.

This, however, does not at all reflect on the nature of the bank, nor of the benefit it would be to the public trading part of the kingdom, whatever it may seem to do on the practice of the present. We find four or five banks now in view to be settled. I confess I expect no more from those to come than we have found from the past; and I think I make no breach on either my charity or good manners in saying so; and I reflect not upon any of the banks that are or shall be established for not doing what I mention, but for making such publications of what they would do. I cannot think any man had expected the Royal Bank should lend money on mortgages at 4 per cent. nor was it much the better for them to make publication they would do so from the beginning of January next after their settlement, since to this day as I am informed, they have not lent one farthing in that manner.

Our banks are indeed nothing but so many goldsmiths' shops, where the credit being high (and the directors as high), people lodge their money; and they, the directory I mean, make their advantage of it. If you lay it at demand, they allow you nothing: if at time, 3 per cent. and so would any goldsmith in Lombard Street have done before; but the very banks themselves are so awkward in lending, so strict, so tedious, so inquisitive and withal so public in their taking securities, that men who are anything tender won't go to them; and so the easiness of borrowing money, so much designed, is defeated; for here is a private interest to be made, though it be a public one; and, in short, it is only a great trade carried on for the private gain of a few concerned in the original stock; and though we are to hope for great things because they have promised them, yet they are all future that we know of.

And yet all this while a bank might be very beneficial to this kingdom; and this might be so if either their own ingenuity or public authority would oblige them to take the public good into equal concern with their private interest.

To explain what I mean:— Banks being established by public authority, ought also, as all public things are, to be under limitations and restrictions from that authority; and those limitations being regulated with a proper regard to the ease of trade in general, and the improvement of the stock in particular, would make a bank a useful, profitable thing indeed.

First, a bank ought to be of a magnitude proportioned to the trade of the country it is in; which this bank is so far from, that it is no more to the whole than the least goldsmith's cash in Lombard Street is to the bank. From whence it comes to pass, that already more banks are contriving; and I question not but banks in London will ere long be as frequent as lotteries. The consequence of which, in all probability will be the diminishing of their reputation, or a civil war with one another. It is true the Bank of England has a capital stock; but yet, were that stock wholly clear of the public concern of the Government, it is not above a fifth part of what would be necessary to manage the whole business of the town; which it ought, though not to do, at least to be able to do. And I suppose I may venture to say above one half of the stock of the present bank is taken up in the affairs of the Exchequer.

I suppose nobody will take this discourse for an invective against the Bank of England. I believe it is a very good fund, a very useful one, and a very profitable one. It has been useful to the Government and it is profitable to the proprietors; and the establishing it at such a juncture when our enemies were making great boasts of our poverty and want of money, was a particular glory to our nation and the City in particular. That when the 'Paris Gazette' informed the world that the Parliament had indeed given the King grants for raising money in funds to be paid in remote years; but money was so scarce that no anticipations could be procured; that just then besides three millions paid into the Exchequer that spring on other taxes by way of advance, there was an overplus stock to be found of £1,200,000 sterling or (to make it speak French) of above fifteen millions which was all paid voluntarily into the Exchequer in less than—.

Besides this, I believe, the present Bank of England has been very useful to the Exchequer, and to supply the King with remittances for the payment of the army in Flanders; which has also, by the way, been very profitable to itself. But still this Bank is not of that bulk that the business done here requires; nor is it able, with all the stock it has, to procure the great proposed benefit, the lowering of interest of money; whereas all foreign banks absolutely govern the interest both at Amsterdam, Genoa and other places. And this defect, I conceive, the multiplicity of banks cannot supply unless a perfect understanding could be secured between them.

To remedy this defect several methods might be proposed. Some I shall take the freedom to hint at.

First, that the present bank increase their stock to at least five million sterling, to be settled as they are already, with some small limitations to make the methods more beneficial.

Five millions sterling is an immense sum; to which add the credit of their cash, which would supply them with all the overplus money in the town, and might probably amount to half as much more; and then the credit of running bills, which by circulating would no question be an equivalent to the other half; so that in stock, credit and bank bills, the balance of their cash would be always ten millions sterling, a sum that everybody who can talk of does not understand.

But then to find business for all this stock which, though it be a strange thing to think of, is nevertheless easy when it comes to be examined. And first for the business. This bank should enlarge the number of their directors as they do of their stock and should then establish several sub-committees, composed of their own members, who should have the directing of several offices relating to the distinct sorts of business they referred to; to be overruled and governed by the Governor and Directors in a body, but to have a conclusive power as to contracts. Of these there should be:—

One office for loan of money for customs of goods, which by a plain method might be so ordered that the merchant might with ease pay the highest customs down, and so by allowing the bank 4 per cent. advance, be first sure to secure the £10. per cent. which the King allows for prompt payment at the Custom-house, and be also freed from the troublesome work of finding bondsmen and securities for the money, which has exposed many a man to tyranny of extents either for himself or his friend, to his utter ruin, who under a more moderate prosecution had been able to pay all his debts, and by this method has been torn to pieces and disabled from making any tolerable proposal to his creditors. This is a scene of large business and would in proportion employ a large cash. And it is the easiest thing in the world to make the bank the paymaster of all the large customs, and yet the merchant have so honourable a possession of his goods as may be neither any diminution to his reputation or any hindrance to their sale.

As, for example, suppose I have 100 hogsheads of tobacco to import, whose customs by several duties come to £1,000. and want cash to clear them. I go with my bill of loading to the bank, who appoint their officer to enter the goods and pay the duties which goods so entered by the bank shall give them title enough to any part or the whole, without the trouble of bills of sale, or conveyances, defeasances and the like. The goods are carried to a warehouse at the waterside, where the merchant has a free and public access to them as if in his own warehouse, and an honourable liberty to sell and deliver either the whole (paying their disburse), or a part without it, leaving but sufficient for the payment; and out of that part delivered, either by notes under the hand of the purchaser, or any other way, he may clear the same without any exactions but of £4. per cent. and the rest are his own.

The ease this would bring to trade, the deliverance it would bring to the merchants from the insults of goldsmiths etc. and the honour it would give to our management of public imposts, with the advantages to the Custom-house itself and the utter destruction of extortion, would be such as would give a due value to the bank and make all mankind acknowledge it to be a public good. The grievance of exactions upon merchants in this case is very great; and when I lay the blame on the goldsmiths, because they are the principal people made use of on such occasions, I include a great many other sorts of brokers and money-jobbing artists, who all get a snip out of the merchant. I myself have known a goldsmith in Lombard Street lend a man £700. to pay the customs of a hundred pipes of Spanish wines. The wines were made over to him for security by bill of sale and put into a cellar, of which the goldsmith kept the key; the merchant was to pay £6. per cent. interest on the bond and to allow £10. premium for advancing the money. When he had the wines in possession, the owner could not send his cooper to look after them but the goldsmith's man must attend all the while for which he would be paid five shillings a day. If he brought a customer to see them, the goldsmith's man must show them. The money was lent for two months; he could not be admitted to sell or deliver a pipe of wine out single, or two or three at a time as he might have sold them; but on a word or two spoken amiss to the goldsmith, or which he was pleased to take so, he would have none sold but the whole parcel together. By this usage the goods lay on hand every month the money remained the goldsmith demanded a guinea per cent. forbearance besides the interest, till at least, by leakage, decay and other accidents, the wines begin to lessen. Then he tells the merchant he is afraid the wines are not worth the money he has lent and demands further security, and in a little while growing higher and rougher the goldsmith tells him he must have his money. The merchant, too much at his mercy because he cannot provide the money, is forced to consent to the sale and the goods—being reduced to seventy pipes sound wine and four unsound (the rest being sunk for filling up)—were sold for £13. per pipe the sound and £3. the unsound, which amounted to £922 together:—

The Cooper's bill came to	£30. 0. 0
The cellarage, a year and a half . . .	18. 0. 0
Interest on the Bond	63. 0. 0
The goldsmith's men for attendance . .	8. 0. 0
Allowance for advance of the money and forbearance	74. 0. 0
	£193. 0. 0
Principal money borrowed	700. 0. 0
	£893. 0. 0
Due to the merchant	29. 0. 0
	£922. 0. 0

By the moderatest computation that can be, these wines cost the merchant as follows:—

First Cost, with Charges on Board

In Lisbon 15 mille reis per pipe is 1500 mille reis exchange at 6/4d. per mille rei . .	£475. 0. 0
Freight to London then at £3. per ton . .	150. 0. 0
Assurance on £500. at 2 per cent . .	10. 0. 0
Petty charges	5. 0. 0
	£640. 0. 0

So that it is manifest by the extortion of this banker the poor man lost the whole capital, with freight and charges and made but £29 produce of a hundred pipes of wine.

One other office of this bank, and which would take up a considerable branch of the stock, is for lending money upon pledges which should have annexed to it a warehouse and factory where all sorts of goods might publicly be sold by the consent of the owners, to the great advantage of the owner, the bank receiving £4. per cent interest and 2 per cent. Commission for sale of the goods.

A third office should be appointed for discounting bills, tallies and notes by which all tallies of the Exchequer and any part of the revenue, should at stated allowances be ready money to any person, to the great advantage of the Government and ease of all such as are any ways concerned in public undertakings.

A fourth office for lending money upon land securities at 4 per cent interest, by which the cruelty and injustice of mortgagees would be wholly restrained and a register of mortgages might be very well kept, to prevent frauds.

A fifth office for exchanges and foreign correspondence.

A sixth for inland exchanges where a very large field of business lies before them.

Under this head it will not be improper to consider that this method will most effectually answer all the notions and proposals of county banks; for by this office they would be all rendered useless and unprofitable, since one bank, of the magnitude I mention, with a branch of its office set apart for that business, might with ease manage all the inland exchange of the kingdom.

By which such a correspondence with all the trading towns in England might be maintained as that the whole kingdom should trade with the bank. Under the direction of this office a public cashier should be appointed in every county to reside in the capital town as to trade, and in some counties more, through whose hands all the cash of the revenue of the gentry and of trade should be returned on the bank in London, and from the bank again on their cashier in every respective county or town, at the small exchange of $\frac{1}{2}$ per cent, by which means all loss of money carried upon the road, to the encouragement of robbers and ruining of the country, who are sued for those robberies would be more effectually prevented, than by all the statutes against highwaymen that are or can be made.

As to public advancings of money to the Government, they may be left to the directors in a body, as all other disputes and contingent cases are; and whoever examines these heads of business apart, and has any judgment in the particulars will, I suppose, allow that a stock of ten millions may find employment in them, though it be indeed a very great sum.

I could offer some very good reasons why this way of management by particular offices for every particular sort of business is not only the easiest, but the safest way of executing an affair of such variety and consequence; also I could state a method for the proceedings of those private offices, their conjunction with and dependence on the general Court of the Directors and how the various accounts should centre in one general capital account of stock with regulations and appeals; but I believe them to be needless, at least in this place.

If it be objected here that it is impossible for one joint-stock to go through the whole business of the kingdom, I answer, I believe it is not either impossible or impracticable, particularly on this one account, that almost all the country business would be managed by running bills and those the longest abroad of any, their distance keeping them out, to the increasing the credit, and consequently the stock of the bank.

Of the Multiplicity of Banks.

What is touched at in the foregoing part of this chapter refers to one Bank Royal, to preside as it were, over the whole cash of the kingdom. But because some people do suppose this work fitter for many banks than for one, I must a little consider that head. And first, allowing those many banks could without clashing maintain a constant correspondence with one another in passing each other's bills as current from one to another, I know not but it might be better performed by many than by one, for as harmony makes music in sound, so it produces success in business.

A civil war among merchants is always the ruin of trade. I cannot think a multitude of banks could so consist with one another in England as to join interests and uphold one another's credit without joining stocks too. I confess if it could be done the convenience to trade would be visible.

If I were to propose which way these banks should be established, I answer; Allowing a due regard to some gentlemen who have had thoughts of the same, whose methods I shall not so much as touch upon, much less discover, my thoughts run upon quite different methods, both for the fund and the establishment.

Every principal town in England is a corporation upon which the fund may be settled which will sufficiently answer the difficult and chargeable work of suing for a corporation by patent or Act of Parliament.

A general subscription of stock being made, and by deeds of settlement placed in the mayor and aldermen of the city or corporation for the time being, in trust, to be declared by deeds of uses, some of the directors being always made members of the said corporation and joined in the trust, the bank hereby becomes the public stock of the town, something like what they call the rents of the town-house in France, and is managed in the name of the said corporation to whom the directors are accountable and they back again to the general court. For example:—

Suppose the gentlemen or tradesmen of the County of Norfolk, by a subscription of cash, design to establish a bank. The subscriptions being made, the stock is paid into the chamber of the city of Norwich and managed by a court of directors, as all banks are, and chosen out of the subscribers, the mayor only of the city to be always one; to be managed in the name of the corporation of the city of Norwich, but for the uses in a deed of trust to be made by the subscribers and mayor and aldermen at large mentioned. I make no question, but a bank thus settled would have as firm a foundation as any bank need to have and every way answer the ends of a corporation.

Of these sorts of banks England might very well establish fifteen at the several towns hereafter mentioned, some of which though they are not the capital towns of the counties yet are more the centre of trade, which in England runs in veins, like mines of metal in the earth:—

Canterbury	Leeds or Halifax or York
Salisbury	Nottingham
Exeter	Warwick or Birmingham
Bristol	Oxford or Reading
Worcester	Bedford
Shrewsbury	Norwich
Manchester	Colchester
Newcastle-upon-Tyne	

Every one of these banks to have a cashier in London, unless they could all have a general correspondence and credit with the Bank Royal.

These banks in their respective counties should be a general staple and factory for the manufacturers of the said county where every man that had goods made might have money at a small interest for advance, the goods in the meantime being sent forward to market to a warehouse for that purpose erected in London, where they should be disposed of to all the advantages the owner could expect, paying only 1 per cent. commission. Or if the maker wanted credit in London, either for Spanish wool, cotton, oil or any goods while his goods were in the warehouse of the said bank, his bill should be paid by the bank to the full value of his goods, or at least within a small matter. These banks, either by correspondence with each other or an order to their cashier in London, might with ease so pass each other's bills that a man who has cash at Plymouth and wants money at Berwick, may transfer his cash at Plymouth to Newcastle in half an hour's time, without either hazard or charge or time, allowing only ½ per cent. exchange; and so of all the most distant parts of the kingdom. Or if he wants money at Newcastle and has goods at Worcester or at any other clothing town, sending his goods to be sold by the factory of the Bank of Worcester, he may remit by the bank to Newcastle or anywhere else, as readily as if his goods were sold and paid for and no exactions made upon him for the convenience he enjoys . . . Daniel Defoe. *Of Banks. An Essay upon Projects* (1697)

---

9 Charles Montagu   The Origin of Exchequer Bills

Charles Montagu, later Earl of Halifax (1661–1715) was Chancellor of the Exchequer from 1694 to 1699 and afterwards First Lord of the Treasury. He was possessed of great administrative and business talents, was a brilliant debater and a lifelong friend of Isaac Newton. It was he who introduced the Tunnage Bill in 1694. He was also the architect of the Great Recoinage begun in 1696; while the provisions for the new currency were being carried out, the credit of the government reached its lowest ebb, with most of the old silver withdrawn and little of the new, as yet, in circulation. Montagu's solution was to exploit a clause grafted onto Harley's National Land Bank Bill of 1696, empowering the government to issue negotiable paper bearing interest at the rate of threepence per day on a hundred pounds; the result was the issue of the first Exchequer Bills.

Everybody being now convinced of the mischiefs that the publick service, and all comerce suffer for want of paper credit, and of the necessity there is of reestablishing it in some manner or other, 'tis probable there will be a great concurrence among most people to advance the currency of Exchequer Bills (which are free from the envy and pique which has destroyed all private Credit) by all means that are not prejudicial to their own private Interest.

The receiving them in all paym.ts is the best means of giving them a currency, and such acceptance will be no prejudice to him who can part with them at the par, when He has occasion.

The occasions of parting with them are either to pay debts, carry on trade, or answer the King's dutys: if therefore by a general consent and agreement among all or the chief merchants and traders they were mutualy received and pay'd, and if his Majesty's officers accepted them in the publick Receipts, every man might dispose of them without loss, and consequently receive them without prejudice.

The King's officers are already commanded to accept them wherever they are tendered.

And 'tis not to be apprehended that there will not be a consent among Merchants in so useful a work, so beneficial to trade in general, and their own private Interest, if a way could be found to make the agreement general and publick whereby they might know one an others mind and mutualy joyn in the undertaking, and so be secure of having those Bills accepted on one hand, which they receive on the other.

In order therefore to give those, who are willing to assist the Goverm.t in this exigency, an opportunity to expresse those intensions 'tis humbly offer'd.

That the form of an instrum.t be prepared and engrossed, whereby the subscribers shall promise and engage that they will freely accept Exchequer Bills in all paym.ts due to them, this would in a manner be an association to stand by one another in accepting them.

But because the engaging to accept them indefinitely may be too hard a condition there should be a Proviso that no Man shall be obliged to take them beyond a certain sum, w.ch sum should be expressed in his subscription.

The subscribers should likewise promise and engage that within − − days after the time of their subscription they will lend into the Exchequer 1/10 of their subscription on credit of the Tallys and Orders in course. By this means £250,000 may be advanced, which will be a sufficient Capital to answer all demands at the Exchequer, if the subscribers circulate them as is proposed.

On the other hand the Lords of the Treasury should consent to allow the subscribers Interest at the rate of 9/14 p.c. for 9/10 of their respective subscriptions.

The subscriptions ought to begin with the Lords Justices, and Council, and by them be recomended to the Lord Mayor, and Court of Aldermen and carryed on in the several wards and companys, but in taking the subscriptions care must be had that no man subscribe above his reputed wealth, and Trade.

Particular reguard should be had of the Jews and Goldsmiths, that they may either come in and assist, or shew their unwillingness to help the Goverm.t.

If the subscriptions amount to the whole or the greatest part of £250,000 the consent of all people which at first made Gold and Silver the medium of Comerce may make those Bills supply their place while the silver is recoyning. Charles Montagu, later Earl of Halifax. *Exchequer Bills.* MS memorandum 65, Goldsmiths' Library

PART TWO

The Mercantilists
on Money

DURING the eighteenth century, writers on money in its more theoretical aspects continued to assume that an increase in its supply was beneficial to economic activity, as their earlier Mercantilist predecessors had done. Apart from this underlying principle, however, it is also possible to detect, from the late seventeenth century, more discussion of the facilities for expanding credit and the relationship of the circulation to the working of the economy as a whole, and less attention being paid to the value of money as such. It has already been noticed that the coincidence of a shortage of currency and a rash of banking proposals at the end of the seventeenth century opened new monetary problems to debate, and brought into being new financial instruments and institutions of unknown potential. Clearly, this provided a considerable impetus towards redirecting the attentions of those who wrote on the subject during the eighteenth century. As one authority has written, 'In this period, economic theory became increasingly interested in the operation and influence of money considered purely as money, rather than as a commodity which might itself possess inherent, definable value.'*

The emphasis on increasing the supply of money and the integration of credit instruments into a larger concept of something like total purchasing power can be noticed in many eighteenth century writers, eg in the work of Berkeley, Vanderlint, Tucker and Gee. At the same time it is possible to differen-

* D. Vickers, *Studies in the Theory of Money 1690–1776* (1960), 6.

tiate two streams of thought on the subject whose policy implications tended to run counter to one another and which were of lasting significance. There was a majority view, at least in so far as policy was concerned, that discussed money in terms of the standard of value and paid particular attention to the stability of the exchanges as an important influence on international trade. For the metallist writers, as they are described here, it was essential that money should consist of, or be adequately covered by some real commodity, usually silver or gold, such that the exchange value or purchasing power of that commodity would always be the same as the exchange value or purchasing power of money. In practice, this meant that a unit of money had to be firmly linked to, and freely interchangeable with, a given quantity of precious metal. Most subsequent writers on money, through the classical period and beyond, held to this fundamental concern with the standard of value and enable us to speak, in general terms, of an orthodox tradition. It is this underlying concern that runs like a thread from the metallist writers who sponsored the banking schemes of the late seventeenth century, and especially those who gave support to the Bank of England, through the authors of the Bullion Report to the Currency School architects of the Bank Act of 1844.

Outside of this tradition were the anti-metallist or cartalist writers who held, in various forms, the increasingly significant view that metallic money was no more than a special case of money in general. Many of these were only active in periods of monetary difficulty, some others were crude inflationists or became such in the course of time. But a few were important in helping to create a lasting tradition of dissent in English monetary thought. It is not always realised how many eighteenth-century writers were concerned to influence the level of employment. Although this concern is particularly clear in the work of the anti-metallists, it has a longer history going back to the Restoration period. From the beginning, devising a policy for unemployment involved some consideration of the theory of money. This can be seen in William Potter's *The Key of Wealth* (1650) and in Sir William Petty' *Treatise of Taxes and Contributions* (1662). In most instances thi line of thought went no further than a simple description of the effects of a monetary expansion, but occasionally there is a clear appreciation of something very like the multiplier. In the case of William Hodges we have a statement of the sequence by which spending on consumption creates income; although it was part of a prescription for a devaluation and there is no mention of saving or investment, it was far in advance of the time (10).

More orthodox writers in the following century were not without an interest in unemployment; on the contrary, they were more conscious of the adverse consequences of inflation and tended to assume that full employment would result from the smooth working of the economic system. It is more than coincidence that most of the land-bank projectors were anti-metallist in persuasion. For having rejected the more orthodox position, that it was the intrinsic value of money that mattered they were naturally more amenable to schemes that they believed would make possible a rational management of money. When one looks in greater detail at the work of those who were mainly responsible for the development of monetary thought from the late seventeenth century on, it is clear that it contains some elements that would be regarded as mercantilist and some as classical. This is the case with Sir William Petty's *Quantulumcunque* (11). It represents the most advanced discussion of the whole subject of money that the seventeenth century produced and includes, in a short space, all the important concepts taken up by monetary theorists during the following century. There is the traditional discussion of intrinsic value, or the metallic content of coins, combined with observations on the contemporary problem of a shortage of money He fully understood the notion of velocity of circulation, the significance of banks and bank-money, as well as the determination of the rate of interest. By contrast with earlier

Mercantilist discussion, which was conducted in terms of the narrow context of specie, Petty was concerned with relating the level of employment to the size of the circulation as well. When one remembers the increased attention given to the effects of paper money and the general impact of credit during the eighteenth century, Petty's encouragement of banking can be seen as a new alternative to the normal Mercantilist solution to the problem of a scarce currency in a country with no domestic production of the precious metals.

As a classical forerunner, Locke's contribution was quite different from Petty's; it is to be found in his two polemical essays published at the time of the recoinage controversy (12). The first statement of the quantity theory of money is usually attributed to him; the general level of prices, he contended, was always in proportion to the quantity of money, including with the latter the 'quickness of its circulation'. This formulation was, of course, a truism, but it did emphasise the function of money as a medium of exchange, though not yet as a store of value, and struck at the heart of the Mercantilist obsession by showing that the absolute size of the money supply as such had little to do with national wealth. Locke's theory of money led him naturally to a discussion of the rate of interest which he saw as being determined by conditions influencing the supply of money in a given demand situation. This led him to oppose any regulation of interest on the ground that this would jeopardise the activities of borrowers and lenders via the market rate, and have an adverse effect on trade.

Another blow to the traditional concern with a favourable balance of trade was David Hume's statement of the specie-flow mechanism in the middle of the eighteenth century (13). He argued that there was a natural distribution of specie taking place automatically between trading nations which tended to balance exports and imports in each country by adjustments to its price level. Thus an increase of gold into a country raises its price level and increases imports until a balance is achieved. On the other hand, any excess of imports results in an outflow of gold to restore equilibrium. The lesson to be drawn from this formulation was that policies aimed at achieving a consistently favourable balance would be self defeating. Hume was also responsible for the final argument against the importance of an abundance of money as such, as distinct from its increase. This view was taken over by Joseph Harris in his *Essay upon Money and Coins* (1757–8), the standard eighteenth-century text on the subject, and helps to explain the secondary role of money in the real analysis of the Classical school from Adam Smith onwards.

It should not go unnoticed that of the three authors chosen here to represent the unorthodox view of money the first two, Barbon and Law, were land-bank promoters, and the third Steuart, was a life-long Jacobite. All three made their theories of money central to their discussion of economic problems, and all showed a fundamental concern with raising the level of employment. Most of the land-bank projectors appear to have been anti-metallists but Barbon was perhaps the first to provide them with a theoretical foundation. Almost alone among his contemporaries he recognised that the stimulus given to employment by increased money expenditures would increase the consumption of commodities via the impact on demand (14). This greater awareness of the factors influencing total demand in the economy is an important feature of all unorthodox writers from Barbon to Law, through Berkeley and Vanderlint, to Steuart. But perhaps Barbon's most important single contribution to monetary theory was his quite new definition of interest, which he saw not as the 'rent of money', but as the 'rent of stock'. Virtually all Mercantilists held a purely monetary theory of interest, even Locke who gave some consideration to the demand side, and for them the important determinant was the supply of funds to the money market. Barbon's view of interest, resurrected by Massie in the mid-eighteenth century,* later became an important constituent in

* Joseph Massie, *Essay on the Governing Causes of the Natural Rate of Interest* (1750).

hat shift to real analysis that enabled the Classical school to lowngrade the monetary aspect of interest in favour of attempts o explain the concept of profit.

Although the link between land banking and anti-metallism :an be traced back to William Potter's *The Key of Wealth* (1650), the great systematic exposition belongs to John Law; he fact that his plan proved to be a prescription for disaster hould not be allowed to detract from his analytical achievenent (15). Before Adam Smith, Law made the only organised attempt to construct a theory of banking. Starting with the ise of land as the collateral for loans, he claimed that notes :ould never be overissued just so long as their amount did not exceed the money value of their collateral. Although he :onsistently used a land base for his currency, his main point was to relate the note issue to the market price of a productive asset, land being the most obvious contemporary example. By :his means, Law became the originator of the idea of a managed :urrency as a method of regulating the economy. His was the irst unequivocal expression of the dominant themes in the anorthodox monetary literature of the eighteenth century—the belief in the beneficent consequences of an expansion of :redit, usually through the issue of paper money—and the possibility of monetary control of the level of employment :hrough the demand for goods. In Law's system cheaper money would lead to an increase in expenditure and a rise in profit margins without raising prices, if the quantity of money was ncreased gradually. Critics of this view saw it as being only a transitional effect, occurring while prices reached a new level. To the extent that a supply response to changes in demand, not being immediate, must involve price increases, then this was valid criticism. But it was less reasonable to object to Law's assumption that idle resources existed in an economy that was certainly underemployed. It is worth noting, finally, that Law's argument concerning the employment effects of paper money issues via a favourable external balance and a subsequent inflow of bullion, anticipates a later doctrine of the Banking

School which was, however, confined to convertible paper only

Sir James Steuart's *Principles* was the only work to attempt a comprehensive treatment of the subject matter of economics before the publication of the *Wealth of Nations*. It is important in the present context because it was founded upon an anti metallist theory of money that synthesised most of the unorthodox monetary thought of the eighteenth century and stands in marked contrast to the ascendant classical position stated by Smith a few years later (16). Steuart's analysis of banking public and private credit, is much fuller than Smith's and of central importance to his object of studying an exchange or money economy experiencing growth. Steuart's emphasis on the economics of control and the role of the policy maker, while it has a decidedly modern ring, was increasingly out of tune in his own day. His use of the term political economy, one of the first instances in English, reflected a Continental view of the subject which saw it as an element of statecraft. Smith also wrote in this tradition of an applied science, though for him the role of the state and the influence of the monetary sector were much less important. Perhaps the most important feature of Steuart's monetary theory arose from his rejection of the Lockean view of money as a mere 'numéraire', a money of account. For Steuart metallic money was only a special case of money in general, and was divorced from commodities. Paper money was therefore a necessary adjunct to specie in the case of a deficient circulation, because only by maintaining the level of the circulation would monetary demand be sufficient to secure full employment. Employment and consumption were the ultimate ends of Steuart's growth theory; in it the supply of money was the central feature linking demand in money terms to the supply of commodities. In Steuart the anti-metallist disregard for inflation can be seen in its most developed form ruling out the possibility of any monetary influence on prices and incomes. Distinguishing sharply between the theoretical contribution of John Law's scheme and its failure in practice Steuart argues that paper money could be based on almost any security, including land, just so long as the asset value of the security remained stable. Having removed the danger of inflationary paper issues, he looked at an underemployed economy and recommended an increase in money incomes in order to induce a higher level of economic activity. Hence his advocacy of banks and government intervention.

As economic life became more complex in the eighteenth century, it necessitated greater use of various kinds of financial instrument to supplement metallic money eg bank credit and bills of exchange. Most writers appreciated their convenience and recognised their function in economising the use of precious metals, though the classic statements were not given until Thorton's *Paper Credit* and Ricardo's *Proposals for an Economical and Secure Currency*. Thus the distinction between the orthodox view and those outside it was not on the grounds of the money-moving functions of banks and paper systems, but on whether or not increases in the volume of money and money substitutes would benefit economic activity. Hence the basically classical view of Hume that a great quantity of money produced nothing beyond a proportionate increase in the price-level; and this despite the importance of his monetary theory for his political economy as a whole, especially the statement of the self-regulating mechanism in international trade.

If the advocacy of increases in the volume of money, in one form or another, was an incorrect prescription for raising the level of economic activity, then how were the monetary requirements of a developing economy to be assessed? One answer, as given by Steuart, was to reject the quantity theory altogether and to make prices depend on the supply of and demand for goods; in this way the likelihood of inflation and an external bullion drain was dismissed to make way for rising paper issues to meet the needs of trade and to achieve the employment objective. The other answer, hinted at by Adam Smith, was what came to be known as the 'real bills' doctrine and later, in a qualified form, as the principle of reflux. This was that the volume of circulation would naturally conform to the needs of

the economy so long as the banks, and in particular the Bank
of England, confined themselves to discounting genuine trade
bills and refused to accommodate speculative dealings. Smith's
version of the doctrine had applied only to fully convertible
notes; even so, the essential fallacy of the theory was later
brought out by Henry Thornton, who showed that the volume
of bills up for discount depended not only upon the state of
trade but upon the rate of interest at which bills were discounted.
Subsequent monetary debate was never to move far away from
the essential issues implicit in Thornton's treatment of the real
bills doctrine—the question of convertibility and the role of the
rate of interest in the control of the monetary system.

10 Sir William Hodges   A Glimpse of the Multiplier

Sir William Hodges (1645–1714) was a London merchant
who made a large fortune in the Spanish trade. He was
involved in the financial transactions of the government on
several occasions during the 1690s, and is reported once to
have accepted a bill for £300,000 and paid it for the use of
the fleet. Apart from his monetary contributions he wrote a
number of pamphlets relating to the working conditions of
seamen. Hodges was the most able of those recommending
devaluation as the solution to the problem of the coinage
during the early 1690s. In the course of his argument he seems
to grasp the multiplier effects of changes in the level of
spending and advocates devaluation in order to maintain the
volume of money in circulation.

It may be observed by all that Receive Money for their
Majesties, or for themselves, either from the Goldsmiths, or in
way of Trade, That the most of the Money that we receive is
Old Money, some broken, and a great deal clipt, and some
half worn out, very seldom our Mill'd Money coming to Hand
in Payments that we Receive: And if any will take the pains to
weigh £10 of Mill'd Money with £15 of the Old, that £10 of
Mill'd Money shall weigh down the £15 of the Old, and that

£100 of mill'd money shall weigh down £150 of the Old, if taken as it is received, but sometimes £4 of mill'd Money shall weigh down £7 of the Old; And there being so many Clippers continually a clipping of our old Money, it will be worse and worse every Year; and there being so many Goldsmiths, or Silver- Wire- Drawers, or others concerned in melting down our New-money, and so many outlandish men concerned in the buying up, and carrying away of our Old mill'd money, we are like to have less and less of it for time to come, if some way be not found out for to prevent it, and while it is so weighty, and at no higher price, no Law can hinder its being melted down, or carried away, except Angels would be at the trouble to execute them; for men that melt it down can do it, and none see them; and they that carry it away, can hide it as none find it, and they will never accuse themselves, except they are distracted: And the reason why we have so little of the mill'd, and do keep their Old, is, because one is too good to keep, and the other too bad to carry away: And we have not half enough of the Old neither; and therefore that which I would propose is, That we might have a new Coinage that might be better by a quarter part than our Old; that is, that £112–10s. of the New might weigh down £150 of the Old money; and that the said £112–10s. should weigh down £100 of our mill'd money that now we have; and in doing so, we should have plenty of good Money quickly, a full fourth part better than what we have, and have the Mint kept in continual supply with Silver; so that they should never need to sit still ten days in a Year, and the profit of £400,000 of that money would call in a £100,000 of Crackt and broken money: And it might be so ordered, That the Gold-smiths should have one and a half present for carrying in a continual supply of money, and not to let any lie in the mint above a month or five weeks; so that they should return their money ten times every Year, and that would be fifteen in the Hundred in a Year; and for the Coinage there might be one per Cent. more or less allowed for Coinage, and so there can never want Silver nor Coiners: And for the other ten per Cent.

G

to go the first £4 or 500,000 to call in as I said, a £100,000 of Crackt Money, and the profit of the rest, and there might be a Million more Coined in every Year. I would humbly propose that there might be £3 or 400,000 worth of crackt and broken, and decayed Money called in every Year, and the profit of the new Coinage will bear the loss of the old, for it cannot be supposed that there can be less than fifteen hundred thousand, or two millions of money Coined every Year, if the Mint be kept in a continual supply, as it will, if there be one and a half, or so allowed to bring in Silver, and the Coiners paid as before-said; and if Silver Rise, then the more Silver Rises, the less to go towards the calling in Crackt money, so that it can never rise so high, but there would be some overplus, and the higher Silver rises, the more plenty we should have brought in: And indeed it may be supposed our Guineas going at about 22s. at Christmas, makes us keep them unmelted, and also in England; and if the Crown-pieces had risen as much in proportion as the Guineas, they would have been preserved: Also if every twenty Shillings had gone for a Guinea, and if every Guinea were settled at 23s. and our Old 20 Shilling pieces at 25s. and the Old 22s. at 27s. they would be daily returned to England again, if they are not melted down: For it is reported that the Jews will bring over our Money again, if they get but four or five per Cent. by it. And indeed our mill'd money having been so good that strangers for some Years have gone from Shop to Shop to buy it up, to carry away: And if they could not have gotten that, they would rather have bought Goods, which they might have had hopes to get by, but would never have carried our old money to lose by: And it hath been judged that for some years, in times of Peace, we had 800,000, or a million of Goods from France, in a Year more than they had of us; whereas if our money had not been so good, they might have been glad to have taken our Goods, as we did theirs; or if not. Let them have kept their Goods, and we kept our money still, and by that means, and the Sweeds, and Danes, and others, we might have transported away several Hundred of Thousands a Pounds-worth of Goods in a Year more than we have done: And indeed, if we consider how great a loss it is to us to have our own money sent away, there is but few can imagine: For first, the most money we receive now is old money, Coined Fifty or a Hundred Years past; and our Trade is double now that it was then, as by the Custom-House Books will appear: And if our money is no more than what we had, then our Payments must be twice so long by Consequence: And indeed every million of money carried out of England, is the hindrance of twenty or thirty millions of Return, and the loss of two or three millions gaining among the Nation. As for Example: money among Tradesmen commonly returns through thirty or forty Hands every year, and that cannot be supposed, that one with another, they can get less than ten per Cent. and to most Lawyers and Doctors of Physick, and all the Clergy, and all Sallaries under their Majesties, the money is all gain, and so that counting one with another there is but ten per Cent. gotten throughout England, by the Return of money, so that a million returned through thirty hands in a Year, gaineth three millions, and the money the same at the Years end: And if it be remembered, after calling in the Parliament-money after 1660, that had been Coining many Years, money was extream scarce, and one effect I suppose of the same was the falling of the Rent of Farms in Essex and Suffolk, and perhaps in most Countreys in England, and the mill'd money Coined, since having been melted down, or carried away great part of it, Money is exceeding scarce now; whereas, were there six or seven millions of mill'd money Coined, as might be, in Three or Four Years, that we might keep when we had it, we might find the sweetness of it quickly, and also our Children after us: And indeed it cannot be supposed in Reason, but that the Cities of London and Westminster, and within the Bills of mortallity, spend as much in One year, as is in Ready money in England, and the rest of the Cities, and the Nation in General spend it five times over, and yet never a Penny the less at the Years end, except it be melted down, or carried away; and indeed the expence of money is the increase of Trade, and the Return of money is the support of Expence and Gain; for there are many thousands that spend a hundred Pound each for many years, that never were worth a hundred Pound a piece in their Lives; and the Return of money being their support; and others getting by them, and so the money of England being returned forty times over in a Year, or fifty times, that is through forty or fifty hands, gaineth the value of it five or six times over, and everybody lives by another; and indeed it may be supposed, that there is as much money owing in England, between Tennants and Landlords, Trades-men and merchants, and Goldsmiths, and every sort of men, as twenty times the money in England cometh to, there being few men but have twenty times more owing to them, than they have ready money; and if care be not taken that we may have money that will stay with us, I fear we shall be like men in Consumptions: For let men feed what they will, if it stayeth not in their Bodies, they cannot be Healthy: And let us Coin what we will, if we keep it not, we shall not grow very rich: For money is so great a Cordial, it is like Blood in the Veins that circulates from the Heart to Head and Feet, and every member, and the Body receiveth Life and Vigour thereby, and Nourishment, and every member the better for it, and the Blood remains still: And so is money in Trade in such a Nation as ours; and we have generally the best Goods in the World to send out into other Nations our Tinn, and Lead, and Woollen-Cloth, and Serges, and other Woollen Manufactory, and divers others Goods to fetch in Goods enough, and money also, if we did not let other Nations carry away our good mill'd money. And indeed, another loss is the melting of it down: And also there is a very great Error, that many Victuallers, Tradesmen, and others have forty or fifty, or a hundred Pound in Plate and Rings by them, which never saw half so much money together of their own in seven Years; and every hundred Pound so lying dead and uncoined, doth lose its being returned through 40 Hands in a Year, which is the loss of the Return of £4,000 and the loss of gaining £2 or 300 among all them it would be returned to; and some are so foolish as to let Plate ly in pawn 5 or 6 years, as a Friend of mine hath had £2, or 300 pounds worth so left with him in Plate 5 Years for £200 the interest of which is £60. And how great a loss is that to the publick, and to the Party, who if they had sold the Plate at first, had saved £60. And if we consider how sad a condition the next Age will be in, if there be not some care taken to leave them better money than our Old money, that is too light by £50 in £150. And if we do not take Care, it will be less, so many hundreds being concerned in the Clipping-Trade: And also it may be considered, That as there is near double the number of Traders now that was fifty years past, so we do need double the money to carry on the Trade: And if Traders should increase a fourth part more in thirty years, we shall need three times the money that was Fifty Years past; and if there be no money coined but what will be melted down or carried away, they will be then in a far worse condition than now we are, which will be bad for Landlords as well as Tennants, and for merchants, as well as Tradesmen and others . . . William Hodges. *An Humble Proposal to their Most Excellent Majesties . . . and to the Two Most Honourable Houses . . .* (1693)

THE ORTHODOX METALLIST TRADITION
11 Sir William Petty   Money and Coin
Petty (1623–87) was a pioneer of the empirical tradition in English political economy. In addition to his work in the application of statistical method to the measurement of economic phenomena, he was Professor of Anatomy at Oxford and a charter member of the Royal Society. His *Quantulumcunque* contains the most advanced discussion of the whole subject of money that the seventeenth century produced and includes, in a short space, all the important concepts taken up by monetary writers in the eighteenth century. The orthodox view of the nature of money is clearly stated, the significance of velocity of circulation and bank-money are perceived, and interest is seen as the rent of money.

Suppose that 20s. of new mill'd Money doth weigh 4 Ounces *Troy*, according to Custom or Statute. Suppose that 20s. of old *Eliz.* and *James's* Money, which ought also to weigh 4 Ounces *Troy*, doth weigh 3 Ounces *Troy*; and very variously between 3 and 4 Ounces, viz. none under 3, and none full 4.

Suppose that much of the new mill'd regular Money is carried into the *East-Indies*, but none of the old light and unequal Money.

QUESTIONS

Qu. 1. Whether the old unequal Money ought to be new Coined, and brought to an equality?

Answ. It ought: Because Money made of Gold and Silver is the best Rule of Commerce, and must therefore be equal, or else it is no Rule; and consequently no Money, and but bare Metal which was Money before it was worn and abused into Inequality.

Qu. 2. At whose Charge?

Answ. At the States Charge, as now it is: Because the Owner was no cause of its Inequality, but the States neglect in (not) preventing and punishing such Abuses, which are remedied by new Coinage.

Qu. 3. Of what weight and fineness ought the new Shilling to be?

Answ. Of the same with the other present new Money, and which the old was of, when it was new: Because all must be like, all according to the Statute; and all fit to pay ancient Debts, according to what was really lent.

Qu. 4. Suppose 20s. of old Money may make but 18s. of new, who shall bear the loss of the two shillings?

Answ. Not the States: Because men would clip their own Money: but the owner himself must bear the loss, because he might have refused light and defective Money, or put it away in time; it being sufficient that he shall have new regular beautiful Money for his own unequal Money, at the States Charge, Ounce for Ounce weight.

Qu. 5. After this Reformation of Coin, Will more Silver be carried out of England, suppose into the East-Indies, than before; and to the Damage of England?

Answ. Somewhat more: But none to the Damage of *England, Eo Nomine*; but rather to its Profit: Because the Merchant will be considered for the Manufacture of the new Money; besides the Metal of it, as he only was when he carried out *Spanish* Reals.

Qu. 6. Whereas the Merchants carries Scarlet and Silver to the Indies, will he not now carry only the new coined Silver?

Answ. The Merchant will buy as much Scarlet as he can for 100 new Shillings, and then consider whether he shall get more Silk in the *Indies* for that Scarlet than for another 100 of the like Shillings: And, according to this Conjecture, he will carry Scarlet or Shillings *in specie*, or part one, part the other, if he be in doubt.

Qu. 7. But will not England be impoverished by Merchants carrying out the said 100 Shillings?

Answ. No, if he brings home for them as much Silk as will yield above 100 Shillings (perhaps 200 Shillings) in *Spain*, and then bring the same 200 into *England*: or, of he bring home as much Pepper as an *English* man will give him 200 of the like Shillings for. So the Merchant and *England* shall both Gain by Exporting the 100 Shillings.

Qu. 8. But if the new Shilling were but $\frac{3}{4}$ths of the weight as formerly, then the Merchant would not meddle with them at all, and so secure this fear of impoverishment?

Answ. The Merchant would Export then, just as before; Only he will give but $\frac{3}{4}$ so much Pepper, or other *Indian* Goods, for the new retrenched Shilling as he did for the old: And would accept in *India* $\frac{3}{4}$ as much Pepper as he formerly had for the old: And consequently there would be no difference, but among a few such Fools as take Money by its name, and not by its weight and fineness.

Qu. 9. If a Shilling was by new Coinage reduced to ¾ of its present weight, should be not thereby have ⅓ more of Money than now we have, and consequently be so much the richer? Answ. You would indeed have ⅓ part more of the new christned Shillings; but not an Ounce more of Silver, nor Money; nor could you get an Ounce more of Forreign Commodities for all your new multiplied Money than before: Nor even of any Domestick Commodities; but perhaps a little at first from the few Fools above mentioned. As for Instance; Suppose you buy a Silver Vessel from a Goldsmith weighing 20 Ounces, at 6s. per Ounce, making 6 Pounds or 24 Ounces of Coined Silver; now suppose that the said 6 Pounds were reduced from weighing 24 Ounces to weigh but 18 Ounces upon the new Coinage; but be still called 6 Pound even by the King's Proclamation; Can it be imagined that the Goldsmith will give his Vessel weighing 20 Ounces of wrought for 18 Ounces of unwrought Silver? For the Workmanship of Money is of little value. Now the Absurdity is the same in all other Commodities, though not so demonstrable as in a Commodity whose Materials are the same with Money.

Qu. 10. Cannot Authority Command that men should give as much Commodity for the new retrencht Money, as for the old which weighed ⅓ part more? Answ. Then the effect of such Authority would also be to take away ⅓ of all mens Goods, which are Commodities beyond Seas, and give the same to Forreigners, who would have them for ¾ of the usual quantity of Silver: And the same Authority would take away from the Creditor ⅓ of the Money which was due before the Proclamation.

Qu. 11. Whereas you suppose retrenching ¼ in the new Coinage; Suppose it was but 1/10, how would the matter be then? Answ. Just the same: For *Magis et minus non mutant speciem*: But it were better you supposed that one Shilling were to be taken for 10 or 20, then the Absurdity would be it self so visible, as to need no such Demonstration, as is needful in such small matters as Common Sense cannot discern: For if the wealth of

the Nation could be *decupled* by a Proclamation, it were strange
that such Proclamations have not long since been made by
our Governours.

Qu. 12. Will not some men, having occasions to buy Commodities in Forreign Parts, carry out all Money, and so not
vend or Export our Own Commodities at all?

Answ. If some *English* Merchants should be so improvident,
yet the Forreign Merchants would buy up such *English* Commodities as they wanted, with Money brought into *England*
from their respective Countries, or with such Commodities as
England likes better than Money. For the vending of *English*
Commodities doth not depend upon any other thing, but the
use and need which Forreigners have of them. But were it not
a folly for an *English* man not to carry Lead into *Turkey*: but go
thither with Money, in his Ballast, and so loose the Freight of
the Lead, which he might sell there; And that a Ship should
come from *Turkey* with Money, in her Ballast also, to fetch
Lead from *England* which might have been carried at first by
the *English* Ship? No: The art of a Merchant is to consider all
those Matters, so as no Prince's Proclamation concerning the
Weight and Denominations of Coins, signifies any thing to
Forreigners when they know it, nor to his own Subjects *pro
futuro*, what e're Disturbances it may make amongst them *pro
prœterito*. We say again: it were better for a Prince owing 20s.
to say he will pay but 15s. than disguishing his own particular
purpose, to say that all landlords shall henceforth take 15s.
Rent for 20s. due to them by their Tenants Leases; and that
he who hath lent a 100*l*. on the *Monday*, (the Proclamation of
Retrenchment coming out on *Tuesday*) may be repaid on
Wednesday with ¾ or 75*l*. on the very Money he lent two days
before.

Qu. 13. Why is not our old worn unequal Money new Coined
and equallized?

Answ. There may be many weak Reasons for it, But the only
good one which I know, is, that bad and unequal Money may
prevent hoarding, whereas weighty, fine and beautiful Money

doth encourage it in some few timorous Persons, but not in the Body of Trading Men. Upon the account of Beauty our *Britannia* Half-pence were almost all horded as Medals till they grew common; For if but 100 of those pieces had been Coined, they would for their Work and Rarity have been worth above 5s. each, which for their Matter are not worth that Half-penny they pass for: For in them, *Materiam superabat Opus*.

Qu. 14. Why hath Money been raised, or retrencht, or imbased by many wise States, and so often?

Answ. When any State doth these things, they are like Bankrupt Merchants, who Compound for their Debts by paying 16s. 12s., or 10s. in the pound; Or forcing their Creditors to take off their Goods at much above the Market rates. And the same State might as well have paid but $\frac{3}{4}$ of what they ow'd, as to retrench their Money in General to $\frac{3}{4}$ of the known weight and fineness. And these practices have been compassed by Bankers and Cashiers, for oblique Considerations, from the Favourites of such Princes and States.

Qu. 15. It is then the Honour of England that no such Tricks have been practiced, though in the greatest Streights that ever that State hath been in.

Answ. It hath been their Wisdom, and consequently their Honour to keep up a Rule and Measure of Trade amongst themselves, and with all Nations.

Qu. 16. But is there no Case wherein Money may be justly and honourably raised?

Answ. Yes, in order to Regulation and Equalising of Species of Coins; As when two Species of one Weight and Fineness are taken at different Rates, then the one may be raised or the other depressed: But this must be rated by the Estimation of the whole World as near as it can be known, and not by any private Nation; and the like may be done between Gold and Silver.

Qu. 17. What do you think of the rising or falling of the Price of Lands, from this following Instance, viz. A piece of Land was sold 60 Years ago for 1000*l*. that is for a 1000 Jacobusses; and the same Land is now sold for 1000*l*. or 1000 Guineas, and the

Guinea is but 5/6 the weight of the Jacobus. Is the Land cheaper now than 60 Years ago?

Answ. It looks like a Demonstration that it is: Yet if Gold be not Money, but a Commodity next like to Money, and that Silver be only Money; then we must see whether 1000 *Jacobusses* would then purchase no more Silver than 1000 *Guineas* will do now: For if so, the Land was heretofore and now sold for the same Quantity of Money, though not of Gold; and is neither risen nor fallen by what hath been instanced.

Qu. 18. What is the difference between retrenching or raising of Money, and imbasing the Metal of the same, as by mixing Copper with Silver?

Answ. The first is the better of the two, if such Mixture be of no use in other things: For if 20s. which contains 4 Ounces of Silver, should be reduced to 3 Ounces of Silver, it is better than to add one Ounce of Copper to the same, in order to make 4 seeming Ounces as before: For if you come to want the said 3 Ounces of Silver mixt with Copper, you must lose the Copper, upon the Test, and the Charge of Refining also, which will amount to above 4 *per Cent.*

Qu. 19. What do you object against small Silver Money; as against Single Pence, Two Pence, &c.?

Answ. That the Coinage of small Pieces would be very chargeable, and the Pieces themselves apt to be lost, and more liable to wearing; for little of our old small Money is now to be seen, and our Groats are worn away to Three half-pence(worth) in Metal.

Qu. 20. What do you say of Money made wholly of base Metal, such as Farthings, &c.?

Answ. That the want of Materials ought to be made up by the fineness of Coinage, to very near the intrinsick Value; or what is gained by the Want of either, to be part of the King's Revenue.

Qu. 21. Which is best, Copper or Tin, for this purpose?

Answ. Copper: Because it is capable of the most imitable and durable Coinage: though the Copper by Forreign, and Tin a

Native Commodity. For suppose Copper and Tin of the same Value in *England*; yet if 100 Weight of Tin sent to *Turkey* will fetch home as much Silk as will fetch above 100 of Copper from *Sweden*, in such case the Difference between Native and Forreign is nothing.

Qu. 22. This Doctrine may extend to a free exportation of Money and Bullion, which is against our Laws: Are our Laws not good?

Answ. Perhaps they are against the Laws of Nature, and also impracticable: For we see that the Countries which abound with Money and all other Commodities, have followed no such Laws: And contrarywise, that the Countries which have forbid these Exportations under the highest Penalties, are very destitute both of Money and Merchandize.

Qu. 23. Is not a Country the poorer for having less Money?

Answ. Not always: For as the most thriving Men keep little or no Money by them, but turn and wind it into various Commodities to their great Profit, so may the whole Nation also; which is but many particular Men united.

Qu. 24. May a Nation, suppose England, have too much Money?

Answ. Yes: As a particular Merchant may have too much Money, I mean coined Money, by him.

Qu. 25. Is there any way to know how much Money is sufficient for any Nation?

Answ. I think it may pretty well be guessed at; viz. I think that so much Money as will pay half a Years Rent for all the Lands of England, and a Quarters Rent of the Houseing, and a Weeks Expence of all the People, and about a Quarter of the Value of all the exported Commodities, is sufficient for that purpose. Now when the States will cause these things to be computed, and the Quantity of their Coins to be known, which the new Coining of their old Money will best do, then it may also be known whether we have too much or too little Money.

Qu. 26. What Remedy is there if we have too little Money?

Answ. We must erect a Bank, which well computed, doth almost double the Effect of our coined Money: And we have in *England* Materials for a Bank which shall furnish Stock enough to drive the Trade of the whole Commercial World.

Qu. 27. What if we have too much Coin?

Answ. We may melt down the heaviest, and turn it into the Splendour of Plate, in Vessels or Utensils of Gold and Silver; or send it out, as a Commodity, where the same is wanting or desired: or let it out at Interest, where Interest is high.

Qu. 28. What is Interest or Use-Money?

Answ. A Reward for forbearing the use of your own Money for a Term or Time agreed upon, whatsoever need your self may have of it in the mean while.

Qu. 29. What is Exchange?

Answ. Local Interest, or a Reward given for having your Money at such a Place where you most need the use of it.

Qu. 30. What is the Trade of a Banker?

Answ. Buying and selling of Interest and Exchange: Who is honest only upon the Penalty of losing a beneficial Trade, founded upon a good Opinion of the World, which is called Credit.

Qu. 31. You were speaking of base Money and Farthings, which are generally below the intrinsick Value, and therefore ought not to be permitted to increase ad infinitum. Is there any way to know how many were enough?

Answ. I think there is: viz. Allowing about 12d. in Farthings to every Family: So as if there be a Million of Families in *England* (as I think there be) then about 50,000*l.* in Farthings would suffice for Change; and if such Farthings were but $\frac{1}{5}$th below the intrinsick Value, the Nation would pay but 10,000*l.* for this Convenience: But if this way of Families be not Limitation enough, you may help it by considering the smallest piece of Silver Money current in the Nation; which how much lesser it is, by so much lesser may the Number of Farthings being but to make up Payments in Silver, and to adjust Accompts: To which end of adjusting Accompts let me add, that if your old defective Farthings were cryed down to 5 a Penny, you might keep all Accompts in a way of Decimal Arithmetick, which hath been long desired for the ease and certainty of Accompts. Qu. 32. What do you think of our Laws for limiting Interest? Answ. The same as of limiting the Exportation of Money, and there may be as well Laws for limiting Exchange also: For Interest always carrieth with it an Ensurance *præmium*, which is very casual, besides that of Forbearance: For Instance, in *Ireland* there was a time when Land (the highest security) was sold for 2 Years Purchase: It was then naturally just to take 20, 30, or 40 *per Cent*. Interest; whereas there the Law allows but 10. And since that time, Land being risen to 12 Years Purchase, responsible Men will not give above 8. And insolvent Men will offer *Cent. per Cent*. notwithstanding the Law. Again, suppose a Man hath 100*l*. of Land worth 20 Years Purchase, and another 100*l*. in Houses, worth 12 Years Purchase, and another 100*l*. in Shipping worth 2 Years Purchase; and another in Horses, worth 6 Months Purchase; Is it not manifest he must have a greater Yearly *præmium* for lending his House than his Land, his Ship then his House, and his Horse than his Ship? For if his Horse be worth 100*l*. he cannot hire him out for less than 10s. *per diem*, whereas the Land will not yield a Groat for the same time; and these Hires are the same with Interest. Sir William Petty. *Quantulumcunque Concerning Money* (1682)

12 John Locke   Defence of the Standard

The philosopher Locke (1632–1704) was consulted by Montagu at the time of the currency crisis. The ruthless logic of his arguments in defence of the standard had the effect of discrediting the alternative scheme of William Lowndes, Secretary to the Treasury. The bill passed in April 1696 for a restoration of the coinage was in substantial accordance with Locke's views. His two essays on the currency problem are best remembered for containing the first full statement of the quantity theory truism, that the value of money varied inversely with its quantity.

The necessity of a certain proportion of money to trade (I conceive) lies in this, that money, in its circulation, driving the several wheels of trade, whilst it keeps in that channel (for some of it will unavoidably be drained into standing pools) is all shared between the landholder, whose land affords the materials; the labourer, who works them; the broker i.e. the merchant and shopkeeper, who distributes them to those that want them; and the consumer who spends them. Now money is necessary to all these sorts of men, as serving both for counters and for pledges, and so carrying with it even reckoning, and security, that he, that receives it, shall have the same value for it again, of other things that he wants, whenever he pleases. The one of these it does by its stamp and denomination; the other by its intrinsick value, which is its quantity.

For mankind, having consented to put an imaginary value upon gold and silver, by reason of their durableness, scarcity, and not being very liable to be counterfeited; have made them, by general consent, the common pledges, whereby men are assured, in exchange for them, to receive equally valuable things, to those they parted with, for any quantity of these metals. By which means it comes to pass, that the intrinsic value, regarded in these metals, made the common barter, is nothing but the quantity, which men give or receive of them. For they having, as money, no other value, but as pledges to procure what one wants, or desires; and they procuring what we want, or desire, only by their quantity, it is evident, that the intrinsic value of silver, and gold, used in commerce, is nothing but their quantity . . .

That, supposing any island separate from the commerce of the rest of mankind; if gold and silver, or whatever else (so it be lasting) be their money, if they have but a certain quantity of it, and can get no more, that will be a steady, standing measure of the value of all other things.

That, if in any country they use for money any lasting material, whereof there is not any more to be got, and so cannot be increased; or being of no other use, the rest of the world does not value it, and so it is not like to be diminished; this also would be a steady, standing measure of the value of other commodities.

That, in a country, where they had such a standing measure, any quantity of that money (if it were but so much, that every body might have some) would serve to drive any proportion of trade, whether more, or less; there being counters enough to reckon by, and the value of the pledges being still sufficient, as constantly increasing with the plenty of the commodity. But these three last, being built on suppositions, that are not like to be found in the practice of mankind, since navigation and commerce have brought all parties acquainted with one another, and introduced the use of gold and silver money, into all trading parts of the world; they serve rather to give us some light into the nature of money, than to teach here a new measure of traffic. Though it be certain, that that part of the world, which bred most of our gold and silver, used least of it in exchange, and used it not for money at all.

That therefore, in any country, that hath commerce with the rest of the world, it is almost impossible now to be without the use of silver coin; and having money of that, and accounts kept in such money, it is impossible to have any standing, unalterable measure of the value of things. For, whilst the mines supply to mankind more than wastes and consumes in its use, the quantity of it will daily grow greater, in respect of other commodities, and its value less.

That in a country, that hath open commerce with the rest of the world, and uses money, made of the same materials with their neighbours, any quantity of that money will not serve to drive any quantity of trade; but there must be a certain proportion between their money and trade. The reason whereof is this, because, to keep your trade going without loss, your commodities amongst you must keep an equal, or at least, near the price of the same species of commodities in the neighbouring countries: which they cannot do, if your money be far less than in other countries: for then, either your commodities must be sold very cheap, or a great part of your trade must stand still,

there not being money enough in the country to pay for them
(in their shifting of hands) at that high price, which the plenty,
and consequently low value of money makes them at in another
country. For the value of money in general, is the quantity of
all the money in the world, in proportion to all the trade: but
the value of money in any one country, is the present quantity
of the current money in that country, in proportion to the
present trade. Supposing then, that we had now in England but
half as much money, as we had seven years ago, and yet had
still as much yearly product of commodities, as many hands to
work them, and as many brokers to disperse them, as before;
and that the rest of the world we trade with, had as much money
as they had before, (for it is likely they should have more by our
moiety shared amongst them) it is certain, that either half our
rents should not be paid, half our commodities not vented, and
half our labourers not employed, and so half the trade be
clearly lost; or else, that every one of these must receive but
half the money for their commodities and labour, they did
before, and but half so much as our neighbours do receive, for
the same labour, and the same natural product at the same time.
Such a state of poverty as this, though it will make no scarcity
of our native commodities amongst us, yet it will have these ill
consequences.

1. It will make our native commodities vent very cheap.
2. It will make all foreign commodities very dear, both which
will keep us poor. For the merchant making silver and gold his
measure, and considering what the foreign commodity costs
him (i.e. how many ounces of silver) in the country where money
is more plenty, i.e. cheaper; and considering too, how many
ounces of silver it will yield him in another country; will not
part with it here, but for the same quantity of silver, or as much
of that silver will buy here of our commodity, which will be a
great deal more than in another place. So that, in all our
exchange of native for foreign commodities, we shall pay
double the value that any other country does, where money is
in greater plenty. This, indeed, will make a dearness, and, in

time, a scarcity of foreign commodities; which is not the worst inconveniency that it brings upon us, supposing them not absolutely necessary. But,

3. It endangers the drawing away our people, both handicrafts, mariners, and soldiers; who are apt to go, where their pay is best, which will always be where there is greatest plenty of money, and in time of war must needs bring great distress.

Upon this measure too it is, that the variation of exchange of money, between several countries, does somewhat depend. For it is certain, that one ounce of silver is always of equal value to another ounce of silver, considered in its intrinsick worth, or in reference to the universal trade of the world: but it is not of the same value, at the same time, in several parts of the world, but is of the most worth in that country, where there is the least money, in proportion to its trade: and therefore, men may afford to give twenty ounces of silver in one place, to receive eighteen or nineteen ounces of silver in another. But this is not all: to this then, (to find out the alteration of the exchange) the over-balance of the trade must be taken into consideration. These two together regulate the exchange, in all the commerce of the world, and, in both, the higher rate of exchange depends upon one and the same thing, viz. the greater plenty of money in one country than in the other: only with this difference, that where the over-balance of trade raises the exchange above the par, there it is the plenty of money which private merchants have in one country, which they desire to remove into another: but, where the riches of the country raises the exchange above the par, there it is the plenty of the money in the whole country. In one, the merchant has more money (or debts, which is all one) in a foreign country, than his trade there will employ, and so is willing to allow upon exchange to him abroad, and that shall pay him ready money at home, 1, 2, 3 &c per cent. more or less, proportionably as his, or his countrymen's plenty of ready money abroad, the danger of leaving it there, or the difficulty of bringing it home in specie, and his present need of money at home, is greater or less: in the other, the whole country has more money, than can well be employed in the trade thereof, or at least the proportion of the money to the trade is greater than in the neighbouring country, where the exchange is below the par.

For, supposing the balance of trade to be equal between England and Holland, but that there is in Holland a greater plenty of money than in England, (which will appear by the lowness of the natural use in Holland, and the height of the natural use in England; and also by the dearness of food and labour in general in Holland, and the cheapness of it in England). If N. has £10,000 in Holland, which the greater advantage he could make of it in England, either by use or purchase, tempts him to transfer into England, it is probable he will give as much to a merchant in England, to pay him £10,000 in England, as the insurance at that time between Holland and England is worth. If this happens to be in a country, where the exportation of bullion is prohibited, he must pay the more: because his venture, if he carry it in specie, will be greater. And upon this ground, perhaps, the prohibiting the exportation of money out of England, under penalties, may be of some use, by making the rate of the exchange greater to those countries, which import upon us more than they export in commodities; and so retain some part of the money, which their over-balance of trade would carry away from us, though, after all, if we are over-balanced in trade, it must go.

But, since the Holland merchant cannot receive N's £10,000 in money in Holland, and pay him £10,000 in England, unless his over-balance of trade make Englishmen indebted to him £10,000 in money, which he is not like to take in commodities; I think the over-balance of trade is that, which chiefly raises the exchange in any country, and that plenty of money, in any country, does it only for so much of the money as is transferred, either to be lett out to use, or to be spent there. And, though, lending to foreigners, upon use, does not at all alter the balance of trade, between those countries, yet it does alter the exchange between those countries for so much as is lent upon use, by not calling away the money, that should follow the over-balance of trade, but letting it rest there, as if it were accounted for; all one as if the balance of trade were for so much altered. But this being not much, in comparison of the general traffick between two nations, or at least varying slower, the merchant too regulating the exchange, and not the userer; I suppose it is the present balance of trade, on which the exchange immediately and chiefly depends, unless some accident shall make a great deal of money be remitted at the same time from one place to another, which will for that time raise the exchange all one as an over-balance of trade; and indeed, when examined, is generally very little different from it.

To be able to estimate the par, with the rise and fall of the exchange, it is necessary to know the intrinsick value, i.e. how much silver is in the coins of the two countries, by which you reckon and charge the bill of exchange. John Locke. *Some Considerations of the Consequences of the Lowering of Interest, and Raising the Value of Money* . . . (2nd Ed 1696)   ———

13 David Hume   Money and the Trade Balance

David Hume (1711–76) the philosopher, historian and economist, published his main economic writings in 1752 under the title 'Political Discourses'. His analysis of money and the balance of trade, spread over a number of essays, marked a shift of attention away from the Mercantilist concern with the nation's supply of money. Hume is generally regarded as the originator of the self-equilibrating, specie-flow mechanism of international trade which Ricardo and J. S. Mill later made a cornerstone of the classical system.

———

Money is not, properly speaking, one of the subjects of commerce but only the instrument which men have agreed upon to facilitate the exchange of one commodity for another. It is none of the wheels of trade; it is the oil which renders the motion of the wheels more smooth and easy. If we consider any one kingdom by itself, it is evident that the greater or less plenty of money is of no consequence; since the prices of commodities are always proportioned to the plenty of money, and a crown in Harry VII's time served the same purpose as a pound does at present. The greater number of people and their greater industry are serviceable in all cases, at home and abroad, in private and in public. But the greater plenty of money is very limited in its use and may even sometimes be a loss to a nation in its commerce with foreigners.

There seems to be a happy concurrence of causes in human affairs which checks the growth of trade and riches and hinders them from being confined entirely to one people as might naturally at first be dreaded from the advantages of an established commerce. Where one nation has gotten the start of another in trade, it is very difficult for the latter to regain the ground it has lost because of the superior industry and skill of the former, and the greater stocks of which its merchants are possessed and which enable them to trade on so much smaller profits. But these advantages are compensated in some measure by the low price of labour in every nation which has not an extensive commerce and does not much abound in gold and silver. Manufactures, therefore gradually shift their places leaving those countries and provinces which they have already enriched and flying to others, whither they are allured by the cheapness of provisions and labour till they have enriched these also and are again banished by the same causes. And in general, we may observe, that the dearness of everything, from plenty of money is a disadvantage which attends an established commerce and sets bounds to it in every country, by enabling the poorer states to undersell the richer in all foreign markets.

This has made me entertain a doubt concerning the benefit of banks and paper-credit which are so generally esteemed advantageous to every nation. That provisions and labour should become dear by the increase of trade and money, is in many respects an inconvenience; but an inconvenience that is unavoidable and the effect of that public wealth and prosperity which are the end of all our wishes. It is compensated by the advantages which we reap from the possession of these precious metals and the weight which they give the nation in all foreign wars and negotiations. But there appears no reason for increasing that inconvenience by a counterfeit money, which foreigners will not accept of in any payment, and which any great disorder in the state will reduce to nothing. There are it is true many people in every rich state who, having large sums of money, would prefer paper with good security as being of more easy transport and more safe custody. If the public provide not a bank, private bankers will take advantage of this circumstance as the goldsmiths formerly did in London or as the bankers do at present in Dublin; therefore it is better, it may be thought, that a public company should enjoy the benefit of that paper credit, which always will have place in every opulent kingdom. But to endeavour artificially to increase such a credit, can never be the interest of any trading nation, but must lay them under disadvantages, by increasing money beyond its natural proportion to labour and commodities, and thereby heightening their price to the merchant and manufacturer. And in this view it must be allowed that no bank could be more advantageous, than such a one as locked up all the money it received, and never augmented the circulating coin, as is usual, by returning part of its treasure into commerce. A public bank, by this expedient, might cut off much of the dealings of private bankers and money-jobbers; and though the state bore the charge of salaries to the directors and tellers of this bank (for according to the preceding supposition, it would have no profit from its dealings), the national advantage resulting from the low price of labour and the destruction of paper-credit, would be a sufficient compensation. Not to mention, that so large a sum, lying ready at command, would be a convenience in times of great public danger and distress and what part of it was used might be replaced at leisure, when peace and tranquility was restored to the nation ... It is indeed evident that money is nothing but the representation of labour and commodities, and serves only as a method of rating or estimating them. Where coin is in greater plenty, as a greater quantity of it is required to represent the same quantity of goods; it can have no effect, either good or bad, taking a nation within itself any more than it would make an alteration on a merchant's books, if, instead of the Arabian method of notation which requires few characters, he should make use of the Roman which requires a great many. Nay, the greater quantity of money, like the Roman characters, is rather inconvenient, and requires greater trouble both to keep and transport it. But notwithstanding this conclusion which must be allowed just, it is certain that since the discovery of the mines in America, industry has increased in all the nations of Europe, except in the possessors of those mines; and this may justly be ascribed, amongst other reasons, to the increase of gold and silver. Accordingly we find that in every kingdom into which money begins to flow in greater abundance than formerly, everything takes a new face; labour and industry gain life; the merchant becomes more enterprising, the manufacturer more diligent and skilful, and even the farmer follows his plough with greater alacrity and attention. This is not easily to be accounted for if we consider only the influence which a greater abundance of coin has in the kingdom itself, by heightening the price of commodities, and obliging everyone to pay a greater number of these little yellow or white pieces for everything he purchases. And as to foreign trade, it appears that great plenty of money is rather disadvantageous by raising the price of every kind of labour.

To account then for this phenomenon, we must consider, that though the high prices of commodities be a necessary consequence of the increase of gold and silver, yet it follows not immediately upon that increase; but some time is required before the money circulates through the whole state and makes its effect be felt on all ranks of people. At first no alteration is perceived; by degrees the price rises first for one commodity then of another; till the whole at last reaches a just proportion with the new quantity of specie which is in the kingdom. In my opinion it is only in this interval or intermediate situation between the acquisition of money and rise of prices, that the increasing quantity of gold and silver is favourable to industry. When any quantity of money is imported into a nation, it is not at first dispersed into many hands, but is confined to the coffers of a few persons, who immediately seek to employ it to advantage. Here are a set of manufacturers or merchants, we shall suppose, who have received returns of gold and silver for goods which they sent to CADIZ. They are thereby enabled to employ more workmen than formerly, who never dream of demanding higher wages, but are glad of employment from such good paymasters. If workmen became scarce, the manufacturer gives higher wages but at first requires an increase of labour; and this is willingly submitted to by the artisan, who can now eat and drink better, to compensate his additional toil and fatigue. He carries his money to market where he finds every thing at the same price as formerly, but returns with greater quantity and of better kinds for the use of his family. The farmer and gardener finding that all their commodities are taken off, apply themselves with alacrity to the raising more; and at the same time can afford to take better and more cloths from their tradesmen, whose price is the same as formerly and their industry only whetted by so much new gain. It is easy to trace the money in its progress through the whole Commonwealth where we shall find that it must first quicken the diligence of every individual before it increase the price of labour . . .

From the whole of his reasoning we may conclude, that it is of no manner of consequence, with regard to the domestic happiness of a state whether the money be in a greater or less quantity. The good policy of the magistrate consists only in keeping it, if possible, still increasing: because by that means he keeps alive a spirit of industry in the nation, and increases the stock of labour, in which consists all real power and riches. A nation whose money decreases is actually, at that time, weaker and more miserable than another nation which possesses no more money but is on the increasing hand. This will be easily accounted for, if we consider that the alterations in the quantity of money, either on one side or the other, are not immediately attended with proportionable alterations in the price of commodities. There is always an interval before matters be adjusted to their new situation and this interval is as pernicious to industry, when gold and silver are diminishing, as it is advantageous when these metals are increasing. The workman has not the same employment from the manufacturer and merchant; though he pays the same price for everything in the market. The farmer cannot dispose of his corn and cattle though he must pay the same rent to his landlord. The poverty and beggary and sloth, which must ensue, are easily foreseen . . .

There are some kingdoms and many provinces in Europe (and all of them were once in the same condition) where money is so scarce that the landlord can get none at all from his tenants; but is obliged to take his rent in kind and either to consume it himself or transport it to places where he may find a market. In those countries the prince can levy few or no taxes, but in the same manner and as he will receive small benefit from impositions so paid, it is evident that such a kingdom has little force even at home and cannot maintain fleets and armies to the same extent, as if every part of it abounded in gold and silver. There is surely a greater disproportion between the force of GERMANY, at present and what it was three centuires ago, than there is in its industry, people and manufactures. The AUSTRIAN dominions in the empire are in general well-peopled and well cultivated and are of great extent; but have not a proportionable weight in the balance of EUROPE; proceeding as is commonly supposed from the scarcity of money. How do all these facts agree with that principle of reason that the quantity of gold and silver is in itself altogether indifferent? According to that principle, wherever a sovereign has numbers of subjects, and these have plenty of commodities, he should of course be great and powerful and they rich and happy, independent of the greater or lesser abundance of the precious metals. These admit of divisions and subdivisions to a great extent and where the pieces might become so small as to be in danger of being lost, it is easy to mix the gold or silver with a baser metal, as is practised in some countries of EUROPE; and by that means raise the pieces to a bulk more sensible and convenient. They still serve the same purposes of exchange, whatever their number may be, or whatever colour they may supposed to have.

To these difficulties I answer, that the effect, here supposed to flow from scarcity of money, really arises from the manners and customs of the people; and that we mistake as is too usual a collateral effect for a cause. The contradiction is only apparent but it requires some thought and reflection to discover the principles by which we can reconcile reason to experience.

It seems a maxim almost self-evident, that the prices of everthing depend on the proportion between commodities and money, and that any considerable alteration on either has the same effect, either of heightening or lowering the price. Increase the commodities they become cheaper; increase the money they rise in their value. As on the other hand, a diminution of the former and that of the latter have contrary tendencies.

It is also evident that the prices do not so much depend on the absolute quantity of commodities and that of money, which are in a nation, as on that of the commodities which come or may come to market, and of the money which circulates. If the coin be locked up in chests, it is the same thing with regard to prices as if it were annihilated; if the commodity be hoarded in magazines and granaries, a like effect follows. As the money and commodities in these cases never meet, they cannot affect each other. Were we, at any time, to form conjectures concerning the price of provisions, the corn which the farmer must reserve for seed and for the maintenance of himself and family ought never to enter into the estimation. It is only the overplus, compared to the demand that determines the value.

To apply these principles, we must consider that in the first and more uncultivated ages of any state, 'ere fancy has confounded her wants with those of nature, men, content with the produce of their own fields, or with those rude improvements which they themselves can work upon them, have little occasion for exchange, at least for money which, by agreement, is the common measure of exchange. The wool of the farmer's own flock, spun in his own family and wrought by a neighbouring weaver, who receives his payment in corn or wool, suffices for furniture and clothing. The carpenter, the smith, the mason, the tailor are retained by wages of a like nature; and the landlord himself, dwelling in the neighbourhood, is content to receive his rent in the commodities raised by the farmer. The greater part of these he consumes at home, in rustic hospitality, the rest perhaps he disposes of for money to the neighbouring town, whence he draws the few materials of his expense and luxury.

But after men begin to refine on all these enjoyments and live not always at home, nor are content with what can be raised in their neighbourhood, there is more exchange and commerce of all kinds, and more money enters into that exchange. The tradesmen will not be paid in corn because they want something more than barely to eat. The farmer goes beyond his own parish for the commodities he purchases, and cannot always carry his commodities to the merchant who supplies him. The landlord lives in the capital or in a foreign country and demands his rent in gold and silver, which can easily be transported to him. Great undertakers and manufacturers and merchants, arise in every commodity and these can conveniently deal in nothing but in specie. And consequently, in this situation of society, the coin enters into many more contracts and by that means is much more employed than in the former.

The necessary effect is that, provided the money increase not in the nation, everything must become much cheaper in times of industry and refinement, than in rude, uncultivated ages. It is the proportion between the circulating money and the commodities in the market which determines the prices. Goods that are consumed at home or are exchanged with other goods in the neighbourhood, never come to market; they affect not in the least the current specie; with regard to it they are as if totally annihilated; and consequently this method of using them sinks the proportion on the side of the commodities, and increases the prices. But after money enters into all contracts and sales, and is everywhere the measure of exchange, the same national cash has a much greater task to perform; all commodities are then in the market, the sphere of circulation is enlarged; it is the same case as if that individual sum were to serve a larger kingdom and therefore, the proportion being here lessened on the side of the money, everything must become cheaper, and the prices gradually fall . . .

Here then we may learn the fallacy of the remark, often to be met with in historians and even in common conversation, that any particular state is weak, though fertile, populous and well cultivated, merely because it wants money. It appears that the want of money can never injure any state within itself, for men and commodities are the real strength of any community. It is the simple manner of living which here hurts the public, by confining the gold and silver to few hands and preventing its universal diffusion and circulation. On the contrary, industry and refinements of all kinds incorporate it with the whole state, however small its quantity may be—they digest it into every vein, so to speak, and make it enter into every transaction and contract. No hand is entirely empty of it. And as the prices of every thing fall by that means, the sovereign has a double advantage. He may draw money by his taxes from every part of the state; and what he receives, goes farther in every purchase and payment . . .

The absolute quantity of the precious metals is a matter of great indifference. There are only two circumstances of any importance, namely their gradual increase and their thorough concoction and circulation through the state; and the influence of both these circumstances has here been explained . . .

Suppose that four-fifths of all the money in Great Britain to be annihilated in one night, and the nation reduced to the same condition with regard to specie, as in the reigns of the Harrys and Edwards, what would be the consequence? Must not the price of all labour and commodities sink in proportion, and everything sold as cheap as they were in those ages? What nation could then dispute with us in any foreign market, or pretend to navigate or to sell manufactures at the same price, which to us would afford sufficient profit? In how little time, therefore, must this bring back the money which we had lost and raise us to the level of all the neighbouring nations? Where, after we have arrived, we immediately lose the advantage of the cheapness of labour and commodities, and the farther flowing in of money is stopped by our fulness and repletion.

Again, suppose that all the money of Great Britain were multiplied five-fold in a night, must not the contrary effect follow? Must not all labour and commodities rise to such an exorbitant height that no neighbouring nations could afford to buy from us, while their commodities on the other hand, became comparatively so cheap that, in spite of all the laws which could be formed, they would be run in upon us and our money flow out till we fall to a level with foreigners and lose that great superiority of riches which had laid us under such disadvantages?

Now it is evident that the same causes which would correct these exorbitant inequalities, were they to happen miraculously, must prevent their happening in the common course of nature and must for ever, in all neighbouring nations, preserve money nearly proportionable to the art and industry of each nation. All water, wherever it communicates, remains always at a level. Ask naturalists the reason; they tell you that, were it to be raised in any one place, the superior gravity of that part not being balanced, must depress it, till it meet a counterpoise and that the same cause which redresses the inequality when it happens must for ever prevent it, without some violent external operation.[1]

[1] There is another cause, though more limited in its operation which checks the wrong balance of trade to every particular nation to which the kingdom trades. When we import more goods than we export, the exchange turns against us and this becomes a new encouragement to export, as much as the charge of carriage and insurance of the money which becomes due would amount to. For the exchange can never rise but a little higher than that sum.

Can one imagine that it had ever been possible, by any laws, or even by any art or industry to have kept all the money in Spain which the galleons have brought from the Indies? Or that all commodities could be sold in France for a tenth of the price which they would yield on the other side of the Pyrenees, without finding their way thither and draining from that immense treasure? What other reason, indeed, is there why all nations at present, gain in their trade with Spain and Portugal but because it is impossible to heap up money more than any fluid, beyond its proper level? The sovereigns of these countries have shown that they wanted not inclination to keep their gold and silver themselves, had it been in any degree practicable.

But as any body of water may be raised above the level of the surrounding element, if the former has no communication with the latter, so in money, if the communication be cut off, by any material or physical impediment (for all laws alone are i neffectual) there may, in such a case, be a very great inequality of money. Thus the immense distance of China, together with the monopolies of our India companies, obstructing the communication, preserve in Europe the gold and silver, especially the latter, in much greater plenty than they are found in that kingdom. But notwithstanding this great obstruction, the force of the causes above mentioned is still evident. The skill and ingenuity of Europe in general surpasses perhaps that of China with regard to manual arts and manufactures; yet are we never able to trade thither without great disadvantage. And were it not for the continual recruits which we receive from America, money would soon sink in Europe and rise in China, till it became nearly to a level in both places. Nor can any reasonable man doubt, but that industrious nation, were they as near us as Poland or Barbary would drain us of the overplus of our specie and draw to themselves a larger share of the West Indian treasures. We need not have recourse to a physical attraction in order to explain the necessity of this operation. There is a moral attraction, arising from the interests and passions of men, which is full as potent and infallible.

How is the balance kept in the provinces of every kingdom among themselves, but by the force of this principle, which makes it impossible for money to lose its level, and either to rise or sink beyond the proportion of the labour and commodities which are in each province? Did not experience make people easy on this head, what a fund of gloomy reflections might calculations afford to a melancholy Yorkshireman, while he computed and magnified the sums drawn to London by taxes, absentees, commodities and found on comparison the opposite articles so much inferior? And no doubt, had the Heptarchy subsisted in England, the legislature of each state had been continually alarmed by the fear of a wrong balance; and as it is probable that the mutual hatred of these states would have been extremely violent on account of their close neighbourhood, they would have loaded and oppressed all commerce by a jealous and superfluous caution. Since the union has removed the barriers between Scotland and England, which of these nations gains from the other by this free commerce? Or if the former kingdom has received any increase of riches, can it reasonably be accounted for by anything but the increase of its art and industry? It was a common apprehension in England before the union, as we learn from L'Abbé du Bos, that Scotland would soon drain them of their treasure, were an open trade allowed; and on the other side the Tweed a contrary apprehension prevailed, with what justice in both, time has shown . . . There is indeed one expedient by which it is possible to sink, and another by which we may raise money beyond its natural level in any kingdom; but these cases, when examined, will be found to resolve into our general theory and to bring additional authority to it.

I scarcely know any method of sinking money below its level but those institutions of banks, funds and paper-credit which are so much practised in this kingdom. These render paper equivalent to money circulate it throughout the whole state, make it supply the place of gold and silver, raise proportionably the price of labour and commodities and by that means either banish a great part of those precious metals, or prevent their farther increase. What can be more short-sighted than our reasonings on this head? We fancy because an individual would be much richer were his stock of money doubled that the same good effect would follow were the money of every one increased; not considering that this would raise as much the price of every commodity and reduce every man, in time, to the same condition as before. It is only in our public negotiations and transactions with foreigners, that a greater stock of money is advantageous and as our paper is there absolutely insignificant, we feel by its means, all the ill effects arising from a great abundance of money without reaping any of the advantages . . .[1]

But as our projects of paper credit are almost the only expedient, by which we can sink money below its level, so in my opinion, the only expedient by which we can raise money above it, is a practice which we should all exclaim against as destructive, namely, the gathering of large sums into a public treasure, locking them up and absolutely preventing their circulation. The fluid, not communicating with the neighbouring element, may, by such an artifice, be raised to what height we please. To prove this, we need only return to our first supposition, of annihilating the half or any part of our cash where we found that the immediate consequence of such an event would be the attraction of an equal sum from all the neighbouring kingdoms. Nor does there seem to be any necessary bounds set, by the nature of things, to this practice of hoarding. A small city like Geneva, continuing this policy for ages, might engross nine tenths of the money of Europe. There seems, indeed, in the nature of man, an invincible obstacle to that immense growth of riches. A weak state, with an enormous treasure, will soon

---

[1] We observed in Essay III ('Of Money') that money, when increasing, gives encouragement to industry, during the interval between the increase of money and the rise of the prices. A good effect of this nature may follow too from paper-credit; but it is dangerous to precipitate matters at the risk of losing all by the failing of that credit as must happen upon any violent shock in public affairs.

become a prey to some of its poorer but more powerful neighbours. A great state would dissipate its wealth in dangerous
and ill-concerted projects and probably destroy, with it, what
is much more valuable, the industry, morals and numbers of
its people. The fluid in this case, raised to too great a height,
bursts and destroys the vessel that contains it; and mixing
itself with the surrounding element, soon falls to its proper level.
David Hume. *Of Money* and *Of the Balance of Trade, Political
Discourses* (1752)

ANTI-METALLISTS AND INFLATIONISTS
14 Nicholas Barbon   Money, Credit and Interest
Barbon (d 1698) is best known as a pioneer of fire insurance
and, in association with Asgill and Briscoe, as a land bank
projector. A supporter of Lowndes in the coinage controversy, Barbon's theoretical contributions were made in his two
Discourses of 1690 and 1696; perhaps the most significant of
these was his non-monetary definition of interest as the rent
of 'stock'.

MONY is a Value made by a Law; And the Difference of its
Value is known by the Stamp, and Size of the Piece.

One use of MONY is, It is the measure of Value, By which the
Value of all other things are reckoned; as when the Value of
any thing is expressed, its said, It's worth so many shillings, or
so many Pounds: Another Use of Mony is; It is a Change or
Pawn for the Value of all other Things: For this Reason, the
Value of Mony must be made certain by Law, or else it could
not be made a certain Measure, nor an Exchange for the Value
of all things.

It is not absolutely necessary, Mony should be made of Gold
or Silver; for having its sole Value from the Law, it is not
Material upon what Metal the Stamp be set. Mony hath the
same Value, and performs the same Uses, if it be made of Brass,
Copper, Tin, or any thing else. The Brass Mony of Spain, the
Copper Mony of Sweden, and Tin Farthings of England, have

I

the same Value in Exchange, according to the Rate they are set at and perform the same Uses, to Cast up the Value of things, as the Gold and Silver Mony does; Six Pence in Farthings will buy the same thing as Six Pence in Silver; and the Value of a thing is well understood by saying, It is worth Eight Farthings, as that it is worth Two Pence: Gold and Silver, as well as Brass, Copper and Tin Mony, change their Value in those Countries, where the Law has no Force, and yield no more than the Price of the Metal that bears the STAMP: Therefore, all Foreign Coins go by Weight, and are of no certain Value, but rise and fall with the Price of the Metal. Pieces of Eight, yield sometimes 4 sh 6 d 4 sh 7 d and 4 sh 8 d as the Value of Silver is higher or lower: And so doth Dollars, and all Forreign Coin, change their Value; and were it not for the Law that fixeth the Value, an English Crown Piece would now yield Five Shillings and Two Pence, for so much is the Value of it, if it were melted, or in a Foreign Country. But the chief Advantage of making Money of Silver and Gold, is to prevent Counterfeiting; for Silver and Gold, being Metals of great Value, those who design Profit by Counterfeiting the Coin, must Counterfeit the Metals, as well as the Stamp, which is more difficult than the Stamp. There's another Benefit to the Merchant, by such Mony; for Gold and Silver being Commodities for other Uses, than to make Mony; to make Plate, Gold & Silver Lace, Silks, &c. And coins of little Bulk, in respect of their Value, the Merchant transmits such Mony from Place to Place, in Specie, according as he finds his Advantage, by the Rise of Bullion; though this may be a Conveniency to the Merchant, it often proves a Prejudice to the State, by making Mony scarce: Therefore, there are Laws in most Countries, that Prohibit the Transportation of Mony, yet it cannot be prevented; for in Spain, though it be Capital, yet in Two Months after the Gallions are come home, there is scarce any Silver Mony to be seen in the Country.

Some Men have so great an Esteem for Gold and Silver, that they believe they have an intrinsick Value in themselves, and

cast up the value of every thing by them: The Reason of the
Mistake, is, Because Mony being made of Gold and Silver,
they do not distinguish betwixt Mony, and Gold and Silver.
Mony hath a certain Value, because of the Law; but the Value
of Gold and Silver are uncertain, & varies their Price, as much
as Copper, Lead, or other Metals: And in the Places where they
are dug, considering the smalness of their Veins, with the
Charges of getting them, they do not yield much more Profit
than other Minerals, nor pay the Miners better Wages for
digging them.

And were it not for the Waste, made of Gold and Silver, by
Plate, Lace, Silks, and Guilding, and the Custom of the Eastern
Princes, to lay them up and bury them, that Half which is dug
in the West, is buried in the East. The great Quantities dug out
of the Earth, since the Discovery of the West-Indies, would
have so much lessened the Value, that by this time, they would
not have much exceeded the Value of Tin, or Copper: Therefore, How greatly would those Gentlemen be disappointed, that
are searching after the Philosopher's Stone, if they should at
last happen to find it? For, if they should make but so great a
Quantity of Gold and Silver, as they, and their Predecessors
have spent in search after it, it would so alter, and bring down
the Price of those Metals, that it might be a Question, whether
they would get so much Over-plus by it, as would pay for the
Metal they change into Gold and Silver. It is only the Scarcity
that keeps up the Value, and not any Intrinsick Vertue or
Quality in the Metals; For if the Vertue were to be considered,
the Affrican that gives Gold for Knives, and Things made of
Iron, would have the Odds in the Exchange; Iron being a
much more Useful Metal, than either Gold or Silver. To
Conclude this Objection, Nothing in it self hath a certain Value;
One thing is as much worth as another: And it is time, and place,
that give a difference to the Value of all things.

Credit is a Value raised by Opinion, it buys Goods as Mony
does; and in all Trading Citys, there's more Wares sold upon
Credit, than for present Mony.

There are Two Sorts of Credit; the one, is Grounded upon the Ability of the Buyer; the other, upon the Honesty: The first is called a Good Man, which implys an Able Man; he generally buys upon short Time; to pay in a Month, which is accounted as ready Mony, and the Price is made accordingly. The other is accounted an Honest Man; He may be poor; he Generally buys for three and Six Months or longer, so as to pay the Merchant by the Return of his own Goods; and therefore, the Seller relys more upon the Honesty of the Buyer, than his Ability: Most of the Retail Traders buy upon this Sort of Credit, and are usually Trusted for more than double they are worth.

In Citys of great Trade, there are publick Banks of Credit, as at Amsterdam and Venice: They are of great Advantage to Trade, for they make Payments easie, by preventing the Continual Trouble of telling over Mony, and cause a great Dispatch in Business: Publick Banks are of so great a Concern in Trade, that the Merchants of London, for want of such a Bank, have been forced to Carry their Cash to GoldSmiths, and have thereby Raised such a Credit upon GoldSmiths Notes, that they pass in Payments from one to another like Notes upon the Bank; And although by this way of Credit, there hath been very Vast Sums of Mony lost, not less than two Millions within five and Twenty Years, yet the Dispatch and Ease in Trade is so great by such Notes, that the Credit is still in some Measure kept up.

Therefore, it is much to be wondered at, that since the City of London is the Largest, Richest, and Chiefest City in the World, for Trade: Since there is so much Ease, Dispatch, and Safety in a Publick Bank; and since such vast Losses has Happened for want of it; That the Merchant and Traders of London have not long before this time Addressed themselves, to the Government, for the Establishing of a Publick Bank.

The Common Objection, that a Publick Bank cannot be safe in a Monarchy, is not worth the Answering; as if Princes were not Governed by the same Rules of Policy, as States are, To do all things for the Well-fair of the Subjects, wherein their own Interest is concerned.

It is True, in a Government wholly Dispotical, whose Support is altogether in its Millitary Forces; where Trade hath no Concern in the Affaires of the State; Brings no Revenue, There might be a Jealousy, That such a Bank might tempt a Prince to Seize it; when by doing it, he doth not Prejudice the Affairs of his Government: But in England, where the Government is not Dispotical; But the People Free; and have as great a Share in the Soveraign Legislative Power, as the Subjects of any States have, or ever had; where the Customs makes great Figures, in the Kings Exchequer; where Ships are the Bullworks of the Kingdom; and where the Flourish of Trade is as much the Interest of the King as of the People, There can be no such Cause of Fear: For, What Objections can any Man make, that his Mony in the Bank, may not be as well secured by a Law, as his Property is? Or; Why he should be more afraid of Losing His Mony, than his Land or Goods?

Interest is the Rent of Stock, and is the same as the Rent of Land: The First, is the Rent of the Wrought or Artificial Stock; the Latter, of the Unwrought, or Natural Stock.

Interest is commonly reckoned for Mony; because the Mony Borrowed at Interest, is to be repayed in Mony; but this is a mistake; For the Interest is paid for Stock: for the Mony borrowed, is laid out to buy Goods, or pay for them before bought: No Man takes up Mony at Interest, to lay it by him, and lose the Interest of it.

One use of Interest: It is the Rule by which the Trader makes up the Account of Profit and Loss; the Merchant expects by Dealing, to get more than Interest by his Goods; because of bad Debts, and other Hazards which he runs; and therefore, reckons all he gets above Interest, is Gain; all under, Loss; but if no more than Interest, neither Profit, nor Loss.

Another use of Interest, is, It is the measure of the Value of the Rent of Land; it sets the Price in Buying and Selling of Land: For, by adding three Years Interest more than is in the

Principle, Makes the usual Value of the Land of the Country; The difference of three Year is allowed; Because Land is more certain than Mony or Stock. Thus in Holland, where Mony is at three per Cent by reckoning how many times three is in a Hundred Pounds, which is Thirty Three; and Adding three Years more; makes Thirty Six Years Purchase; the Value of the Land in Holland: And by the same Rule, interest being at six per Cent in England, Land is worth but Twenty Years Purchase; and in Ireland, but Thirteen; Interest being there at Ten per Cent: so that, according to the Rate of Interest, is that Value of the Land in the Country.

Therefore, Interest in all Countrys is settled by a Law, to make it certain; or else it could not be a Rule for the Merchant to make up his Account, nor the Gentleman, to Sell his Land By. Nicholas Barbon. *A Discourse of Trade* (1690)

15 John Law   The Benefits of Paper Money

After a successful gambling career on the continent, Law (1671–1729) impressed the French Regent, the Duke of Orleans, with his financial ability and in 1716 founded the Banque Générale. The success of this venture later led him into the ill-fated Mississippi colonisation scheme. In 1718 Law's bank was converted into the Banque Royale, the notes of which were to be guaranteed by the Crown. During the credit inflation that followed Law rapidly lost control of the situation and in May 1720 the French government repudiated its obligations.

There are several Proposals offer'd to Remedy the Difficulties the Nation is under from the great scarcity of Money.

That a right Judgement may be made, which will be most Safe, Advantageous and Practicable; it seems Necessary, 1. That the Nature of Money be inquired into, and why Silver was us'd as Money preferable to other Goods. 2. That Trade be considered, and how far Money affects Trade. 3. That the

Measures which have been us'd for Preserving and Increasing Money, and these now propos'd, be examin'd . . .

Domestick and Foreign Trade may be carried on by Barter; but not for so great Value as by Money, nor with so much convenience.

Domestick Trade depends on the Money: A greater Quantity employs more People than a lesser Quantity. A limited Sum can only set a number of People to work proportion'd to it, and 'tis with little Success Laws are made, for employing the Poor or Idle in Countries where Money is scarce; good Laws may bring the Money to the full Circulation 'tis capable of, and force it to those Employments that are most profitable to the Country: But no Laws can make it go further, nor can more People be set to work, without more Money to circulate so, as to pay the Wages of a greater number. They may be brought to work on Credit; and that is not practicable, unless the Credit have a Circulation, so as to supply the Workmen with Necessaries; if that's suppos'd, then that Credit is Money, and will have the same effects, on Home and Foreign Trade . . .

The first Branch of Foreign Trade, which is the Export and Import of Goods, depends on the Money. If one half of the People are imploy'd, and the whole Product and Manufacture consum'd; more Money, by imploying more People, will make an Overplus to Export: If then the Goods imported ballance the Goods exported, a greater Addition to the Money will employ yet more people, or the same People before imployed to more Advantage; which by making a greater, or more valuable Export, will make a Ballance due. So if the Money lessens, a part of the People then imployed are set idle, or imployed to less advantage; the Product and Manufacture is less, or less valuable, the Export of Consequence less, and a Ballance due to Foreigners . . .

Some Countries have rais'd Money in the Denomination, when others have lower'd it; some have allay'd it, when others who had allay'd it have rectified it; some have prohibited the Export of Money under the severest Penalties, when others have by Law allowed it to be exported; some thinking to add to the Money, have obliged Traders to bring home Bullion, in proportion to the Goods they imported. Most Countries have try'd some or all of these Measures, and others of the same Nature, and have try'd contrary Measures at one time, from what they us'd immediately before, from the Opinion, that since the Method used had not the Effect design'd, a contrary would: Yet it has not been found, that any of them have preserved or increased Money; but on the contrary.

The Use of Banks has been the best Method yet practis'd for the Increase of Money . . .

Banks, where the Money is pledg'd equal to the Credit given, are sure; for, tho' Demands are made of the whole, the Bank does not fail in Payment.

By the Constitution of this Bank (Amsterdam), the whole Sum for which Credit is given ought to remain there, to be ready at demand; yet a Sum is lent by the Managers for a Stock to the Lumbar, and 'tis thought they lend great Sums on other Occasions. So far as they lend they add to the Money, which brings a Profit to the Country, by imploying more People, and extending Trade; they add to the Money to be lent, whereby it is easier borrowed, and at less Use; and the Bank has a Benefit: But the Bank is less sure, and tho' none suffer by it, or are apprehensive of Danger, its Credit being good; yet if the whole Demands were made, or Demands greater than the remaining Money, they could not all be satisfied, till the Bank had called in what Sums were lent.

The certain Good it does, will more than balance the Hazard, tho' once in two or three years it failed in Payment; providing the Sums lent be well secured: Merchants who had Money there might be disappointed of it at Demand, but the Security being good, and Interest allowed, Money would be had on a small Discompt, perhaps at the Par . . .

National Power and Wealth consists in Numbers of People, and Magazines of home and Foreign Goods. These depend on

Trade, and Trade depends on Money. So to be powerful and wealthy in Proportion to other Nations, we should have Money in proportion with them; for the best Laws without Money cannot employ the People, improve the Product, or advance Manufacture and Trade . . .

Credit that promises a Payment of Money, cannot well be extended beyond a certain Proportion it ought to have with the Money. And we have so little Money, that any Credit could be given upon it would be inconsiderable.

It remains to be considered, whether any other Goods than Silver can be made Money with the same Safety and Convenience . . .

Silver Money is more uncertain in its Value than other Goods, so less qualified for the Use of Money . . .

Most Goods have encreas'd in Quantity, equal or near as the Demand for them has encreas'd; and are at or near the Value they had 200 Years ago. Land is more valuable, by Improvement producing to a greater Value, and the Demand encreasing, the Quantity being the same. Silver and Money are of lesser Value, being more encreas'd in Quantity than in Demand . . .

Land will continue to rise in Value, being yet capable of Improvement, and as the Demand encreases, for the Quantity will be the same.

Silver will continue to fall in Value, as it encreases in Quantity, the Demand not increasing in proportion; for the Increase does not depend on the Demand. Most People wont allow themselves to think that Silver is cheaper or less valuable, tho' it appears plainly, by comparing what Quantity of Goods such a Weight of fine Silver bought 200 Years ago, and what Quantity of the same Goods it will buy now . . .

What I shall propose, is to make Money of Land equal to its Value; and that Money to be equal in Value to Silver Money, and not liable to fall in Value as Silver Money falls . . . Land is what in all Appearance will keep its Value best, it may rise in Value, but cannot well fall: Gold or Silver are liable to many Accidents, whereby their Value may lessen, but cannot well rise in Value . . .

The Paper Money propos'd will be equal in Value to Silver, for it will have a Value of Land pledge equal to the same Sum of Silver Money, that it is given out for . . .

This Paper Money will not fall in Value as Silver Money has fallen or may fall: Goods or Money fall in Value, if they increase in Quantity, or if the Demand lessens. But the Commission giving out what Sums are demanded, and taking back what Sums are offer'd to be returned; this Paper Money will keep its Value, and there will always be as much Money as there is Occasion or Imployment for, and no more . . .

Money is not the Value for which Goods are exchanged, but the Value by which they are exchanged: The Use of Money is to buy Goods and Silver, while Money is of no other Use.

Tho' Silver were our product, yet it is not so proper to be made Money as Land. Land is what produces everything, Silver is only the Product . . .

Goods will continue equal in Quantity as they are now to the Demand, or wont differ much; for the Increase of most Goods depends on the Demand. For example, if the Quantity of Oats be greater than the Demand for Consumption and Magazines, what is over is a Drug, so that Product will be lessen'd, and the Land imployed to some other use: if by a Scarcity the Quantity be lesser than the Demand, that Demand will be supply'd from Magazines of former Years; or if the Magazines are not sufficient to answer the Demand, that Scarcity cannot well be suppos'd to last above a Year or two . . .

Most People think scarcity of Money is only the Consequence of a Ballance due; but 'tis the Cause as well as the Consequence, and the effectual Way to bring the Ballance to our side, is to add to the Money . . .

It cannot well be known what Sum will serve the Occasions of the Nation, for as Manufacture and Trade advance, the Demand for Money will increase; but the many Poor we have always had, is a great Presumption we have never had Money enough. John Law. *Money and Trade Considered with a Proposal for Supplying the Nation with Money* (1705)

___

16 Sir James Steuart   Money and Economic Growth

Steuart (1713–80) espoused the Jacobite cause on his Grand Tour and was personally responsible for attempting to negotiate a French invasion in 1745. He was subsequently exiled in France and Germany, where he wrote the 'Principles'. He returned to Scotland in 1763 and finally completed the work. Apart from its unprecedented scope, perhaps the most distinctive features of Steuart's writings on economics was the emphasis he laid on the beneficial effects of government intervention and the importance he attached to banking institutions.

___

I. He [the statesman] ought to form to himself a clear and distinct idea of the nature, properties and effects of circulation; a word frequently made use of without much meaning and in a vague and undeterminate sense.

The term, circulation, is perhaps one of the most expressive in any language and is therefore easily understood. It represents the successive transition of money, or transferable commodities, from hand to hand and their return, as it were, in a circle to the point from which they set out. This is the rough idea which every one, who understands the word at all, must form of its meaning. But a statesman's perceptions should be more accurate as well as more complex.

He must combine the consequences which result from this successive transition, and attend to the effects produced by it. He must not consider the money only, which is a permanent value, passing from hand to hand, but weigh the consequences of the variety of consumption which it draws along with it in its progress.

Before a guinea can travel from London to York, it may be the means of consuming a thousand times its value, and as much more, before it can return to London again. Every stop the guinea makes in its course, marks a want of desire to consume, in him who possesses it, for the time. If, therefore, in any country, there were but one guinea in circulation, all consumption would stop (or barter would take place) the moment it fell into the hands of a miser. This leads us to the second object of a statesman's attention.

II. He ought at all times to maintain a just proportion between the produce of industry and the quantity of circulating equivalent, in the hands of his subjects, for the purchase of it; that by a steady and judicious administration, he may have it in his power at all times, either to check prodigality and hurtful luxury, or to extend industry and domestic consumption, according as the circumstances of the people shall require the one or the other corrective, to be applied to the natural bent and spirit of the times.

For this purpose he must examine the situation of his country relatively to three objects, viz. the propensity of the rich to consume; the disposition of the poor to be industrious and the proportion of circulating money, with respect to the one and the other.

If the quantity of money in circulation is below the proportion of the two first, industry will never be able to exert itself; because the equivalent in the hands of the consumers, is then below the proportion of their desires to consume and of those of the industrious to produce. Let me illustrate this by a familiar example taken from a party at quadrille.

When, on dealing the cards, every one puts in a fish into the stake, according to the old English fashion, a very few fishes are sufficient for the circulation of the game; but when you play the aces, the consolation and the multiplication of beasts according to the French custom, you must have a box with contracts, fishes and counters; so reducing all to the lowest denomination, every player has occasion for above five hundred marks. It is therefore plain, that the number of marks ought to be in proportion to the circulation of the game. But at play, as in a state, circumstances render this circulation very irregular.

Fortune may run so equally among the players, during a considerable time, that none of them may have occasion to pay away above the value of a hundred counters, and while this equality continues, there will not be found the smallest interruption in the circulation. But let one of the players have a run of good luck, you will soon see three of the boxes empty and all the circulating marks heaped up before the winner. Fortune at quadrille, forms stagnations of the circulating equivalent, as industry and frugality form them in a state. At this period of the game, must not the players stop, or must they not fall upon a way of drawing back their marks into circulation? If they borrow back from the winner, this represents loan. If they buy back their marks with money from their purses, it represents what I call throwing solid property into circulation.

From this familiar example, we may judge how necessary it is that the circulating fund be constantly kept up to the proportion of the occasions for it. It is impossible to determine the proportion of coin necessary for carrying on the circulation of a country, especially one where neither loan, nor paper credit, that is, the melting down of solid property are familiarly known. Here is the reason; the solution of the question does not depend upon the quantity of coin alone, but also upon the disposition of those who are the possessors of it; and as these dispositions are constantly changing, the question thereby becomes insoluble.

It is, therefore, the business of a statesman, who intends to promote circulation, to be upon his guard against every cause of stagnation; and when he has it not in his power to remove these political obstructions, as I may call them, by drawing the coin of the country out of its repositories; he ought (in proportion as the other political interests of his people are found to require it) to facilitate the introduction of symbolical money to supply its place . . . A statesman who allows himself to be entirely taken up in promoting circulation, and the advancement of every species of luxurious consumption, may carry matters too far, and destroy the industry he wishes to promote.

This is the case when the consequence of domestic consumption raises prices and thereby hurts exportation.

A principal object of his attention must therefore be, to judge when it is proper to encourage consumption in favour of industry, and when to discourage it in favour of reformation upon the growth of luxury.

If the country he governs be in a state of simplicity, and that he wishes to awaken a taste for industry and refinement, he must, as has been said, encourage domestic consumption, for the sake of multiplying and giving bread to the industrious; he must facilitate circulation by drawing into the hands of the public what coin there is in the country in case he finds any part of it locked up, and he must supply the actual deficiency of the metals, by such a proportion of paper-credit, as may abundantly supply the deficiency.

In every country where simplicity prevails and where there is any quantity of coin, a great proportion of it must be locked up, because there the consumption must be small, consequently little circulation; consequently, either little coin or many treasures. In such cases therefore, a statesman must engage the possessors of these riches to part with them, at the desire of those who can give security for their worth; and he must establish the standard of an annual retribution for the loan. If this be difficult to be brought about from the want of confidence in the moneyed men, he may, in their favour contrive expedients to become the borrower himself, at the expense of the alienation of certain rights, or the creation of new privileges, in lieu of interest; and when he has engaged them to part with their coin, he may lend it out to such as have both solid property and a desire to consume, but who, for want of a circulating fund to purchase superfluities, have hitherto lived in simplicity.

The introduction, therefore, of loans upon interest, is a very good expedient to accelerate circulation and to give birth to industry.

Objection. But here it is objected, that such a plan is looked upon by some nations to be contrary to the precepts of the

Christian religion and therefore a statesman cannot permit it.

To this I can make no answer because I am no casuist; but I can propose an expedient which will supply the defect of borrowing at interest and, as it may serve to illustrate the principles I am now upon I shall here introduce it.

The intention of permitting loans upon interest, is not to provide a revenue to those who have ready money locked up, but to obtain the use of a circulating equivalent to those who have sufficient security to pledge for it. If the statesman, therefore, shall find himself withheld by the canons of the church, from drawing the coin of his subjects into circulation, by permitting the loan of it upon interest, nothing is more easy than to invent another specie of circulation, where no interests at all is necessary.

Let him open an office, where every proprietor of lands may receive, by virtue of a mortgage thereon, a certain proportional value of circulating paper of different denominations, the most proper for circulation. He may therein specify a term of payment in favour of the debtor, in order to give him an opportunity to call in his obligation and relieve the engagement of his property. But this term being elapsed, the land is to belong to the creditor, or the paper to become payable by the state, if required, which may in consequence become authorised either to sell the land engaged, or to retain a proportional value of the income, or of the property of the land itself, as shall be judged most expedient.

Further, let him constitute a real security for all debts upon every species of solid property, with the greatest facility in the liquidation of them, in favour of those who shall have given credit to the proprietors for merchandise of any kind. To compass this, let all entails, substitutions, and 'fidei commissa' or trusts, restraining the alienation of land property be dissolved; and let such property be rendered as saleable as house-hold furniture. Let such principles influence the spirit of the government; let this sort of paper-credit be modified and extended according to circumstances and a taste for consumption will soon take place.

The greatest of all obstacles to industry in its infancy, is the general want of credit on both sides. The consumers having no circulating value, the difficulty of liquidating what they owe by the alienation of their lands, prevents their getting credit; and the many examples of industrious people giving way, on account of bad payments, discourages others from assisting them in the beginning of their undertaking.

From these principles we may gather, that a statesman who intends to increase industry and domestic consumption, should set out by providing a circulating fund of one kind or other, which ought always to be ready and constantly at the command of those who have any sort of real equivalent to give for the consumption they incline to make, for as specie may oftentimes be scarce, a contrivance must be fallen upon immediately to supply the want of it.

The utility of this kind of credit, or paper-money, is principally at the instant of its entering into circulation; because it is then only that it supplies the want of real specie, and by this invention the desire to consume creates, as it were, the circulating equivalent, without which the alienation of the produce of industry would not have taken place; consequently, the industry itself would have suffered a check.

But in the after-circulation of this paper-money from hand to hand, this utility comes to cease; because the subsequent consumer who has another man's paper to give in exchange, is already provided with a circulating equivalent and therefore, were it not for the wearing of the specie, or difficulty of procuring it, it is quite indifferent both to the state as well as to circulation whether this paper continue to pass current, or whether it be taken up and realised by the debtor and gold and silver be made to circulate in its place.

Let me now endeavour to make this whole doctrine still more plain, by an example.

Suppose a country where there is a million of pieces of gold employed necessarily in carrying on the ordinary circulation, a million of pieces of the same value locked up, because the proprietors have no desire to spend them. Suppose the revenue of the solid property of the country to be worth also a million a year; and that if the fund itself could be sold, it might be worth twenty millions of the same specie. Suppose no such thing as credit or paper-money be known and that any man who inclined to make any consumption, must be previously provided with a part of the circulating million, before he can satisfy his inclination.

Under these circumstances, the statesman resolves to establish industry and finding that by his people's taking a taste for a greater consumption, the million which was formerly sufficient for carrying on circulation is no longer so; he proposes to those who have the other million locked up, to borrow it from them at 5 per cent. and the better to engage them to comply with his proposal, he offers to impose duties upon the whole of the inhabitants to the annual amount of fifty thousand pieces of gold, to be paid annually to the creditors, in return for their treasure. If this scheme be adopted he may, upon good security, lend out his million in small sums to everyone who inclines to borrow; or by premiums and other encouragements given to his infant manufacturers, he may throw it into the hands of the public, that is, into circulation. Here is one method for increasing the quantity of a circulating fund when an augmentation upon the consumption of the produce of industry comes to demand it.

But let us now suppose this regular plan of borrowing to be contrary to what is called the constitution of the state, to religion, or to the spirit of the people, what must be done to supply the place of such a scheme?

The statesman must then fall upon another contrivance, by extending the use of pledges and instead of moveables, accept of lands, houses etc. The Monte Pietà at Rome issues paper money upon moveable security deposited in their hands. Let the statesman, without exacting interest, do the same upon the

K

lands of his subjects, the best of all securities. While the lands subsist, this paper-money must retain its value; because I suppose the regulations to be such as to make it convey an indisputable right to the lands engaged. The advantage of such an establishment will be, that as formerly no man could purchase the smallest produce of industry without having a part of the circulating million pieces of gold, everybody now who has an inclination to consume, may immediately procure paper-money in proportion to his worth and receive in return whatever he desires to possess.

Now let me suppose that this paper-money shall in time, and from the growing taste for superfluities, amount to the value of five millions of pieces of gold. I ask, whether the real value of this paper is any way diminished, because it exceeds, by far, all the gold and silver in the country, and consequently cannot all at once be realized by the means of the coin? Certainly not: because it does not draw its value from any representation of these metals, but from the lands to which it conveys a right. Next, I ask, if the country is thereby become any richer? I answer, also, in the negative: because the property of the lands, if sold being supposed worth twenty millions, the proprietors of the paper are here supposed to have acquired, by their industry, five millions of the twenty and no more than the remaining fifteen millions belong to the landlords.

Let us now suppose a million of this paper-money to fall into the hands of those who have no inclination to spend it. This is the case of the frugal, or money-hoarding persons; will they not naturally choose to realise their paper, by taking possession of the lands represented by it? The moment this operation takes place, the million of paper-money is annihilated and the circulating capital is reduced to four millions of paper and one million of specie. Suppose on the other hand that those who have treasures which they cannot lend at interest, seeing a paper-money in circulation, which conveys a right to solid property, shall first purchase it with their million pieces of gold and afterwards lay hold of a proportional part of the land; what effect will this double operation produce upon the circulating fund? I answer that the currency, instead of being composed, as formerly, of one million of coin and five millions of paper, will at first, on the buying up of the paper consist of two millions of coin and five millions of paper and so soon as the million of paper bought up comes to be realised upon the land, it will be thereby extinguished; consequently the circulating coin will be raised to two millions and the paper will be reduced to four. Here then is a very rational method of drawing all the coin of the country from the treasures of the frugal, without the help of interest. Let me take one step farther and then I will stop, that I may not too far anticipate the subject of the fourth book.

I suppose that the statesman, perceiving that the constant circulation of coin insensibly wears it away and reflecting that the value of it is entirely in proportion to its weight and that the diminution of the mass must be an effectual diminution of the real riches of the country, shall call in the metals and deposit them in a treasure and shall deliver, in their place, a paper-money, having a security upon the coin locked up. Is it not plain that, while the treasure remains, the paper circulated will carry along with it as real (though not so intrinsic) a value as the coin itself could have done? But if this treasure comes to be spent, what will the case be then? It is evident that the paper conveying a right to the lands and issued, as we have supposed, by the proprietors of them, would have lost its value had an earthquake swallowed up, for a foreign conqueror seized the solid property engaged in security for it.

The expedient, therefore, of symbolical money, which is no more than a species of what is called credit, is principally useful to encourage consumption and to increase the demand for the produce of industry. And bringing the largest quantity of coin possible into a country, cannot supply the want of it in this respect; because the credit is constantly at hand to every one who has property, and the other may fail them on a thousand occasions. A man who has credit may purchase at all times, though he may frequently be without a shilling in his pocket.

Whenever, therefore, the interest of a state requires that the rich inhabitants should increase their consumption, in favour of the industrious poor, then the statesmen should fall upon every method to maintain a proportion between the progress of industry and the gradual augmentation of the circulating fund, by enabling the inhabitants to throw with ease their solid property into circulation whenever the coin is found wanting. Here entails are pernicious.

On the other hand, when luxury begins to make too great a progress and when it threatens to be prejudicial to foreign trade, then may solid property be rendered more unwieldy, and entails may then become useful; all moveable debts, except Bills of Exchange in foreign circulation may be stripped of their privileges and particularly, as in France, of the right of arresting the person of the debtor. Usury ought then to be punished severely; even something like the Senatus Consultum Macedonianum which made the contract of loan void on the side of the borrowers, while they remained under the power of their fathers, may be introduced. Merchants' accounts should no more be allowed to enjoy a preference to other debts; but on the contrary, be made liable to a short prescription. In a word, domestic circulation should be clogged and foreign circulation accelerated. When foreign trade again comes to a stop, then the former plan may be taken up anew and domestic circulation accelerated and facilitated, in proportion as the produce of industry and taste for superfluity require it . . .

I have laid it down as a principle that it is the complicated operation of demand and competition which determines the standard price of everything. If there be many labourers and little demand, work will be cheap. If the increase of riches therefore have the effect of raising the demand, work will increase in its value, because there competition is implied; but if it has only the effect of augmenting demand, prices will stand as formerly. What then will become of the additional quantity of coin or paper-money? I answer that, in both cases it will enter into circulation in proportion to the rise or augmentation of demand; with this difference, that in the first case, it will have the effect of raising prices; because the supply is not supposed to augment in proportion. In the second, prices will stand as they were because the supply is supposed to augment in proportion. These are the consequences of the augmentation of wealth, when it has the effect of either raising or augmenting demand. But if upon the increase of riches it be found that the state of demand remains without variation, then the additional coin will probably be locked up, or converted into plate because they who have it, not being inspired with a desire of increasing their consumption and far less with the generous sentiment of giving their money away, their riches will remain without producing more effect than if they had remained in the mine. As for paper-money, so soon as it has served the first purpose of supplying the demand of him who borrowed it (because he had at that time no coin) it will return upon the debtor in it and become realised, because of the little use found for it in carrying on circulation.

Let the specie of the country, therefore, be augmented or diminished in ever so great a proportion, commodities will still rise and fall according to the principles of demand and competition and these will constantly depend upon the inclinations of those who have property or any kind of equivalent whatsoever to give, but NEVER upon the quantity of COIN they are possessed of.

Let the quantity of coin be ever so much increased, it is the desire of spending it alone which will raise prices. Let it be diminished ever so low, while there is real property of any denomination in the country, and a competition to consume in those who possess it, prices will be high, by the means of barter, symbolical money, mutual prestations and a thousand other inventions . . . Sir James Steuart. *An Inquiry into the Principles of Political Oeconomy* (1767), chaps xxvii and xxviii

PART THREE

Private Banking and the Money Market to 1825

THE late seventeenth century saw an increase in commercial expansion and industrial growth that set up fresh demands for capital at a time when the needs of war were laying a much heavier burden on national resources than ever before. Long-term lending through the mortgage market was beginning to be significant, but there were few signs of a money market that was capable of making available a sustained expansion of credit. However, some of the tools of such a market were already in existence. Inland bills of exchange and promissory notes were in use and even circulated from hand to hand to some extent, though they were less acceptable than the foreign bill before 1705. At the national level the flow of funds consisted in the main of the transmission of government revenues, arising out of Customs and Excise duties and the Land tax, to the metropolis. Much of this involved a straightforward drain of specie from the provinces, but some dues were remitted in the form of obligations. There were certainly also significant private capital transfers to London from elsewhere in the country.

This was the background against which the first banks came into existence. Yet although there was clearly a need for a more systematic method of making commercial payments, as many contemporaries noticed, the London goldsmith-bankers and the early provincial, private banks that made a slow appearance after them, seem to have done little to obviate the difficulty. The goldsmiths, from those ranks came many London bankers, generally contented themselves with handling the local business of their clients (17). In the country districts a unit system of private banking made slow progress before the middle of the eighteenth century. In part this was a result of a lack of specialisation among merchants and manufacturers whose banking requirements were often not great in comparison with their need for other financial services. But to a large extent it was the consequence of restrictive legislation. From the beginning, the Bank of England has always had few branches; as late as 1844 it had only twelve so that other banks had to be able to receive deposits and grant credits. However, as a result of the Bank's acquisition of a virtual monopoly early in the eighteenth century, only private banks with a maximum of six partners were free to develop, and all partners were charged with complete personal liability for the firm's debts. It is not surprising that the firm of Thomas Smith of Nottingham appears to have been the only provincial bank dating from before 1700.

Only after 1750 can one begin to speak of a nationwide banking system. It was a very loosely co-ordinated and highly unstable structure, based upon the influence exerted by the London money market over a growing number of country banks. In rural areas, like East Anglia, bankers tended to accumulate funds in excess of the requirements of their own locality, and looked increasingly to the London money market for the employment of these surpluses. In the growing industrial regions of the north and west, where there was normally a net demand for funds, bankers again turned to London to meet their needs. In this way the London money market acted, to some extent, as an intermediary linking demand with supply. The money market was dominated by the Bank of England, whose primary occupation was the financing of public expenditure by drawing upon the wealth of the Home counties. It also included the London private bankers who, by the middle of the century, were both more experienced and more specialised than their country brethren, whose banking function was only now becoming distinct from their trading activities.

The connection between the Bank of England, the London banks, and indirectly, the country banks, lay in the nature of bank assets. These consisted of government stocks and short-term paper, bills of exchange and bankers' drafts; in addition most of the London business of the country bank was handled by a London bank, which acted as agent and regularly corresponded. This arrangement brought country bankers into contact with the London market, and the London account provided them with a relatively well-managed liquidity reserve to be drawn upon in time of need. Normally this reserve consisted of a permanent deposit upon which no interest was earned, in effect a payment for agency services.

In addition, there was a current account which did carry interest; sometimes a commission was paid or a combination of interest-free deposit and commission. Especially after 1780 this association was strengthened by country bankers actually buying into London firms or establishing their own houses. Younger London banks were prominent in interlocking partnerships and a few can be found working this kind of relationship in reverse, in order to gain access to lucrative country business (19).

The chief function of the provincial banker, until at least the second quarter of the nineteenth century, was to assist in the provision of a means of payment and his notes circulated freely in his area. He also undertook transfer and remittance activities with other country banks for customers, and had to stand ready to exchange the notes of other bankers for his own. Together with drafts and bills, the note issue helped to make up for the deficiencies of the Mint, in respect of coin, and the uneven circulation of the Bank of England note. In London, of course, where private notes had virtually disappeared by the 1770s, the Bank of England circulation was supreme. In Lancashire also, country notes were unimportant; the bill of exchange predominated there even for small day-to-day transactions (21). It was through their note issues that the banks touched the lives of the majority of people, and for this reason bank failures were always likely to be a subject of public concern. This feeling

of unease was heightened during the Suspension of Cash
Payments after 1797 when country bank issues rose rapidly and,
at their height, were providing about as much of the ordinary
currency of the country as the Bank of England and the Mint
together. Between the 1790s and the 1830s the Bank of England
note and the country note were the most widely utilised means
of payment over the country as a whole; even the advent of
joint-stock banks, and the impetus they gave to deposit banking,
did little at first to alter this situation, since most of the early
joint-stock banks issued their own notes. Note issues provided
a large part of a country banker's profits and enabled him to
influence the supply of credit. This explains the reluctance to
relinquish them in the face of mounting criticism that they were
inflationary and made economic crises more acute (23).

There was much contemporary confusion concerning the Bank
of England's control of internal credit, particularly during the
Suspension when convertibility into gold as the mainstay of
the monetary system was removed. Domestic inflation and the
deterioration of the foreign exchanges naturally directed
attention to the policy of the Bank of England with regard to
the price of gold. Although prior to 1797 the Bank had tended
to regulate its issues with reference to the state of the exchanges,
it subsequently grew lax and came in for much criticism (22).
There was a widespread belief that country issues were regulated
by those of the Bank, which deflected the blame away from
bankers for a time. After the Suspension, there was a tendency
to argue for having country note issues regulated by the foreign
exchanges as well as by those of the Bank. Most bankers on
the other hand failed to see any connection between their
activities, changes in the price level, and the balance of payments. They catered for the demands of trade, and it was difficult enough for them to see how the Bank's circulation was
relevant to their own, when there was frequently no apparent
similarity in their movements. The actual link which sub-
ordinated the country banks to Bank of England policy was, of
course, through the ultimate dependence of the country banker

upon his London balances which, in turn, were controlled through the Bank of England's discount policy. This came to be appreciated only slowly, long after the Suspension period (25).

Such terms as 'bill', 'draft' and 'note' were used at this period as interchangeable descriptions of private bank paper. This practice provides a clue to the origin of bank money in other credit instruments like bills of exchange and promissory notes, which also required consideration in any treatment of the means of payment. Early country notes were not always payable on demand; as with bills, they might be payable after some period had elapsed and bore interest. Demand notes came into their own during the Suspension and, until 1829, could be issued for as little as £1. This fact undoubtedly aided the expansion of country banking, particularly in the remoter rural regions where industrial activity was scattered, such as the South West and Yorkshire; later, private demand notes became confined to agricultural districts. By contrast, the bill of exchange proper was very much a commercial instrument and, by the eighteenth century, had long been used in international transactions. Though not without defects, the bill was developed within a legal framework that was generally sympathetic to the needs of merchants, into a form of currency that was suitable even for small transactions (18). In some areas it was regarded as a superior means of payment, preferred over other constituents of the money supply and reaching a high velocity of circulation in many instances. The growing popularity of the bill of exchange as an instrument of internal credit was considerably augmented after the middle of the eighteenth century by the development of a nationwide banking system. It rapidly became a convenient repository for bank funds looking for investment on the one hand, and on the other, the most common method by which bankers granted accommodation to their customers. In the deployment of their resources country bankers had, of course, to have some regard for their cash ratios. These, however, tended to vary greatly, depending on the nature of a bank's business and changes in the economic climate, and could be anything from 5 to 40 per cent for most of the century with a decline taking place during the Suspension period. In addition, bankers invested their funds in government securities, bills and drafts on London, and in balances with their London agents. After the liquidity requirement, the most important factor influencing banking behaviour was the extent of local investment opportunities. These were more numerous in industrial than in agricultural areas, and this was normally reflected in the practice of rural bankers holding more London assets and making correspondingly fewer local advances than their counterparts in manufacturing areas.

The very rapid expansion of country banking during the later decades of the eighteenth century and the high incidence of failure in periods of crisis, can only partly be attributed to the mismanagement of bankers and the defects of the banking structure. The period was one of general economic growth with spectacular booms in key industries like cotton; with so many outlets for funds, investment intentions changed quickly, speculation was rife, credit was vulnerable. The manner in which unsound accommodation by some sections of the mercantile community could react on the whole financial structure can be clearly seen in the crisis of 1793 and required emergency action and a ready assumption of ultimate responsibility by the Bank of England and the Government when it occurred (20).

Along with the increased activities of country bankers during the Napoleonic war, there was another feature of great significance for the future evolution of the money market. This was the emergence of a comparatively new group of financial specialists—the bill brokers. By negotiating bills of exchange for the banks, the bill broker was beginning to draw the banking system more closely together, and his activities anticipate the emergence of the discount market later on. Eighteenth century traders had often dealt in bills, in a limited way and simply as intermediaries, as an adjunct to their normal business. And at least until 1815 the first specialist brokers were working as agents, and not principals, in the purchase and sale of bills. The

London banker continued to remain the chief agent for the London business of his country bank clientele, so that the appearance of a large bill broker like Thomas Richardson in the early years of the nineteenth century should not be over-emphasised (24). His kind of specialisation was very much a product of the Suspension period and the size of his business was almost certainly not representative. It arose, primarily, out of the high interest rates brought about by the war; as London agents and other net savers in the community began to invest more in the national debt via the stock exchange, incidentally side-stepping the effect of the Usury laws, so the supply of discounts for country bankers was reduced. Bill brokers now moved in to supply the country banker's cash requirements, thereby enabling him to build up the necessary drawing rights with his London agent. At first, the country bankers had turned to the Bank of England, but by the end of 1795 the demand for discounts had risen to such an extent that rationing had to be introduced. Furthermore, the Bank refused to discount bills that had more than sixty-five days to run, whereas bill brokers were usually more concerned with the quality of the bill—the people who had endorsed it—than with its usance—the time left to maturity. Long-dated bills were plentiful but they offended against the London bankers' view of what was good self-liquidating paper; the purism of the banker was the bill broker's opportunity. The development of this new function after 1815 was uneven, expansion occurring when interest rates were low.

By comparison with the very rapid growth in the number of provincial banks at the end of the eighteenth century, the number of London banks increased fairly steadily over the century. The London banking fraternity had a hundred years of experience behind it before the country banks came to influence the working of the money market in any significant way. Their tradition was not an entirely continuous one, however; the ranks of the Restoration goldsmith-bankers had been decimated during and after the South Sea Bubble, and much new blood came into banking in the early 1770s. Nonetheless, three characteristics set London banks apart from those in the provinces. Firstly, their much earlier growth as deposit banks which was a reflection of the wealth, and sheer economic and political weight, of London in the nation's economy. Secondly, the foundation of the Bank of England with the bulk of its lending going to the government, and its growth as a note-issuing institution. Finally, the revolution in government finance after 1688 and the emergence of new securities for investors. The combined effect of these factors was to accelerate an earlier tendency to leave off the goldsmith's trade and concentrate on banking. The speculative climate existing between the Revolution of 1688 and the South Sea Bubble, while it encouraged private banking in the capital, also made the Bank of England more eager and the government more amenable to a monopoly of joint-stock banking. Following a number of ill-fated financial projects in the first decade of the eighteenth century, the Bank was granted and confirmed in a banking monopoly that was to last for more than a century. It is arguable how far the Act of 1708, conferring the privilege of exclusive banking, retarded the growth of banking techniques in London and in the manufacturing areas later in the century. The restriction of banks to six partners had not prevented the introduction of one element of specialisation becoming evident as early as 1720. On the one hand were the City bankers who kept mercantile accounts and engaged in discounting. On the other were the West End banks, many of them well documented like Hoares, Childs and Coutts, whose business tended to be more substantial and was concentrated on the landed classes, receiving rents and making mortgage loans.

After 1750, as the number of country banks increased, it is noteworthy that the new agency business was taken by the new City banks with existing trading connections in many cases. Many West End banks did have country connections, of course, but these appear to have been long-established and the bulk of the agency business went to firms like Down, Esdaile, Masterman and Barclay. This growth of country business was one factor leading to the establishment of the London Clearing House in 1773. It facilitated a growing volume of inter-bank payments by economising on the time taken and the cash required to transact day-to-day business. At the same time, another striking feature was the greatly increased use of cheques in London private banking after 1750. This took place side by side with a decline in their note-issues, and against the background of the rising circulations of the Bank of England and the country banks (27). By the end of the eighteenth century the various elements of the money market had developed a working relationship with the Bank of England as a central organ beginning to assume some central banking functions. Yet industrialisation was starting to reveal the inadequacies of what was still a small private banking system. There was an alarming increase in the number of bank failures in the first quarter of the nineteenth century, and in 1826 Lord Liverpool told Parliament that the existing system 'would permit every description of banking except that which is solid and secure'. Those who sought reform observed that the problems which afflicted English banking from the 1790s to the 1820s did not show themselves in Scotland to any degree, and comparisons favourable to the Scottish system of joint-stock banks and branches were increasingly telling (26). After the crisis of 1825 the advent of joint-stock banking in the provinces placed private banking in a defensive position. The subsequent growth of deposit banking, which threatened at first to make the bill brokers of the London money market redundant, eventually brought about a change of practice on the part of the London bankers, towards keeping more money at call in bills of exchange. This enabled a proper market in discounts to develop, especially after 1844. Finally, the London Clearing House, which had been jealously guarded by the private banks for so long, allowed six joint-stock banks to partake of its facilities in 1854.

_____

17 Anonymous   The Goldsmith Bankers

The relations of the Crown with the goldsmiths of Restoration London was an important influence on the growth of banking in the metropolis. The financial requirements of government spurred the transition of the goldsmiths' trade in plate to the practice of essential banking functions. Between 1640 and 1670 the goldsmiths turned increasingly to foreign exchange dealing, to the acceptance of deposits and the payment of interest upon them, and ultimately to the issue of assignable receipts or promissory notes. The pamphlet reproduced below is perhaps the most important single piece of evidence relating to the transition to private banking in London.

Sir. Since you are pleased to demand my advice in the disposal of your Son to the Goldsmiths Trade, and my opinion of the Trade itself; I must trouble you more than I was willing to set down what I have observed of the Goldsmiths since I have Traded, and the steps of their Rise and Progress, and leave the judgment of the whole to your Self; tis but fit that a Son should owe the good choice of his imployment and way to his fortunes to the prudence and love of his Father.

If I could now discourse you, I ought to be satisfied whether you have thoughts to put your Son to a Goldsmith of the Old or New Fashion, those of that profession having of late years wholly changed their way of Trading. In my time their whole imployment was to make and sell Plate, to buy forreign Coyns and Gold and Silver imported to melt and cull them, and cause some to be coyned at the Mint, and with the rest to furnish the Refiners, Plate-makers, and Merchants, as they found the price of gold and silver to vary, and as the Merchants had occasion for Forreign Coyns.

But about Thirty years since, the Civil Wars giving opportunity to Apprentices to leave their Masters at will, and the old way having been for Merchants to trust their Cash in one of their Servants custody, many such Cashiers left their Masters in the lurch and went to the Army, and Merchants knew not how to confide in their Apprentices; then did some Merchants begin to put their Cash into Goldsmiths hands to receive and pay for them, (thinking it more secure) and the trade of Plate being then but little worth, most of the Nobility and Gentry, and others melting down their old Plate rather than buying new, and few daring to use or own Plate, the Goldsmiths sought to be the Merchants Cash-keepers to receive and pay for nothing, few observing or conjecturing their profit they had for their pains.

It happened about that time that the then Parliament had coyned out of Plate, and otherwise seven Millions in Half-Crowns, and no Mills being then used in the Mint, the Money was of a very unequal weight, sometimes two pence or three pence in an ounce difference, & the French and others then changing the value of their Coins often, which made silver and gold of much greater value abroad than at our English Mint: The Goldsmiths found a new Mischeivous trade to send all the money trusted in their hands into their Cocklofts, where they had Scales and various Weights adapted for their pourpose, and servants constantly weighed every half-crown (at least) and sorted them to melt for Two pence or three pence, or sometimes less gain by the ounce, and sometimes their advantage being greater by the accidents of the rise or fall of the exchange, those heaviest Coins were sent away in specie, several French men and other Merchants making it their whole and only business weekly to transport the gold and silver so culled, either melted down or in specie; and from hence the Goldsmiths set up another new Trade of buying the old English gold coin at a rate much above its Lawful coyned value, buying and selling it at five, seven, eight and ten pounds in the hundred more than it was coyned for, still sending it away so fast, or supplying those with it whose business was to Transport it, that by a modest computation eight parts of ten of the coyn'd Gold was suddenly consumed, and two shillings a piece was commonly given for gold, when a penny a piece was often given before to exchange gold into silver; the Seven Millions also of silver new Coyned, was apparently reduced to less than one Million, and the people so abused in their money, that there was little Coin passed in trade but overworn, washed, and clipt, to the great vexation and loss of the Traders.

These unlawful practices and profits of the Goldsmiths, made them greedy to ingross all the Cash they could, and to combine with all mens servants who continued to keep any Cash, to bring their moneys to them to be culled, and to remain with them at four pence the day interest per centum without the Masters privity: And having thus got Money into their hands, they presumed upon some to come as fast as others was paid away; and upon that confidence of a running Cash (as they call it) they begun to accommodate men with moneys for Weeks and Months upon extraordinary gratuities, and supply all necessitous Merchants that over traded their Stock, with present Money for their Bills of Exchange, discounting sometimes double, perhaps treble interest for the time as they found the Merchant more or less pinched.

Profit arising by this Trade, some of them who had the highest Credit, undertook to receive Gentlemens Rents as they were returned to Town, and indeed any Man's money, and to allow them some intrest for it though it lay for a month only, or less, the Owners calling for it by a hundred or fifty pounds at a time as their occasions and expences wanted it; this new practice giving hopes to everybody to make Profit of their money until the hour they spent it, and the conveniency as they thought, to command their money when they pleased, which they could not do when lent at intrest upon personal or reall Security; These hopes I say, drew a great Cash into these new Goldsmiths hands, and some of them stuck to their old Trade, but every of them that had friends and credit, aspired to this new Mystery to become Bankers or Casheers, and when Cromwell usurped the Government, the greatest of them began to deal with him to supply his wants of Money upon great Advantages especially after they had bought these Dollars whereof he robb'd the Spaniards to about the value of £300,000.

After the King's return he wanting money, some of these Bankers undertook to lend him not their own but other mens money, taking barefaced of Him ten pounds for the hundred, and by private contracts many Bills, Orders, Tallies, and Debts of the King's, above twenty, and sometimes thirty in the hundred, to the great dishonor of the Government.

This Prodigious unlawful Gain induced all of them that could be credited with moneys at intrest to become lenders to the King to anticipate all the Revenue, to take every Grant of the Parliament into pawn as soon as it was given, I had almost said, before the Act was passed for it, and to outvie each other in buying and taking to pawn, Bills, Orders, and Tallies, in effect all the King's revenue passed their hands, and if Solomon be in the right, that the Borrower is a Slave to the Lender, the King and Kingdom became Slaves to these Bankers, and the Kingdom gave no small share of their Taxes to them, paying double and treble Intrest, as if they had not been able to raise Money for the publick Service at the times it was requisite.

But the number of these Bankers increased so fast, and the money at Interest come so much into their hands, that the King and His Farmers, and all Tallies of Anticipation and Orders, could not secure all the money they had to lend. Hereupon they sought out according to their several natural wits and capacities, how to dispose of money for more than lawful Intrest, either upon Pawns or Bottom, Reason or unreasonable discounts of Intrest for Bills, or upon notorious usurious Contracts, or upon personal Securities from Heirs whose Estates are in expectancy, or by sudden advance of money to Projectors, who drawn into Projects many Responsible Men to the ruin of their Families; These Goldsmiths however getting £10 or £15 per Centum, and sometimes more, only for the present advance of the money, besides the future Intrest, These and a hundred other practices they have used and do still continue in contempt of Law and Justice, whereof they are so conscious to themselves, that most of them do once a year (at least) sue out their general Pardon to avoid the penalty of those wholsom Laws made to prevent such Frauds, Oppressions, contempt of Government, and mischeives to the Publick as they are dayly guilty of: Tis also suspected that their original Trade of culling the heavy Money is not deserted by some of them; also how come all clipt and washt money to pass so currant at their Shops, and so little appearance in payments of all the new coyned Money since the King's return, so many £100,000's of the Parliaments Coin, besides Bullion imported having been new coyned, and how comes Guinies also to be bought and sold by them so much above the Coynage rate, that upon their account only, and by their means, they pass currant in payments for more than they are really worth from some of their Shops: I am sure some Merchants are supplyed with Gold and Silver English Coyn, to transport upon the advantage of the exchange, or making their present Bargains in France and elsewhere, for importing Prohibited Goods.

Sir, I Have given you my Remarques upon the Rise and growth of these new kind of Goldsmiths, and I take them to have been in their highest Ascendant or State about the time that our Ships were burnt at Chatham by the Dutch: that cold Storm of the Peoples fears that their money was not safe in the Bankers hands blighted them, and since being in their declension, the Famous stop upon the Exchequer almost blasted their very root, men being unwilling to trust money in their hands to lend his Majesty, so long as they hear the deplorable Cryes of the Widdow and the Fatherless, whose money they say at Feasts, they lent the King, and cannot repay them, no nor their Intrest to buy them Bread.

Now admitting that all the Creditors of the Bankers can no more think it safe that their money should be lent to the King since Tallies, Orders, and the Great Seal itself, are found to be no security, I cannot imagine how Bread should be got by their trade of borrowing money upon lawful Intrest to lend upon unlawful to private persons, though they can silence their consciences and forget Christianity, and neither regard their neighbours welfare, nor the good of the whole Kingdom, but seek by Usurious unlawful Bargains, and oppressive Exactions from the needy and men in streights, and by hook and by crook to make the most of their Cash.

I dare take it for granted that the men now of that Trade are not men of greater natural Abilities nor acquired parts, than other Tradesmen of their age and degree, nor are they better instructed than others to imploy greater Stocks in an advantagious Trade, nor have they greater Stocks of their own to hazzard to remote places, from whence most profit may be hoped for; Neither have these men greater skill in Law than other Citizens, to judg of Securities to be taken for Money, nor have they more knowledge of Men to guess at the value of their Bonds; how then should they be able to make more Intrest of money than other Traders; yet the profit that may satisfy other Traders, cannot be sufficient for them to keep open their Shops; they must have a great dead stock of Cash to answer all Payments, and be always ready occasionally to advance great Summs: their Servants and Shops must be maintained for no use but Payments and Receipts, and deducting dead Stock and Charges, if they do not take nine per Cent. intrest for what they Lend and dispose of, they cannot make one of one, much less subsist. Besides there must be allowance for Charges to defend themselves against Informers for their usurious Contracts, and procuring frequent Pardons, and for hazard of loss of their Money lent upon unlawful Intrest, every borrower having it in his power to plead their usury against them in lue of their Debts. All these things, and many more being duly considered, I suppose people will suddenly come to their wits, and begin to examine why a Goldsmith-banker should be better Security than another man, or fitter to be trusted for ten times more than he is worth: They give only personal Security, and many times their Notes for £500, £1,000 or more, when they owe before they give that Note, twenty times the value of their own Estates, and yet these free Lenders will scarce be satisfied with two or three Mens Bonds £1,000 that are known to be worth £5,000 a Man; doubtless I say, People will think at last that a Banker ought to give as good Security for money he borrows as another man, especially since he runs the greatest hazards in his disposing of Money for excessive Gain or intrest.

I leave it then to your self to judg whether Banking be like to continue half your Son's Apprenticeship, and whether all the Arts that they can teach him can be worth one of the £200 you design to give with him; I presume upon your Pardon for my plainness and tediousness; Yet I am prompted to say something more in point of Conscience, doubting whether it be Lawful to exercise any Trade in a constant avowed breach of the Laws of the Kingdom, as all Bankers do, these Laws being made for the good of the Society, to which the Scripture commands obedience for Conscience sake, where they are met contrary to the Laws of God.

Perhaps it is worth the inquiry upon that account, whether any man that hath exercised the Mystery of Banking, hath living or dying, gone off the stage with a clear good Estate, all his Creditors being paid, fully paid. But I judg no Man. I submit these thoughts and my Self to Your Prudent Censure, and remain, Sir, Your Humble Servant J. R. Anonymous. *The Mystery of the New Fashioned Goldsmiths or Bankers* (1676)

18 William Forbes   Credit Instruments

William Forbes (d 1745) was an advocate and the first Professor of Civil Law in the University of Glasgow from 1714. He was the author of a number of treatises on Scots law as well as being a pioneer in the comparative law of England and Scotland. His *Methodical Treatise*, first published in 1703, is a very useful digest of the custom of merchants relating to exchange matters and was based upon a thorough knowledge of the European authorities on the subject.

Persons take and give money upon exchange, either by

concerting the matter betwixt themselves; or through the assistance and mediation of a set of men abroad, called Agents, or Brokers of Exchange, whereof some interpose without any authority, others are sworn persons authorised for that effect, and allowed for their pains a certain reward . . . In other countries when the Remitter is not acquainted with him, who would take up Money per Exchange, or doubts his credit; the Drawer is ordinarily either put to make his Bills payable to a known substantial man, and to get them by him indorsed to the Remitter or his order; or else to procure some such sufficient Person to subscribe the second or third Bill under his own subscription, who thereby becomes equally liable with the principal Drawer to the Remitter, or him to whom the so subscribed Bill is made over . . . Persons going to a strange place, where probably they may have use for money, and not thinking fit to take Bills with them; ordinarily provide themselves with Letters of Credit. These are either general or special. The last are open letters, addressed to a Factor or Correspondent, bearing Orders to furnish such a man, with such a sum at one or several times, upon his Bills of Exchange, or Receipts: And to charge it to his Accompt who gives the Letter of Credit. General Letters of Credit, are ample letters directed to some particular Correspondent, or to all Merchants and others, that shall advance money thereon, to the person or persons thereinmentioned, without restriction, as to Time, or Place, or Sum, or other Circumstances; obliging the writer for re-payment.

Men write general letters of credit, commonly for their own Account, or Concernments in the Course of Trade: And when such are given to any friend, 'tis only to put Honour upon him . . .

Sometimes Bills of Exchange are made by Procuration, as when any Merchant, by Letters of Factory under his hand, impowers one to draw and accept bills in his name; which being registered and intimated to those he has to do with, in business of that nature, the factor by drawing and accepting bills subscribed with the quality of factor for such a man, doth effectually bind his constituent, tho' the factor be minor or under age, without any obligement upon himself, and this is called drawing, and being drawn upon in commission. The deed of a factor for two or more persons that are in partnership or joint-traders, will oblige each of 'em *in solidum*. A power to draw bills in the name of another, doth imply also a power to draw in and indorse all such as are payable to the principal, or to him or his order . . .

In in-land bill dealing, as when bills are drawn and payable in the Bank, or when the place of payment is not far distanced from where the bill was made; the deliverer gets but one bill: But if it be at some considerable remove, or in the case of foreign bills, he will not hold himself content with one bill, 'tho payable at sight; because one may be lost. It is not determined how many bills should be given for one parcel, but commonly two, and sometimes three, are taken of the same date, and alike in all respects, except the distinction of first, second, &c. each carrying this qualification, *My other Bills of the same Date not being paid*: Wherefore it is that payment of any one of them annuls the rest . . .

A drawer who fears his bills may be refused, will recommend it by a Letter of Advice to some other friend or correspondent at the place of acceptance, to prevent the dishonour of his bills . . .

When the design'd accepter is an out-dweller, i.e. dwells not at the place where the bill is to be paid; the remitter usually gets with the bill an address and direction from the drawer; or after acceptance, from the accepter; where, and to whom the possessor must apply for payment. And when no such direction is given, the possessor must timely advertise the accepter whom he is to pay to, that he may make due Provision for it.

The drawer to prevent forgeries and imposters, and that he who is drawn upon, may not be surpriz'd with the draught, must inform and advise him on whom he draws, by a letter, (called a letter of advice) concerning the sum drawn for, the species of money, time and place of payment, person payable to, who is to be debited for it; and (unless he be creditor to the person drawn upon) the fund design'd for his reimbursement, with all the other circumstances of the bill. But the drawer of a bill, for his own or some third person's account, lies under no necessity to advise the person drawn upon, concerning the exchange; unless the bill be expressly payable in a species of money, not current at the place of payment . . .

It is usual in bills of exchange, to write the sum to be paid in figures at the top of the bill; and in the body of it in words at length. But if it should happen the sum in figures, to differ from that expressed at length; the sum in the body of the bill is to be the rule, even though the first agree with the letter of advice. Because over and above that a man is more apt to mistake in writing a figure, than in writing a word . . .

Bills are either made payable simply, or conditionally, as after the accepter has sold off a certain cargo, or after he has got in certain effects of the drawer's, &c. but whether the bill be simple or conditional, it may be payable either at sight, or so many days sight, or on a certain fix'd day, or so long after date, or at such usance . . .

. . . But by the general custom of merchants, it is arbitrary to the parties to appoint any term of payment, as they can agree, without respect to local distance. For what is more ordinary than to make bills payable at usance, or at double or treble usance? And usance is frequently taken for sometime after sight.

Usance differs in different places. For by usance from Scotland, England, France and Ireland, Brabant, Flanders, and any town in Holland and Zealand, to Amsterdam, and from thence to all these places except France, we mean one full month after date; whether it consist of 31, 30, or 28 days: And so double or treble usance is as who should say, two or three months after date; and for half usance we reckon 15 days . . .

Again, the ordinary way of dealing in bills being by delivery of value at the time of the draught, present value receiv'd is presum'd, betwixt persons not otherwise concerned together than by such bills; because that is presumed which is most ordinary . . .

If value in money, or money-worth, or value in accompt be given for bills, or if value be discounted, they use to bear value received; or value of such a one, as when bills are payable to one, for value received of another; or a simple order to pay, which imports value received. By the term Discount is understood the diminution that is agreed upon between the parties to be made in a sum of money payable only at a certain term, upon condition to pay the remainder in ready money e.g. One merchant who has an accepted bill upon another for a certain sum of money, payable in three months, wanting ready money, offers to the accepter to make a certain rebatement of so much per cent. for present payment, which diminution or rebatement, if agreed to by the accepter, is called the discount. And if the accepter do not agree to pay ready money upon the consideration of that rebatement, the bearer of the bill sells it to any banker, who, deducing the ordinary allowance for the discount, will pay the remainder in ready money. This discount differs in different countries, by reason of the different interest of money in several places: But no government allows the discompt of bills of exchange to be higher than the interest is in the country . . .

Tho' the value and the bill be reciprocally the causes one of another; yet sometimes more is given by way of value than the sum contained in the bill, less again at other times; which ballance is term'd the Exchange. If these be equal, the exchange is said to be at par; but when the creditor in the bill receives less than the value paid in to the drawer, exchange is above the par; and below it when he receives more. Par is the equality of the real intrinsick value of the species, and not the equality of the number of pennies, stivers, solses, &c. For if e.g. 60 pence English for 80 French solses be given by the buyer of a bill upon Paris, the exchange is above the par: The par between England and France being 54 English pence for a French crown in specie of 60 solses, now that the extrinsick value of the crown is rais'd in France far beyond its intrinsick. Yet some are of opinion, that there can be no certain rate set on the par in exchange, to answer the just value of foreign coins; by reason of their diversity and different intrinsick values. In Russia, Turky, and Persia, the exchange is kept above the par: By which politick, there is no trade with them in money, but only in goods, and the exportation of their money, and the over-ballancing of foreign commodities with theirs, is effectually prevented . . .

The possessor of a bill may, for his own conveniency, transfer or assign it by a short writing, called an Indorsement, because it is commonly put on the back of the bill.

Indorsement of a bill, (called also re-drawing) is a sign'd mandate to pay the contents, for some cause, to such a one, or his order; to whom the subscriber term'd, the indorser, becomes as liable as the drawer. So that if a bill should be indorsed, and pass through a thousand hands, every indorser is an accumulate security, and liable *in solidum*, to the porteur of the bill, called the indorsee. But if one of more indorsers commit an error in the indorsing, that must ly at his own door only, and cannot be charged upon the rest . . .

Acceptance of a bill of exchange is an obligement to pay it; and the person thus oblig'd is call'd, the Accepter. Acceptance is either verbal, or written: But the first is not so safe or convenient as the other . . .

For determining the time allotted for presenting of bills, we may consider two cases. 1. If no lawful impediment interveen, so much time only should be allowed for presenting, as the possessor may conveniently go or send to him, on whom the bill is drawn. 2. If the possessor be necessarily detain'd and with-held by an accident, or *casus fortuitus*, from going or sending to get his bill accepted; he ought to be excus'd, and not to be put to account for what may happen to the person drawn upon, during the just and legal impediment . . .

Protesting, in general, is a profitable remedy, whereby we commonly preserve our right entire. And in bills of exchange 'tis an essential piece of diligence, that cannot be dispensed with, or supplied by witnesses, or oath of party, or by any other act. Bills are either protested for not acceptance, or for not payment, or the like. The design whereof is only to signify to the drawer, that the possessor the bill did his duty in duly requiring acceptance or payment; but that the person drawn upon was either unwilling, or not to be found, or insolvent; and thereby to make the drawer liable. For there is always action competent to the creditor in the bill against the accepter, whether it be protested or not: Tho' without that formality he cannot have summary diligence . . . In England the person to whom a bill is payable, his servant, agent, or assigns, causeth it to be protested by a notary publick; and in default of such notary, by any other substantial person of the place, in the presence of two or more witnesses betwixt sun and sun, or sun rising and setting, when shops are generally open, or the Courts of Justice sitting . . .

In all instruments of protest, the bill protested must be prefixed; with all the indorsements, if there be any, copied and transcribed *verbatim*: And an account of the reasons given by the party, why he does not honour the bill.

The common reasons for not acceptance, are, because he hath no advice thereof, or no effects of the drawer's, or no order from the third person for whose account the bill is drawn, or the like. But acceptance cannot be refused, upon pretence that the presenter of the bill hath no right thereto; for as much as that may be made up at any time before payment is required. And the naked having of the bill without any further title is sufficient in order to protest for not acceptance . . .

Bills, if acceptance be refused upon the first representing, ought instantly to be protested, (no Days of Grace being allowed for accepting of bills), but yet the possessor is sometimes in use to gratify the desire of the person drawn upon, in allowing a short time to consider upon the acceptance, till the next post day.

The suffering a bill to be protested for not acceptance, doth not touch the reputation of the person upon whom it was drawn; unless he had of the drawer's effects; but it wounds one's credit to have his accepted bill protested for not payment, because that which at first was *actus voluntatis*, becomes *necessitatis* after acceptance . . .

Some allow no dealing in exchange to be lawful, but what is expede by foreign bills, i.e. such as are drawn in one country, to be paid in another: Which was indeed the first and most ancient way. So, if a bill be drawn in Amsterdam, by one person upon another, payable in the same place, or at Rotterdam, or any other part within the Province of Holland; 'tis no more privileged than a common obligation. And in Castile they have a law, discharging all persons to make a profit by advancing money upon exchange from one place to another within the kingdom, under the pains of forfeiting the money, and being punished as usurers; tho' that statute be not rigidly observed. Others, as those in France, do not dispute the lawfulness of inland exchange, provided it be from and to distant places within the same kingdom or province; still holding that local distance is essential to an exchange contract, without which it degenerates into usury. But our custom is more liberal, in allowing bills to be made payable after a certain time, even in the same place where they are drawn or indors'd . . .

Inland bills of exchange had not in England, before the year 1697, any manner of force or credit. But, at length, seeing great damages frequently happened in the course of trade, by reason of the delays of payment, and other neglects of such bills; these bearing value received, were ordained to be summarily negotiated by protesting, accepting, and giving advice thereof, &c. provided the bills be drawn for £20 sterling or upwards . . .

Promissory Notes, (called in France, Billets de Change, or Notes of Exchange) whereby any person promises in writing to pay to one or his order, any sum of money thereinmentioned, have the same effect both in France and in England, as inland bills of exchange, as to indorsement thereof, and maintaining action thereon, for payment of the sum, with costs and damages. Only there is this difference, that, whereas a bill must be protested, the party failing to pay a note, must be summoned to a court. William Forbes. *A Methodical Treatise concerning Bills of Exchange* . . . (1718 edition)

19 The State of Commercial Credit 1793   Report

Your Committee have thought it incumbent on them, in proceeding to execute the Orders of the House, to direct their Attention to Three principal Points:

First.—Whether the Difficulties at present experienced, or the Probability of their Continuance and Increase, are of such urgent Importance to the Public Interest, as to require the Interposition of the Legislature.

Secondly.—On the Supposition that such Interposition should be deemed necessary, what is the most practicable and effectual Plan which can be adopted for giving Relief.

Thirdly.—What Means can be suggested for preventing the Renewal of similar Inconveniencies.

The Consideration of the First and Second Head appeared in some Measure blended together; and the Third, though of great Importance, appearing to be less urgent in Point of Time, your Committee have thought it proper to submit to the House such Considerations as occurred to them upon the Two First Points, reserving the latter for a separate Report.

Under the First of these Heads, the Notoriety of Failures to a considerable Extent, the general Embarrassment and Apprehension which has ensued, a Consideration of the necessary Connection between different Mercantile Houses, and their Dependence on each other, and the Influence which the State of Commercial Credit must have upon the Trade, the Revenue, and general Interests of the Country, appeared sufficient, without minute Examination, to satisfy your Committee that the present Situation strongly called for an immediate and effectual Remedy, if any practicable Plan could be suggested for that Purpose.

In Addition to this, the Committee had an Opportunity of

collecting, from several of their own Members, Information, grounded either on their general Observation upon the Subject, or on their own immediate and personal Knowledge.

Your Committee, understanding that some Suggestions on this Subject had been laid before the Chancellor of the Exchequer, on the Part of several Persons of great Eminence and Respectability in the City of London, were of Opinion that a Communication of these Suggestions, would be very material to the Objects of their Enquiry, with a View of ascertaining the Opinion of Persons of this Description, both with respect to the Necessity of some Remedy, and to the particular Mode in which it might be applied.

The Chancellor of the Exchequer accordingly laid before the Committee a Paper which had been delivered to him on the 23rd Instant, by the Lord Mayor and Mr. Bosanquet; which is inserted in the Appendix to this Report: He also stated to the Committee, the Circumstances which had led to this Paper being drawn up.—That he had received Representations from many different Quarters, which induced him to believe, that the Failures which had taken place, had begun by a Run on those Houses who had issued Circulating Paper without being possessed of sufficient Capital, but that the Consequences had soon extended themselves so far as to affect many Houses of great Solidity, and possessed of Funds ultimately much more than sufficient to answer all Demands upon them, but which had not the Means of converting those Funds into Money, or Negotiable Securities, in Time to meet the Pressure of the Moment.—That the sudden Discredit of a considerable Quantity of Paper which had been issued by different Banks, in itself produced a Deficiency of the Circulating Medium, which in the ordinary Course of Things could not be immediately replaced, and that this Deficiency occasioned material Inconvenience in Mercantile Transactions.—That in Addition to this immediate Effect, these Circumstances also were represented to have induced Bankers and others to keep in their Hands a greater Quantity of Money than they thought necessary in the usual Train of Business, and that large Sums were thus kept out of Circulation, and great Difficulty arose in procuring the usual Advances on Bills of Exchange, particularly those of a long Date.—That many Persons were said to be possessed of large Stocks of Goods, which they could not at present dispose of, and on the Credit of which they could not praise Money—That this occasioned an Interruption of the Means by which they were enabled to make their Weekly Payments, tended to prevent the Employment of a Number of Persons engaged in different Manufactures.—That these Evils were represented as likely rapidly to increase to a very serious Extent, if some extraordinary Means were not adopted to restore Credit and Circulation.—That in consequence of these Representations, he had desired a Meeting of different Gentlemen, in order to obtain the best Information in his Power, respecting the Extent of the Evil, and the Possibility and Propriety of any Measure to remedy it.—That after much Discussion, all the Gentlemen present seemed to agree in a very strong Opinion of the Extent of the Evil, though many Objections at first occurred to any Plan for remedying it.—That in the Result, it was agreed to desire the Gentlemen whose Names were mentioned in the Paper now delivered, to meet the next Day at the Mansion House, to consider more particularly the Proposal for the Issue of Exchequer Bills to a certain Amount, to be advanced under proper Regulations, for the Accommodation of such Persons as might apply for the same, and likewise the Objections to which such a Proposal might be liable; and that the Paper which he had laid before the Committee, contained the Opinion of this Second Meeting.

The Chancellor of the Exchequer also gave an Account to the Committee of an Application that had come within his Knowledge for the Accommodation and Support of a House connected with a very important Manufacturing District, that the Sum wanted for the Support and Accommodation of this House was comparatively small, and the Security proposed, as he had understood from very good Authority, was admitted to be unquestionable, but that the Application had hitherto been ineffectual.

The Lord Mayor informed the Committee, That in Conformity to the Statement mentioned by the Chancellor of the Exchequer, Eleven Gentlemen met at the Mansion House on the 23rd, selected principally from that Part of the preceding Meeting, who had expressed the greatest Difficulties in finding out a Remedy; and after a long Discussion upon the Subject, they unanimously were of Opinion, that the Interposition of Parliament was necessary, and that an Issue of Exchequer Bills, under certain Regulations and Stipulations, was the best practicable Remedy.

Your Committee also received Information from Mr. Thornton, Mr. Alderman Anderson, and Mr. Chiswell, Members of this Committee, with respect to Instances which had fallen under their personal Observation, to the following Effect:

Mr. Thorton represented, That he was at this Time acquainted with the Situation of Five or Six Mercantile Houses, who were in the Possession of large Quantities of Goods, the Produce of which would give them effectual Relief, but that owing to the Stagnation of Trade, and the Impossibility of converting these Goods into Money, the Houses in Question were under very great Apprehension of being shortly obliged to stop Payment.

He informed the Committee, That he was lately appointed a Trustee for liquidating the Concerns of a House in London, with Extensive Connections in the Country, that had been obliged to suspend its Payments; that after the Intervention of about Three Weeks it had been enabled to pay its Acceptances, and within Twelve Months would discharge all its Debts, and that the Partners had a reasonable Expectation of retaining a Surplus of One hundred thousand Pounds, and if they had had the Opportunity of raising only a moderate Sum of Money on the Securities which they held, the Calamity that befell them and their Connections might have been averted.

Mr. Alderman Anderson informed the Committee, That it had fallen under his own personal Knowledge that Seven

Mercantile Houses, of known and undoubted Property, and with a large Quantity of Goods on Hand, now not saleable, are brought to very great Distress from the Scarcity of Money, and will not be able to make good their Payments if not assisted, which would prove of very serious Consequence to many other Merchants and Manufacturers to whom they stand indebted.

Mr. Chiswell stated, That the present Mercantile Distress arose from an alarming Stagnation of Credit, which, on his Knowledge, had reduced Eight Houses of known and large Property to stop their Payments—That he also knew others of the same Description who have had temporary Assistance from him and others, but which will be ineffectual if they are not further relieved in a short Time.—He also stated, That various Applications had been made to him from different Houses of undoubted and very considerable Capitals, which in ordinary Times, or even in Times of Pressure, he would have assisted, and that he is now only withheld by the Uncertainty to what Extent the Mischief may increase, from the present unexampled general Alarm and Want of Credit.—He also farther stated, That if those Houses were not assisted, the Consequence would be the immediate Failure of many others of good Credit and Fortune dependent on them.

Your Committee understanding that Mr. Gilbert Innes, a Director of the Royal Bank of Scotland, was at present in London, desired his Attendence, and received Information from him to the following Effect:

That, as a Director of the Royal Bank of Scotland, he has had many Occasions to judge of the present State of Commercial Credit in Scotland:

That the Country is in very great Distress, and the Two Chartered Banks will not be able much longer, with Prudence to themselves, to furnish the Accommodation and Support, necessary to different Mercantile and Manufacturing Houses, nor to the Country Banks, and, if something is not immediately done by Government, a very general Failure may be expected; and that many Houses with undoubted Effects, and who would

M

ultimately pay all Demands against them, will be involved, unless they can obtain a temporary Relief.

There have been several Failures, and a very considerable one lately, which is connected with Manufacturers who may ultimately be involved, and where Seven or Eight hundred Persons are now employed.

The Effect of these Failures, in his Opinion, must occasion many Manufacturers to be thrown out of Employment, and he had heard some were already dismissed; and such is the Pressure of the Times, that the Distress, if not Ruin, of several principal Manufacturing Houses may ensue.—Many Manufacturers would have been dismissed but for the liberal Support their Employers have received from the Royal Bank, but that Assistance cannot, without Imprudence, be continued without extraordinary Aid.

This Prospect of Distress to the Manufacturers, in his Opinion, arises not so much from a Failure of the usual Markets for the Goods, as from the Difficulty in discounting, in London and in Scotland, the long-dated Bills received for the Goods.

Great Quantities of manufactured Goods belonging to Manufacturers in Scotland, are now in London, for which when sold, Bills are granted for a small Part at Three Months, and the Remainder from Six to Fourteen Months, the greatest Part of which Goods have been formerly sold for long-dated Bills, but are not so now from the Difficulty of obtaining Discounts; and he has heard Manufacturers say, they were willing to sell their Goods with a considerable Loss to obtain Relief, by Sales for ready Money.

Manufacturers frequently borrow Money for the Purposes of their Trade on Personal Bonds, great Part of that Money has been called for at Whitsunday next, 15th May, and from the State of Credit in Scotland he has Reason to think the Manufacturers will not be able to answer these Demands by borrowing on the former Securities.

The Manufacturers keep as little Stock in their Warehouses as they can, and as Fashion varies, he should think the Mercantile Interest would be more benefited by depositing the raw Materials on Pledge than the Manufacturer, who, however, might indirectly be benefited by the Advance.

He certainly thinks that Paper issued on Government Security, and advanced upon the Deposit of Goods or other unquestionable Private Security, would, when properly understood, be a material Relief in the present Distress of Scotland; and he has no Doubt several Persons might be found to concur in giving a joint Security for the Support of Co-partnerships, with perfect Safety to the Public.

He believes the Quantity of Paper circulated by the Country Banks, has of late been considerably diminished, and their Discounts on Bills of Exchange greatly so, since these Troubles began: With regard to the Royal Bank, the Circulation is nearly the same, and the Assistance given to the Country greatly superior to what it has given at any former Period.

In Addition to these Statements, your Committee, when they were on the Point of concluding their Report, had the Opportunity of receiving further Information from Mr. Macdowall, a Member of this House, who stated, that he is Representative in Parliament, for the City of Glasgow, from whence he had, this Morning, returned, and that he had there found all the Commercial Houses and Manufacturers in the greatest Distress from the late Stagnation of Commercial Credit and total Want of private Confidence.

The present Distress does not appear to him to arise from a Want of Property or Funds, but from the Stop which has been lately put to discounting Bills at any of the Glasgow, Paisley, or Greenock Banks, who have not for some Time past discounted to any Extent, from their Notes being poured in upon them for Gold, and from the Alarm which the present Situation of Credit in London has occasioned.

The Manufacturers have plenty of Goods on Hand in London, and in Glasgow, which they cannot sell but at so reduced a Price as renders it perfectly absurd for them to think of disposing of their Goods, in order to obtain immediate Relief:

The Manufacturers, and those who have Cotton Mills, have begun to discharge the Workmen employed by them during the last Fortnight; and, by a Letter received from the Lord Provost of Glasgow, by him, this Morning, he learns that the Manufacturers have discharged a very great Number of Workmen.— There are employed in Glasgow, Paisley, and their Dependencies, in different Parts of Scotland, about One hundred and Sixty thousand Men, Women, and Children: Any Relief to be administered must be given immediately to render it effectual.

The Result of the Information thus obtained confirms your Committee in the general Impression which they have already stated, and seems to preclude the Necessity of requiring further Evidence as to the Extent of the Evil, and the Necessity of a Remedy; and the Urgency of the Occasion appears to render it highly desirable to avoid all unnecessary Delay.

Your Committee, therefore, think it proper to state what has occurred to them under the Second Head of Enquiry, without detaining the House by Observations of any considerable Length, on Circumstances which appear of themselves sufficiently clear and forcible. They think it however material to remark, that if the present Distress were confined in its Effects to Individuals, however they might regret the Extent of Private Calamity, they should not consider the Case as justifying an extraordinary Public Interposition, much less should they recommend such a Measure, if the Pressure had been felt only by Houses of doubtful Credit, or who had suffered from the Consequences of rash and unwarrantable Speculations:—But it appears to your Committee, that the Embarrassments arising from the Want of Credit, have already affected Houses of undoubted Solidity and sufficient ultimate Resources; and that there is too much Reason to apprehend that these Embarrassments may extend in a Degree which no Individual Exertions can counteract, with sufficient Expedition and Certainty, to prevent Consequences of the most serious National Importance.

In proceeding to examine the Second Head of Enquiry, it was on every Account a great Satisfaction to your Committee, to have the Advantage of the Suggestions contained in the Plan, which had been delivered to the Chancellor of the Exchequer, and which has been already referred to.

On the best Consideration which your Committee could give to the Subject, the principal Objects to be attended to in any Measure for affording Relief, appeared to be, to enable those who have Securities ultimately good, but which would not be available till too distant a Period, to receive such Advances as might enable them to support the Pressure to which they might be exposed in the Interval—To furnish some Medium of Circulation which might, either directly or indirectly, replace the Quantity of Currency suddenly withdrawn—and, by the Effect of these Measures, to afford such Assistance to Individuals, as might revive Confidence and Credit.

Such a Measure, under proper Regulations, appears to be capable of producing very rapidly an Effect far beyond the Amount of the Sum directly advanced, by setting at Liberty and restoring to Circulation Sums to a much larger Amount, which are rendered in a Manner useless by the present Stagnation.

It appeared to your Committee, That this Object could not be effectually attained, but by Advances issued under the Authority, and resting upon the Security, of the Public.

In adopting such a Measure, it is obviously necessary to keep in View, that the Assistance to be given must be considered as merely temporary, and arising out of the very peculiar Circumstances of the Case; and also to establish such Regulations as may prevent, as far as possible, the Accommodation intended to be afforded from being applied to any Persons but those who, on the one Hand, stand in Need of it from a real Pressure arising out of the present Circumstances, and, on the other, can give sufficient Security for the Repayment of it. The latter Circumstance is entitled to peculiar Attention, for the Purpose of confining this Accommodation to the Description of Persons, to whom alone it can be permanently useful, or can be afforded with Safety to the Public.

Another Consideration of equal Importance is, that it should be so regulated to furnish the Opportunity to Individuals to render their own Exertions ultimately effectual, without, at the same Time, giving such a Degree of Facility to their Transactions as might lead to a Relaxation or Suspension of those Exertions.

The next material Object which suggests itself, is to provide, as far as the Nature of the Case will permit, that the Distribution of this Assistance should be conducted in such a Manner as may best secure the safe and impartial Application of it.

On a Consideration of the Plan above referred to, it appears to your Committee, that it contains the Outline of Provisions adapted to all these Objects; they have therefore made it the Basis of the Proposal which they think it their Duty to suggest to the House, and have added such Observations as appear to them to be necessary, upon any of the particular Points, in the Order in which they occur in the Plan.

With respect to the Amount of the Sum to be issued, the Committee are of Opinion, that it will be adviseable to extend it to £5,000,000 instead of £3,000,000 as originally suggested. They are induced to do so, not only from wishing to leave a considerable Latitude, in order the better to insure that the Relief proposed shall be effectual, but also from having thought it right that the Advances should be made on the Deposit of Goods in certain principal Out Ports as well as in London, and from having had under their Consideration the Information received with respect to Scotland.

The Interest to be allowed on the Exchequer Bills proposed to be issued, ought, in the Opnion of the Committee, to be fixed at Two Pence Half-penny per Cent per Day (being at the Rate of about £3.16s. per Cent per Annum) instead of Two Pence per Cent per Day, which would be only about Three per Cent per Annum; and they have been informed, that the Gentlemen who originally suggested the Plan, concur in the Propriety of this Alteration. The Committee approve of the Principle on which a Difference has been proposed to be made between the

Rate of Interest to be allowed on the Exchequer Bills, and that of Five per Cent which, according to a subsequent Part of the Plan, is proposed to be paid to the Public by the Parties to whom the Advances shall be made: They conceive this to be expedient, not so much because the Difference will furnish a Fund for defraying the Expence of the Commission, as because it has a Tendency to prevent any Persons from taking Advantage of this Accommodation, who are not of the Description intended to be assisted. The Difference, however, between £3.16s. and £5 per Cent together with the Chance of some Discount on these Exchequer Bills, even at the increased Rate of Interest, seems sufficiently to secure the Object last stated, without rendering the Terms of the proposed Assistance more dis-advantageous than is desirable.

The Committee are of Opinion, that the Exchequer Bills should be made out in Sums of £100, and of £50; and, possibly, some Proportion of them in Sums of £20.

The Periods fixed for the Discharge of the Exchequer Bills in equal Proportions, appear to be highly expedient, with a View to the Object before described, of affording Means 'to Individ-uals to render their own Exertions ultimately effectual, without, at the same Time, giving such A degree of Facility to their Transactions as might lead to a Relaxation or Suspension of those Exertions.'

It may deserve Consideration, whether some Provision should not be made to enable Persons to repay the Sums advanced to them at an earlier Period than they originally stipulated.

With respect to the Appointment of Commissioners, the Manner of selecting proper Persons for that purpose, must remain for the Consideration of Parliament, if the Measure in Contemplation should be adopted; but the Committee are inclined to think, that the Number to be appointed should not exceed Twenty; and they have Reason to believe, that respect-able Persons will be found, who will give the Public the Benefit of their Services, without receiving any Emolument.

An Augmentation has been already suggested of the Total

Amount of Exchequer Bills to be issued; but an Issue of One Fourth Part of this augmented Sum, in the first Instance, instead of One Half of the Sum originally proposed, may, it is conceived, be sufficient, as there will be the Means of making further Issues in Case of Necessity.

The Security on the Deposit of Goods, which in the Plan is confined to Goods actually in London, may, in the opinion of Committee, be safely and properly extended to a few other principal Ports—Bristol, Hull, and Liverpool, may be sufficient in England; and Leith and Glasgow in Scotland. Subject to this Alteration, the Committee agree in the Propriety of confining the Advances to the Species of Security, and in the Proportion stated in the Plan, for the Purpose already mentioned, of confining the Aid to those Instances where it may be safely and usefully given.

With respect to the Apportionment of the Sums to be advanced, it would have been very satisfactory to the Committee, if it had appeared possible to subject it beforehand to fixed Rules; but, upon the fullest Consideration, they are decidedly of Opinion, that, from the Nature of the Subject, it is impossible to frame any Rules which will be found applicable to the various Cases which must occur, without such a Knowledge of those Cases, and of the Nature, Circumstances, and Amount of the different Demands, as can only be obtained from the Applications to be brought under the Consideration of the Commissioners.

The Nature of the Securities being already fixed, and the Proportion of the Advances limited, the Regulation of further Details must, it is conceived, be left to the Judgment of the Commissioners; but it appears at the same Time highly expedient that they should be required, as proposed, to take the earliest Opportunity of laying down general Rules for their own Guidance, which should never be deviated from in particular Cases, but be subject to Revision on general Grounds, as Occasion may require . . . *Report of the Select Committee on the*

State of Commercial Credit, House of Commons Journal, XLVIII,
702–7

20 Henry Thornton   The Money Supply – Its Definition and Increase

Henry Thornton (1760–1815) was a member of the London
bank of Downe & Co from 1748, and MP for Southwark
from 1782. He became the foremost monetary authority in
Parliament and was, with Horner and Huskisson, one of the
most influential members of the Bullion Committee. A great
philanthropist, he supported many overseas missionary
activities and was, with Wilberforce, a leader of the Clapham
Sect.

Have you Reason to think there has been a great Increase
in the whole Scale of Publick Income and Expenditure?

Undoubtedly.

Has not a similar Increase taken Place in the Scale of Private
Expenditure?

If you include several Years past, it certainly has.

Has there not been of late Years a Rise in the Price of Provisions and of Labour?

Certainly.

Has there not been a great Extension in the Manufactures
and Commerce of the Kingdom?

Undoubtedly.

Have not the Circumstances, stated in the preceding Questions and Answers, occasioned a Demand for additional Means
of Circulation?

Before I reply to that Question, it may be proper to express
distinctly what I shall understand by Means of Circulation. I
conceive it to mean, First, Coin of every Sort; Secondly, Notes
to Bearer payable on Demand, whether issued by the Bank of
England or by Country Bankers, which I consider as exchange-
able at all Times for Cash; and Thirdly, Bills of Exchange. In
calling Bills of Exchange a Means of Circulation, I do not

consider them equally so with the other Two Articles I have mentioned, since they ostensibly serve the Purpose of ascertaining Debts between Buyer and Seller, and of pledging the Acceptor to a punctual Payment, and are often created chiefly with that View, and are used but sparingly and occasionally as a Means of Circulation. I conceive that the Number of Bills of Exchange which may happen at any time to exist, bears no necessary Proportion to the Magnitude of the existing Trade, although, I conceive, that the Use of them in Payment does bear a pretty regular Proportion to the Quantity of Commerce. For instance, at Liverpool and Manchester all Payments are made either in Coin or in Bills of Exchange. The Holders of these Bills (since they themselves profit by the Detention of them, the Bills growing more valuable in Proportion as they become nearer due) keep them in their Possession in larger Quantities than they would Notes to Bearer on Demand, the Profit of the Detention of which last goes to the Bank which issues them, and not to the Person who has them in his Possession.

I would now reply to the Question put to me, by answering, that I conceive the increased Trade of the Country has undoubtedly caused a Necessity for an increased Use, either of Bills or Notes to Bearer in Payment; and also that the increased Scale of Expenditure of the Country must have caused, as I conceive, an increased Use chiefly of Notes to Bearer upon Demand, though partly also of Bills of Exchange, and likewise, in some Degree, perhaps of Cash, especially in those Times when Notes to Bearer on Demand come into Discredit. In general, I consider Guineas as furnishing the Means of paying small or broken Sums; and as bearing much the same Relation to Notes which Shillings do to Guineas, and that the Occasion for the Increase of their Quantity does not necessarily keep Pace with the other increased Means of Circulation.

How far have the additional Means of Circulation, stated in the last Answer to have become necessary, been furnished in the Metropolis, either by an increased Proportion of Bank Notes in Circulation, or by any other Means, so as to keep pace with the enlarged Scale of Expenditure, and with the increased Employment of acting Capital?

No Notes pass currently in Payment in the Metropolis except those of the Bank of England; nor is it usual there to make use of Bills of Exchange in Payment, as is done often in the Country. Of the Quantity of Bank of England Notes which may have been issued now and at former Periods, I can have no authentic Information; it is commonly understood, however, to have lately decreased; and I should conceive that the high Rate of Interest for Money amounting from Eight to Ten, and even Eighteen per Cent which has been evident in the Price of Exchequer Bills, India Bonds, and other such Securities, soon convertible into Bank Notes, has arisen in a great Measure from the Scarcity of Bank Notes, the Price paid (if I may so express it) for the Purchase of Bank Notes naturally increasing in Proportion as those Notes are few in Number and in great Demand. In consequence of the assumed Scarcity of Bank Notes, it has been in the Contemplation of several Persons, and particularly of Bankers, to endeavour to provide some additional Means of Circulation for the Metropolis; which it has been thought, that if the Bankers would agree to take, they might become generally current in the Metropolis; but some Doubts have been entertained whether a Project of this Sort would answer, unless the Bankers should guarantee the Notes of each other; in which Case it is a Question, whether it might not be an Infraction or Evasion of the Bank Charter, I consider these Circumstances as Proofs that the Bank Notes in Circulation have not borne a due Proportion to the Wants of the Public.

If, instead of a Decrease of Bank Notes in Circulation, assumed by the last Answer to have taken Place, the Quantity of those Notes had remained as they were, without material Increase or Decrease, would not the Inconveniences resulting from the forced Sale, and consequent Depreciation of other Securities, have then also prevailed, though in a less Degree?

I conceive they would; and that the increased Transactions of Commerce in the Metropolis must have required an Increase

of the Bank Notes issued. These being the only Means of
Circulation in the Metropolis; excepting Guineas which cannot
be used in any considerable Dealings.

What Effect would any considerable Augmentation in the
Quantity of circulating Bank Notes in the Metropolis have
produced?

I conceive that the Increase of their Quantity ought to
depend not only on the increased Quantity of Trade in the
Metropolis, but also on the Occasion for them which might arise
from other Causes.

If, for Instance, general Credit should be impaired while
Bank Notes sustain their Credit, it follows that there would be
a Disposition in many People to hold Possession of Bank Notes,
although at some Loss to themselves, who at other Times
might be satisfied with the Possession only of Bills of Exchange;
for, the Convertibility of Bills of Exchange into Bank Notes
being more doubtful, prudent Persons would provide themselves
if possible with Bank Notes for their expected Payments, at a
Time perhaps much antecedent to the Time of Payment. I
conceive, therefore, the Quantity of Notes which it may be
proper at any time to issue, to depend much on the State of the
Public Mind, that is, on the Dispositions of Persons to detain
them. If indeed, a much larger Quantity were issued than
would remain in Circulation, I should imagine that the Effect
of such excessive Emissions might be to draw Guineas out of
the Bank of England.

How far are you of Opinion, that an Increase in the Quantity
of circulating Bank Notes, adequately proportioned to the
increased Wants and Demands above described would, or would
not, have tended to an increased and inconvenient Call upon
the Bank for the Issue of Cash?

I think that an increased Quantity of Notes, proportioned
to the increased Occasion for them, must tend to prevent a
Demand for Guineas rather than to promote it; and if the
Quantity of Notes issued should be very considerably less than
the Occasion of the Mercantile World requires, I should think

a Run upon the Bank for Guineas would be the Consequence; for when Trade is much distressed and Failures are expected, a general Distrust is apt to be excited; and as the Cause of such expected Failures is not distinctly known to be the Diminution of the Bank of England's circulating Notes, there are likely to be at least some Persons in the Country who may wish not only to be possessed of Bank Notes for their Security, but even of Guineas. I further think, that a Scarcity of the circulating Medium of the Metropolis tends to induce some of the Country Bankers, who are the most opulent and respectable, to forbear from issuing their Bank Notes, through the Apprehension of Mercantile Distress: And their Forbearance to issue Country Bank Notes is naturally followed by a considerable Increase in the Use of Guineas, all which are drawn out of the Bank of England.

Is it not for the Interest of the Bank of England, as well as of every private Banker, to issue as many Notes as they possibly can, consistently with due Attention to their Credit and Stability?

I conceive that to be self-evident.

Will you proceed to state how far any additional Means of Circulation have been furnished by the Country Banks to keep Pace with the increased Demand described in the preceding Questions and Answers?

I have no distinct Information as to the Quantity of Bills of Exchange used in the Country, and which, as I have before stated, in many Cases, answer the Purpose of Notes to Bearer on Demand, and in some Degree also may spare the Use of Guineas. I conceive, however, that the Use of Notes and Bills of Exchange depending in a great Measure on the Custom of each particular Place, which does not often vary, the Circulation of Notes and Guineas when combined must, generally speaking, supply the Means of Circulation in those Parts where Notes and not Bills of Exchange have been ordinarily current, as a Means of Circulation. I am well assured, that in many Parts the Notes of Country Bankers have, since the Year 1793, diminished rather than increased, and that they are in particular much decreased at this Time. I infer, therefore, that the Means of Circulation have been supplied, to a considerable Extent, by Guineas . . .

You have stated, that in Time of general Mercantile Difficulty and Apprehension of Failures, it is the Custom of the respectable and prudent Country Bankers to lessen or suppress the Quantity of their Notes payable on Demand, what is the Reason that, on the same Principle, the Bank of England ought not to lessen their circulating Notes at the same Time?

I take the Case of a Country Banker and of the Bank of England to be in several Respects extremely different, and that the Explanation of the Differences I allude to in their Circumstances, will best furnish an Answer to that Question.

First, I would observe, That a Country Banker who issues Notes to Bearer on Demand has, in many Cases, also several other Branches of Business which he follows, and which are very important to him. He has perhaps large Deposits in his Hands from his own immediate Customers, amounting in some Cases possibly to many Times the Sum in Notes which he has in Circulation; and he is liable to be called upon at any Time for immediate Payment of the whole Amount of these Deposits. His Customers, however, having Confidence in him, and being personally known to him, are not very likely to take Alarm, unless some special Cause of Alarm should be given them; his Notes on the contrary circulate through the Hands of Strangers, and, consisting in small Sums, they are often in the Hands of the lowest Class of People. These Notes, moreover, are often confounded in the Minds of the Holders of them, with the Notes of other Bankers of less Credit; insomuch, that in the Event of the Failure of any neighbouring Bank, it is probable that the most respectable Banker in the Country would suffer some Run upon him from the Holders of his Notes. In order, therefore, to prevent his Credit from being wounded in that Part where it is most vulnerable, a prudent Country Banker, in Times of apprehended Danger, is apt to lessen or suppress his Notes to

Bearer on Demand, for the Sake of better securing his Credit in other Respects. This is one Circumstance in which a Country Banker differs from the Bank of England. The Bank of England Notes possess undoubted Credit in the Metropolis and its Neighbourhood, where alone they chiefly circulate, and are not confounded with the Paper of other Banks. It is obviously not through any Distrust of the Bank of England Notes that any considerable Quantity of Guineas has been demanded for them, and that there is no Occasion, therefore, in Times of Danger to suppress them, for the Reason operating in the Minds of the Country Bankers which I have just stated. I would remark that, in the next Place, the Country Banker withdraws his Notes in a Time of Danger, partly because they expose him to a sudden Demand for Guineas in the following Manner: Rival Banks, when in want of Guineas, have only to possess themselves of his Notes, in order to obtain a Supply of Cash for themselves, which, when his Notes are every where in Circulation, are easy to be obtained, and he is thus exposed both to the Expence and the Risk of supplying Guineas to other Banks who have not sufficiently supplied themselves. If he withdraws his Notes, the rival Banks cannot so easily obtain Guineas from him by the Means of Guineas paid for the Deposits of his Customers; for his Customers will not assist them in any such Attempt. In this respect, the Case of the Bank of England is widely different. I here assume indeed, that the Bank of England will in no Case totally suppress their Paper Circulation; and, if they do not, it is obvious that any one who has Property which he can sell for what is called ready Money, (that is Bank of England Notes,) may possess himself of Guineas; and thus the Bank of England, as long as they issue Notes at all, are liable to be drained of their Cash just as much as any Country Bank that is the most exposed by his Paper Circulation. Moreover, the Bank of England are liable to have Cash demanded of them for the Amount of whatever may be their Deposits, and for all the Sums which they discount also, assuming that they continue to discount at the Rate, for Instance, of £100,000 a Day, they are liable to a daily Demand for Guineas to that Amount; and this Demand may be made upon them by Persons immediately connected with Country Banks who want those Guineas, without the Bank being able to prevent it; for, from the Extent of their Transactions, and from the Effect of the general Rules which they lay down, from the little private Attachment which can be supposed to be between them and their Customers, and, above all, from their being considered as the chief Repository of Cash on which every Individual in the Country supposes himself to have a Right to draw, they are, through the Necessity of their Situation, obliged to furnish Guineas to all the Persons who may be in Want of them. As no Reduction of their Notes can remove from them his Hardship, they have in this Particular no such Inducement to lessen their Paper Circulation, as the Country Banker has.

In the next and last Place I would remark, that when a Country Banker lessens or suppresses his Notes payable to Bearer on Demand, either some other Kinds of Paper or Guineas naturally supply their Place, and no general Distress results from such Conduct of one individual Banker: He may contribute possibly, by too great a Reduction of his Business, to produce general Commercial Difficulty, but the Advantage in the Way of Ease and Security, and, perhaps, of Profit also, which he individually derives from the Suppression of his own particular Notes, may be greater than his Share of the Disadvantage which results from his own particular Conduct. In this respect, the Case of the Bank of England is totally different. When the Bank of England materially lessens or suppresses its Notes, there are no other Notes, as I said before, which can supply their Place. Their Place, indeed, may be supplied partly by Guineas; but these Guineas must be furnished by the Bank of England itself; the Distress which the Suppression of Bank of England Notes, to any considerable Degree, causes in the Metropolis, produces Distress through the whole Kingdom: It is the Means, as I before explained, of producing the Suppression of much of the Paper of the Country, and a consequent

Demand for Guineas from the Bank; in short, the Suppression of the Bank of England's Paper, to any considerable Extent, must, unless some other Paper is substituted, in my Opinion, pull down the Price of Exchequer Bills, of India Bonds, and other Government Securities, which will be sold by those who possess them, in order to secure a sufficient Quantity of Bank Notes to carry on their Payments, and which a Variety of Bankers will be selling at the same Time, each endeavouring, though in vain, to possess himself of the notes held by the others. It must produce, therefore, Discredit to the Government, a consequent Distrust in the Minds of the Public, who will not understand the Cause of this Depreciation of the Stocks; it must produce, at the same Time, Commercial Failures, and an Appearance of Bankruptcy, even in Times when the Individuals in the Nation, and the Nation itself, might be rich and prosperous; and in the general Alarm and Difficulty which must ensue, the Demand for Guineas must of course rise, and perhaps to a considerable Height: in this Manner I think that the Bank of England, by its powerful influence on the Affairs of the Country, must, by the Suppression of its Notes, both prejudice the Country, and materially involve itself.

I conceive that the Principle of lessening the Paper Circulation of the Bank, in Proportion as Difficulties threatened it, and as Guineas were drawn out, may possibly at its first Origin have been a prudent Principle, for the same Reason that it is now a prudent Principle in the Country Bankers; but that since the Bank of England have obtained the Monopoly of supplying the Metropolis with its whole Means of Circulation, and have, by their superior Credit, excluded entirely all other Paper, and have also bound themselves, as far as long Custom can bind them, to a Number of General Rules, such as that of discounting daily for the Public; and since they have also become so considerable, that their individual Conduct operates upon the Credit of the whole Nation; it is no longer prudent in them to attempt to pursue their own individual interest, by any Means which are contrary to the general interests.

N

Do Country Bankers, notwithstanding the peculiar Difficulties which you have stated they are exposed to, usually proportion the Number of their Notes to the Demand which they know is likely to be made for them in Payment of Rent and other large Remittances?

In ordinary Times, I conceive they do.

Evidence of Henry Thornton. *House of Lords Committee of Secrecy on the Bank of England* Journal, 186–262

_____

21 Sir Francis Baring   The Bank of England in Crisis
Baring (1740–1810) was the founder of the famous merchant banking house of London which earned for him the title of 'the first merchant in Europe'. He was also chairman of the East India Company 1792–3. In the 'Observations' of 1797 his explicit recognition of the role of the Bank of England as lender of last resort was coupled with criticism of country bankers for issuing notes payable on demand.

_____

As the circulation of the Bank of England, although the most important, doth not form the largest part of that of the country in general, it becomes necessary to take a more comprehensive view of the subject, in order to entertain a correct opinion of the whole. The establishment of Country Banks is of modern date and within my recollection; but I believe there was no material convulsion, with regard to circulation, from the Rebellion, until that which happened by the failure of the Air Bank in the year 1772. This failure was accompanied with others of great extent at the same time in Holland;—but as it was evidently a partial and not a general convulsion, the Bank of England acted very wisely, by affording even a liberal support to those houses whose solidity was unquestionable, leaving others which were rotten, to fall; and as they were swept away, confidence was gradually restored. The next check to commercial credit arose from the failure of a circulation established between Lancashire and London, well known in the courts of law by the case of Gibson v. Johnson, which has been so often tried; but, although the amount was large, it moved in so narrow a line, that it produced no general effect on the country. What happened in the beginning of 1793 was, however, very different; far beyond any thing which preceded, or has followed it, in magnitude, it pervaded, more or less, every part or place in both islands and affected very description of property. The last and most important event in one respect, is that which compelled the Bank of England to suspend their payments.

During the interval between the failure of the Air Bank and the distress of 1793, a very material change had taken place in regard to the general circulation; Banks had been established in almost every town, and even in villages, throughout the country; and in the larger towns rival establishments were formed. These produced a most important, and whilst it was secure, a beneficial change to the country, by increasing its circulation; but unfortunately the principles on which those Banks were usually established, were insecure, in their being compelled at all times to invest or employ the deposit left in their hands, and thereby rendering themselves incapable of facing a sudden storm, or, as it is called, answering a run upon them, which, from natural events, must, in a course of time, arise. A Banker in London never allows interest to his customers, and can afford to reserve a proportion of his deposits, to enable him to answer sudden demands, or a run on his house; as he thereby sustains no real loss, but only diminishes the amount of his profit. The country Banker is in a very different situation, for he allows interest on deposits, and therefore he cannot afford to suffer even a small sum to remain dormant and unproductive; for every £100 which he suffers to remain in that predicament, is a loss of the interest which he pays to his customer and which interest he must get reimbursed (by investing the money) before he can realise any profit for himself. Thus it will appear, that whilst the circulation was greatly increased, and its beneficial effects enjoyed, by the commerce, manufactures, agriculture &c. of the country, it was founded

on the most insecure principle, and liable to almost instantane-
ous convulsion, by unforeseen, and even trifling circumstances.
This might be promoted, more or less, by the practice of
particular establishments; for if Country Banks, whose principals
are men of large unquestionable property, should fail, the
contagion will immediately spread, and the consequences are
incalculable. Thus, for instance, in the beginning of the year
1793, and of the present year, the Banks of Newcastle stopt
payment, whilst those of Exeter and the West of England
stood their ground. The partners in the Banks of Newcastle
were far more opulent, but their private fortunes being invested,
could not be realised in time to answer a run on their Banks.
Their Notes allowed interest to commence some months after
date, and were then payable on demand; by which means
they had not an hour to prepare for their discharge. The Banks
at Exeter issued Notes payable twenty days after sight with
interest to commence from the date of the Note, and to cease
on the day of acceptance. There can be no doubt but the
practice of the Banks at Newcastle is more lucrative, whilst it
must for ever be liable to a return of what has happened. The
twenty days received at Exeter furnishes ample time to communicate with London and receive every degree of assistance
which may be required. It is therefore most earnestly to be
wished, that a law should pass to prevent Country Banks from
issuing Notes payable on demand, as they never can be in a
situation to pay without some notice; and the country ought
to be protected against those convulsions which have arisen
and will continue to arise from such a practice.

Another circumstance contributed very materially to produce
the distress of 1793, which was the sudden, unexpected declaration of war. That dreadful calamity is usually preceded by some
indication which enables the commercial and monied men to
make preparation. On this occasion, the short notice rendered
the least degree of general preparation impossible, and which
may be ascertained by the prices of stocks in the preceding
month of October, and various collateral circumstances. The

foreign market was either shut or rendered more difficult of access to the merchant; of course he could not purchase from the manufacturer; and an important variation in the rate of exchange on the Continent, furnished a pretence to foreigners to withhold their remittances from both. The manufacturers in their distress applied to the Bankers in the country for relief; but as the want of money became general, and that want increased gradually by a general alarm, the country Banks required the repayment of old debts, being utterly incapable of increasing them, and which of course brought their own situation to the test.

In this predicament the country at large could have no other resource but London; and after having exhausted the Bankers, that resource finally terminated in the Bank of England. In the mean while, the alarm in the country continued to increase; confidence in their Banks vanished; every creditor was clamorous for payment, which he insisted should be made in gold and which was complied with, until the Bankers in London were exhausted. At first the Bank accommodated themselves to the circumstances, and furnished large supplies; but unfortunately the Directors caught the panic; their nerves could not support the daily and constant demand for guineas; and for the purpose of checking that demand, they curtailed their discounts to a point never before experienced, and which placed every part of the commerce of the country in a considerable degree of danger. This dreadful convulsion (for it really was so at the time) was occasioned by the erroneous principle upon which country Banks are established, and that principle operated upon in the manner I have described. I can readily believe, that under all circumstances it might then have been right for the Bank to lessen the amount of their discounts, or to lessen the amount of the accommodation which individuals had been accustomed to receive, but then it ought to have been gradual; their determination, and the extent to which it was carried, came like an electrical shock.

In such cases the Bank are not an intermediate body, or

power; there is no resource on their refusal, for they are the 'dernier resort'. The laws against usury effectually destroy every other means of relief in this country, whilst experience has proved, at Hamburgh, at Amsterdam and other places, that the most effectual mode of keeping the rate of interest low, is to leave it free from every restriction. But this point has been very fully discussed by Mr. Bentham, in a small tract entitled 'A Defence of Usury' which has never been answered, because in truth it is unanswerable. As the determination of the Bank was founded upon the demand which came from every quarter of the country for guineas, I must beg leave to add some remarks on that subject. I do not mean to offer those remarks for the information of the Directors, as they are no doubt well informed on the subject; nor do I pretend to arraign their conduct, as circumstances may have existed to justify their proceedings, although it may be improper to disclose them publicly. I can only reason upon what is generally known, and upon those principles in which I am persuaded the Directors will agree.

For the present purpose, it may be sufficient to confine the considerations, as to the cause of the demand for guineas, to three heads:

First, as a Medium of Remittance to foreign parts, to supply the want of Bills of Exchange

Second, For the purpose of Hoarding in the country, from want of confidence in the Government, and in the circulating paper.

Thirdly, To enable Country Banks to discharge their demands, whilst confidence in the Government, and in the Bank of England remained entire and perfect.

The first is the most dangerous, as being the most injurious to the country; every measure ought to be taken to palliate or prevent it, prohibitions or bankruptcy excepted; but it is inevitable, if we shall continue for a long time to have more to pay to foreigners than we receive from them; or, in other words, if the Balance of Trade is against us.

The second is the only circumstance which can in any

measure justify the late bankruptcy; but I wish to reserve this point for future consideration.

The third ought to be viewed, not with perfect indifference but with a disposition on the part of the Bank to supply almost their last guinea; as they cannot be sent abroad, but must return again to their own coffers, as proved to be the case in the year 1793.

It was notorious, at the time, that large quantities of gold and silver were received from France; of course none could be sent thither. Sir Francis Baring. *Observations on the Establishment of the Bank of England and on The Paper Circulation of the Country* (1797), 13–25

_____

22 M. Dorrien Magens   Attack on Country Note Issues
M. Dorrien Magens was a banker and sometime MP for Carmarthen and Ludgershall. He contributed to the debate on legal tender during the Suspension period and published 'Thoughts upon a new coinage of Silver . . .' (1797). He is sometimes confused with Nicholas Magens, author of 'The Universal Merchant' (1753).

_____

Currency then, consisting of the coin itself, by which every commodity is valued, or a circulating note, purporting to command at pleasure, the quantity of this coin, as expressed on the face of it; the inquiry of course will be made, how these notes, or piece of paper, become so valuable, and who are the persons to coin and issue them? They cannot be issued by every body thinking it a convenient way to raise money. Such notes, if taken at all, would only pass through one or two hands, and be returned again: the credit, or, perhaps, even the name of the issuer, would be known to so few persons, that any one into whose hands they might accidentally fall, would forthwith realize them in money, for fear the party might become unable to pay them. The sphere in which similar notes to the above can circulate, even if attempted to be issued, must be so con-fined, as to defeat the intention. We next find a partnership of

4, 5 or 6 persons, exerting their influence and credit to coin notes to pass as currency, and, in proportion to their influence, connections, and credit, do these notes circulate in the district where they are in repute, and form, jointly with every note issued by other persons in different parts of the kingdom, a currency, performing all the operations attainable by actual gold and silver. Paper of this description being peculiarly in use in great Britain and Ireland, the present observations are meant to apply principally to these united Kingdoms; leaving the currency among other nations to consist, as it always has done, for the most part, of actual money.

The notes above-mentioned affording local convenience, are yet very much limited, as few of them will pass beyond the district where they are issued, and none of them in London, the Bank of England nearly engrossing all circulating notes there: and though it contains numerous banking-houses of the utmost respectability, the circulation of a note in the Metropolis, any other than of the Bank of England, does not take place; so that while the country banker is circulating his paper for several thousand pounds, as coined money, the full supply of notes by the Bank of England renders the practice to the London banker, as currency there unknown. Opulence and credit, therefore, are not along sufficient for this purpose; there must be local circumstances, and tacit acquiescence also, to enable the issue; for if, as in London, persons were disposed to call nothing money, but coin, or Bank of England notes, none could be circulated; or, if the nation were inclined to agree that nothing but coin should circulate, no note whatever would pass. Mr. Thornton (page 54) observes, 'There is a further objection to the same remark of Dr. Smith, (as mentioned in page 53.) It would lead an uninformed person to conceive, that the trade of the country, and of this country in particular, circumstanced as it now is, might be carried on altogether by guineas, if bank notes of all kinds were by any means annihilated.' To form some opinion upon such a material point, let us ask how it is in other countries? Are there any bank notes there? is there any circulating medium there? Do not Holland and Hamburgh, in proportion to their population and extent, carry on as much trade as Great Britain; and have they any substitute for money? If it should prove that they have not, and that other countries, with few exceptions, have not, may we not pause, before we maintain the *necessity* of circulating paper; though we may approve it in many cases, for various reasons, and find great advantage from its convenience. In Holland, or Hamburgh, if you take your bill of exchange for payment, should you not keep an account at the Bank, the coin is always ready for you; no note, no bill, but actual specie. What, if you have an account at the bank? The amount is transferred from the account of the person paying the bill to your's; and the actual money lies there at your disposal, as compleatly as if under your own lock and key. No notes circulate there; a receipt along is given, acknowledging the deposit, to be re-delivered at your option; which will not pay for commodities from hand to hand, but can only accomplish a payment being made over in the bank books to another person; by which alone, the transport of the money is saved. It will be remarked, How can such arguments be used? Was it not notorious that there was not a ducat in the bank when the French entered Holland? Perfectly true; but what was the consequence? Is it not equally notorious, that bank money was at a discount, and continued so until every guilder was replaced by the city of Amsterdam in actual specie? The Bank of Amsterdam (and Hamburgh is upon the same plan) furnishes no additional circulating medium; it is only a warehouse; and the commission paid for every transfer, &c. may be considered as warehouse-rent; so that no receipt or paper is issued of any kind, but has its corresponding value actually lying in the vaults of the Stadt House at Amsterdam, unless, as it has been seen, can be done in times of distress, which acting paramount to all other objects, induced the directors to dispose of it in such a manner, as might save it from the enemy, they conceived ready to wrest it from them; exactly as an individual, whose house is threatened with an attack from banditti, would hastily remove the whole of his valuables: all which must be admitted to be rational policy: but the burgher of Amsterdam, knowing this in common with others, calculates the risk of the money not returning, and occasions of course, as it lately did, the bank money to be at a discount. An effect, however, universally allowed to be so detrimental to their commerce, was not permitted to exist a moment longer than the necessity required; and the actual specie was replaced the moment sufficient light dawned upon them to prevent the alarm of seizure from unbounded power; with this measure confidence in the bank money returned as before. It may be fair, however, to doubt if the credit of the Bank of Amsterdam rests upon the same solid foundation in the public mind as before, or if it ever will.*

Having stated who the persons are that issue notes, it now becomes a consideration for what they issue them, what value they receive in return, and what benefit attaches to the circula-

---

* In February, 1795, there was a publication from authority, of the state of the Bank of Amsterdam, by which it appeared, that the bank held securities in bonds upon the East India Company, and the different states of the Republic, for money advanced; and it said further, that the city of Amsterdam was responsible for the whole, not only as guarantee, but as an actual debtor to the bank. It is very well known that, until the peace of Amiens, the foreign exchanges with Holland were all calculated in currency, and bank money was at a discount; but, at the beginning of 1802, about the time of the ratification of the treaty of peace, the sound sense, and mercantile knowledge of the Dutch, induced them to make every effort to re-establish the credit of their bank; and the city of Amsterdam as guarantee, decreed a tax upon the property and income of the citizens, for the sole purpose of supplying the bank with bullion, and restoring it to the credit which it formerly maintained in foreign countries; and, in effect, from the time appointed, which was in the following summer, all foreign bills of exchange were paid in bank money, which bore an agio of four and five per cent as before the shutting. The remark which arises upon this is, that the Dutch, knowing the necessity of supporting their credit as a commercial people, lost no time, and spared no expence, to put their national bank upon its former footing; and in their decree, they declare that no circumstance whatever, can excuse the removal of the bullion so paid in.

tion. The object of every one engaging in a circulation of this kind, is to get as many of them to pass current as possible; but will he, in consequence, give every body who asks him a note for that purpose? It would be absurd to suppose it; he must then have something given to him to induce him to make out the note. We will suppose a gentleman receives 500l. from his tenant in the country, which he considers as a larger sum than he wishes to keep in his house; he therefore takes the whole, or a part of it, to this person, or to a bank, and says, being friendly to the parties, and inclined to encourage the institution, 'I do not like to keep so much money at home; let me have your notes for it from time to time, as I may require it, and I will lodge it with you.' The notes are given, the money remains. Another person, a manufacturer, comes to this same establishment, and says, 'I have large out-goings in my business, which require a great deal of ready money to buy the raw materials, and to pay the workmen; while at the same time, I have a great many persons dealing with me, who are in some degree dependent upon me; if you will accommodate me with a loan of one, two or three thousand pounds of your notes, I will take care to encourage and keep them in circulation among my connections as much as I can, and will give you my buildings as a security for the repayment of the money.' The notes are lent. A farmer comes, and makes a similar application, and upon the same grounds, his great daily expences, his extensive connections in helping to circulate the notes, and the badness of the present markets for realizing his stock; he therefore begs a loan, and gives in his produce, or other things, as security, and obtains an issue of the notes. A grazier also applies, and, by similar engage-ments, a large circulation of notes ensues. This coinage becomes currency, and commands the same powers as the same quan-tities of gold and silver would do. It is matter of great convenience to the district, the notes are regularly paid when brought back to the bank, every body is satisfied, and every body is pleased. A line of canal is projected to pass through this part of the country; it is considered advantageous, the subscription fills, the bank itself takes a few shares, their friends take many more; the stated periods for payment come round, the shares are pledged, the notes are received for it, and the business of the bankers increases rapidly.

In this state of prosperity let us review their situation; the firm consists of four persons; the acting partner honest and industrious, but with inconsiderable property; the tradesman with a fair capital, principally engaged in his particular business; the manufacturer, of extensive concerns, and with money, but very much employed in his works; and a neighbouring country gentleman of landed estate; or more frequently the attorney of the place: the firm so constituted, is undoubted in security, and of great respectability. This description of partnership, or others nearly similar, established in every large town, and many smaller ones, it is, that now supplies the currency in the country. In London, the whole is furnished by the Bank of England, which issues its notes in proportion to the quantity the circulation will bear. A subscription of proprietors originally gave rise to this institution, and a large sum has been subscribed at different times, till it has increased to its present magnitude. From its first establishment, it has always paid ample dividends; and upon the report of its condition in 1797, it was made evident, that it possessed immense property, in addition to the subscriptions received, which have been lent to Government. Its issue of notes being from sixteen to eighteen millions sterling, what securities does it obtain in exchange for them? It makes out notes for the individuals who lodge their money there, as they would do at a private banker's, it sends them into circulation for all the bullion it buys, for the purposes of coining, or otherwise; it gives notes to bankers and merchants who discount bills, with it; it pays with notes for the purchase of exchequer bills, and Government floating paper, as also for the advances made to the nation upon the land and malt taxes, and other loans furnished from time to time upon Parliamentary grants; and for renewals of its charter, &c. This is the paper which it is conceived, in conjunction with what gold and silver coin there is in the kingdom, forms the actual circulation of the country, passing from hand to hand, at a known and invariable value, never less, never more; but always the same, and without fluctuation . . . M. D. Magens. *An Inquiry into the Real Difference between actual money . . . and paper money* (1804), 30–9 and 57–61

23 Thomas Richardson   The Rise of the Bill Broker

Thomas Richardson (1771–1853), a Yorkshire Quaker whose establishment in London was financed by his cousin Edward Pease. Richardson became manager for Smith, Wright and Gray, the Quaker bankers of Lombard Street, and in 1806 started a bill-broking business with another Yorkshireman, John Overend. With the involvement of Samuel Gurney the firm rapidly became the largest bill-brokers in the City, and Richardson was able to lend financial support to the railway enterprises of George Stephenson and the Pease family. The concern later became Overend, Gurney & Co and was forced to stop payment in the crisis of 1866.

I believe you are a Bill Broker?
> Yes.

You are also an agent for country banks?
> Yes.

Have the country banks increased in number since the restriction on the Bank of England?
> Very considerably.

Can you tell in what proportion?
> No. I never made any calculation.

Do you know how many country banks there are?
> No. I do not; it might be easily ascertained from the printed Lists of Country Bankers.

Are you aware that the notes of the country bankers in circulation are much increased?
> I have no doubt of it; very considerably.

Are those Notes which are made payable in London increased?
> Yes, I should think very much.

Do you mean the notes of country banks generally are increased?

Yes, both descriptions; those made payable in London, and those which are not.

What means have you of knowing they are increased?

General observation.

What is the nature of the agency for country banks?

It is two-fold; in the first place to procure money for country bankers on Bills when they have occasion to borrow on discount, which is not often the case; and in the next place, to lend the money for the country bankers on Bills on discount. The sums of money which I lend for country bankers on discount are fifty times more than the sums borrowed for country bankers.

Do you send London Bills into the country for discount?

Yes.

Do you receive Bills from the country upon London in return, at a date to be discounted?

Yes, to a very considerable amount, for particular parts of the country.

Are not both sets of Bills by this means under discount?

No, the Bills received from one part of the country are sent down to another part for discount.

And they are not discounted in London?

No. In some parts of the country there is but little circulation of Bills drawn upon London, as in Norfolk, Suffolk, Essex, Sussex, etc. but there is there a considerable circulation of country bank notes, principally optional notes. In Lancashire there is little or no circulation of country bank notes; but there is a great circulation of Bills drawn upon London at two or three months date. I receive bills to a considerable amount from Lancashire in particular, and remit them to Norfolk, Suffolk, etc. where the Bankers have large lodgments, and much surplus money to advance on Bills for discount.

Do you not send bills drawn in London by one merchant upon another to be discounted in the country?

Yes, to a considerable amount.

Are not bills of that description called notes in London?

Generally so.

How do you get your remittances for those Bills that you so send to be discounted?

In bills that have three or four days to run, or by orders for cash on bankers in London.

What part of the country are they sent into?

Norfolk, Suffolk etc. and small sums into some parts of Yorkshire.

Are not the returns sometimes made in Bills at two months or other dates?

It is very seldom the cases, unless it be in exchange for a bill of a much longer date.

Do not transactions of this nature take place to the amount of several hundred thousand pounds a year?

I have never had any transaction of the sort last described. In modes of discounting previously mentioned, many millions go through my hands in a year.

How many millions pass through your hands in the course of the year?

I should certainly speak within bounds if I say seven or eight millions.

Do the country bankers in general keep agents in London exclusive of the bankers on whom they draw?

No, not of the description of which I am.

Are not the agents principally employed for the prupose of lending the money of the country bankers on discount on bills accepted in London?

We are employed both by those who have money to lend and those who want to borrow money.

You have stated that seven millions of money pass through your hands annually; what proportion of that may you have lent for country bankers on discount?

A million and a half. I speak of the sum outstanding upon discount at one time, on account of country bankers, which, multiplied about four or five times in the year, owing to the bills being from two to three months, will amount to the aggregate sum which I have mentioned.

Then it follows that the seven millions which have passed through your hands, have been lent for country bankers on discount?

Yes. I have no transactions whatever but which relate to discount.

Do you know in point of fact, whether such transactions as you have now described, were in practice previous to the suspension of the cash payments of the Bank?

Yes, they were.

Do you know whether they were practised to a similar extent?

No, they were not.

In what proportion, compared with the present time?

I cannot form any exact criterion.

Can you state to the Committee the cause of such difference?

I believe it to be on account of the increase of country paper.

Are the bills so discounted on behalf of the country banks, such as the Bank of England would refuse to discount?

At least two-thirds of them, on account of their having more than 65 days to run.

Are there any other reasons for which you think the Bank would refuse discounting such bills?

Yes.

State them.

Some houses have more occasion for discount than others; the Bank only take a limited amount. The business of some houses arises principally at one period of the year when they make their sales; they then want larger accommodations than the Bank would afford them, and many of the Bills being indirect, by which I mean not discountable at the Bank without two London endorsements.

Do you ever discount Bills for London bankers through the medium of your country correspondents?

I do not believe that it is a general practice for the London
bankers to apply for any such discounts.

Will you state what sum of money belonging to country bankers
has been employed by you in the last year in the purchase of
Exchequer bills, and other Government securities?

In Exchequer bills I do not think £1,000.

In what other securities?

Occasionally we buy stock for country bankers, but only
to a very limited amount.

Do you guarantee the bills you discount and what is your
charge per cent?

No, we do not guarantee them; our charge is one-eighth
per cent, brokerage upon the bill discounted—but we
make no charge to the lender of the money.

Do you consider that brokerage as a compensation for the skill
which you exercise in selecting the bills which you thus get
discounted?

Yes, for selecting of the bills, writing letters and other
trouble.

Does the party who furnishes the money give you any kind of
compensation?

None at all.

Does he not consider you as his agent, and in some degree
responsible for the safety of the bills which you give him?

Not at all.

Does he not prefer you on the score of his judging that you
will give him good intelligence upon that subject?

Yes, he relies upon us.

Do you then exercise a discretion as to the probable safety of
the bills?

Yes, if a bill comes to us which we conceive not to be safe,
we return it.

Do you not then conceive yourselves to depend in a great
measure for the quantity of business which you can perform on
the favour of the party lending the money?

o

Yes, very much so. If we manage our business well, we retain our friends; if we do not, we lose them.

Is not the quantity of business which you can do, limited in a great measure by the amount of ready money which you are enabled to supply?

Yes, no doubt of it.

Does not then the quantity of discountable bills transmitted to you, depend on the quantity of ready money which you are able to furnish?

Yes, but we find that the better our bills, the more readily we obtain money on discount, as more people are induced to take bills on discount instead of buying Exchequer bills, or vesting money in the funds.

Do you not then conceive that the quantity of discountable bills that is drawn depends on the extent of the supply of ready money which the country bankers issuing country bank notes are able to furnish?

No, I do not; for when the country bankers are poor, the London bankers are often full of money.

Do you not conceive, then, that it depends on the quantity of ready money which the country bankers and the London bankers together are able to furnish?

I have no doubt in many instances it does; but if a manufacturer has sold his goods at six months, and learns that money is plentiful in London and that he can have his bill discounted, he will send it to be discounted.

Does not that accommodation tend to increase the business of the country manufacturer?

Yes, no doubt of it; he goes to market again with his ready money.

Can you state what it may cost to raise money by discount in the manner you have described?

It will cost six and a half per cent per annum to the merchant, supposing the transaction to take place four times in the year, the banker five and a half per cent per annum.

Will you explain that difference?

> The merchant pays from one-eighth to one-fourth per cent for obtaining the bill on the banker in London; the country banker, unless he draws upon his London banker, pays no commission, as he pays away the bill he receives and endorses it.

Have there been many losses incurred upon bills thus discounted?

> No, there have not by us, except to a small amount indeed.

Were there any losses incurred upon such bills, before the restriction upon the cash payments in the bank?

> Yes, many more in the same proportion.

Were not many losses incurred in the year 1793?

> To a very large amount.

How do you account for the greater proportion of losses before than since the restriction of the Bank?

> I think that many of the country bankers have many losses by taking bills themselves; but those who do their business in London by means of a broker, who understands it, have but few losses.

Do you therefore assign the discretion of the agent in London to be the only cause why there have been fewer losses sustained since the restriction on the Bank than before it?

> Yes; I should think it much depends upon the discretion of the agent in London.

Is not the present system of discounting, as carried on by the Agents in London for the country banks, a great and mutual accommodation to the country and London bankers?

> I think it may to the country bankers, but not to the London bankers.

Is it not a great convenience to the London bankers, in times when money is in plenty, to lend on discount on the Bills which the agents of the country banks carry to them?

> Yes, it is.

You state that you send long dated bills into the country (say six months to run) to be discounted?

Yes.

Is it not sometimes the practice for the country banker, to remit in payment a bill at two months upon his banker in London, that it may be there discounted, deducting of course the proportion of the discount money, namely, for the two months action?

> Yes, it is the practice in some parts of Westmoreland and at Manchester but those are transactions in which we have no concern, they are done by corresponding with the party directly.

Not to a large amount?

> No, I believe not; business of this sort was done to a great extent, when a considerable number of West India bills at from twelve to thirty-six months date were in circulation.

Can you state to the Committee the causes which periodically produce an abundance or scarcity of money in London?

> No. It is beyond my conception.

Do you think from the appearance of the bills which have come into your hands to be discounted, that many bills are now drawn solely for the purposes of raising money, and not for real business done?

> No. I believe a very small proportion indeed that are not for real business pass through my hands.

Are there any other persons in London whose transactions are considerable in this line?

> Yes, several, but I believe no one house that carries on agency to the same extent as we do; I do not think they altogether carry it on to one-third of the extent we do.

Are there not some who carry on similar transactions for mercantile houses in London and obtain money on discount from London bankers?

> A great many.

Can you state what may be the comparative extent to the latter class?

> I should think to a much greater extent for the merchants, than for the country bankers.

Can you distinguish between those bills which are properly called bills of accommodation, and those for real mercantile transactions?

> No. I wish I could; it would be of great use to me in my business.

Do not the bills drawn from the country necessarily partake in some measure of both characters?

> Yes. I have no doubt it is sometimes the case; I have heard it stated that a merchant in London shall buy £1000 worth of goods in the country and that the seller shall draw for two; but to distinguish from the bill whether such transactions are real or not is impossible.

Is not the sufficiency of the acceptor, drawer and indorser, the principal rule by which you necessarily judge?

> No, not at all times; there is a great influx of a particular description of paper in the market at times which we must avoid, let the parties be ever so good. Particular businesses get into disrepute, the Spanish wool trade for instance. When an article is very high, both drawer, acceptor and indorser get into bad credit and we are then cautious of taking such bills.

Can you generally obtain as many bills founded on real transactions in commerce, as you are able to get discounted?

> Yes. Nine months out of the year we can.

Can you obtain more of such bills than you are able to discount?

> Yes. Particularly for the last four months.

Supposing the supply of cash to increase through the increase of country bank notes, do you conceive that you could obtain a proportionable increase in the supply of bills founded on real transactions of commerce?

> Yes, to more than double the amount of the increase, by taking bills which have from three to six months to run.

Has your business gradually increased to the great extent at which it is now?

> Yes, for about the last four or five years it has . . . Evidence

of Thomas Richardson. *Select Committee on the High Price of Gold Bullion* (1810), 177–84 and 228–31

_____

24 Vincent Stuckey   Country Banking in the Suspension Period

Vincent Stuckey (1771–1845) was a country banker of Somerset and the grandfather of Walter Bagehot. Stuckey early recognised the advantages of joint stock banking and was one of the first to take advantage of the Act of 1826. In that year he became the first chairman of Stuckey's Banking Company of Langport, Somerset.

_____

You are a country banker?—I am.

With what country banks are you connected?—Bristol, Langport and Bridgewater, in the county of Somerset.

Are you generally connected with all the country banks at those places?—We have an establishment at each place. Our banking establishment at Langport has existed for nearly fifty years.

Are there other country banks besides those with which you are connected?—Several in the County.

Have there been great fluctuations in the amount of the paper issued by the country banks with which you are connected since the bank restriction?—When the bank restriction took place in 1797, I was at the head of the bill department in the Treasury, and of course saw a good deal of important transactions; soon after that period I succeeded to the principal management of a considerable country bank; in consequence, the subject of currency has very much engaged my attention. I now hold in my hand the scale of our circulation for the last four years.

So far as you recollect, what has been the case since 1797?— Soon after that year, if I recollect right, the circulation was very low; it gradually got up again, till some time before the year 1810; in 1811 it was very low; it began to increase again in 1812, and continued increasing till the latter end of 1815;

in 1816 it became low again; since that it has been gradually increasing, in the following ratio:

March 1816	10
1817	12
1818	16
1819	$17\frac{1}{2}$

I think the circulation generally may be taken for the last twelve months to have been nearly stationary; but ours has increased lately, in consequence of a neighbouring bank getting out of credit.

So far as you know of other establishments, do you think the amount of their circulation has varied in pretty much the same proportion?—Yes, of banks in good credit, I should conceive so.

Do you mean to apply your observation, of the increase and diminution of other banks being similar to yours, to the whole circulation of the country?—I think, as before stated, the whole circulation of the country has been about stationary for the last twelve months.

Do you think the diminution arising from the discredit of another bank has been such as to vary the general proportion of the circulation in that part of the country?—No.

On what do you think the fluctuations in country bank paper mainly depend?—A good deal depends upon their credit, and also the prices of different articles: if articles are very dear, it requires, in my judgment, a larger circulation to carry on the business of the country than it would when articles are cheaper.

Do not you think the price of articles is rather the effect of an increase or decrease of country bank paper than the cause of them?—I think the price of articles might be affected by the great increase, but I consider that country banks generally follow the Bank of England; if they increase their circulation, it has been commonly found that the circulation of the country banks increase.

Do not you think the high prices are caused by the increase of country bank paper?—A country bank well regulated of course takes care not to issue but on a fair demand; we endeavour not to lend on any speculation; but it is found that if articles are dear, a larger circulating medium is required.

In what way do the issues of the country banks with which you are connected take place?—Various. For instance; many of the respectable farmers in our country keep accounts at our bank, and at one period of the year they frequently leave cash with us, which of course they draw out in our notes; at another period, we are in the habit of accommodating them; many gentlemen of the country also keep their cash at our bank; and when they receive their rents, it is paid into our bank, and we transfer the amount to the London banker, if they have one; if not, when the gentlemen themselves are in London, we order their checks to be paid by our London banker, carrying it to their account in the country. Much in that way, nearly the whole revenue in the county of Somerset, is collected and paid.

In what way do you issue your paper to those persons who have no deposits; What is the nature of the security you require? —Our established rule is to require two securities; we sometimes lend to two farmers on their joint note, in most instances for two months; another mode in which the established country banker gets his paper into circulation is as follows. The county of Somerset is a grazing and an agricultural country, our graziers are in the habit of sending their cattle to Smithfield market; the money they sell for is paid into our London bankers, by their agent in London; they then come to our country bank, and receive the amount in our notes; the same with dealers in corn: a miller is generally a large circulator of country bank notes; he opens an account with his country banker, and the notes he is in the habit of receiving he brings to his banker in the country, and receives his own banker's notes in exchange; we also now and then discount; but in a country situation, such as Bridgewater and Langport, there is not much dis-counting; part of that district is a clothing country, and we discount the clothier's bills on his agent in London, at two months.

At what rate?—Invariably five per cent: another mode by which we get our notes in circulation, is, that persons who keep accounts with us, generally pay away our notes.

In what does the country gentleman make his deposit?—In what he receives for his rents.

In what are his rents paid?—Perhaps in our own notes, or probably the notes of others; probably there is £1,000 paid in, and he takes it out gradually in £100 at a time; country notes are deemed by gentlemen in their own neighbourhoods to be preferable to the Bank of England notes.

Do you allow interest on the deposits made with you?—Yes, we do; for the last thirty years, invariably three per cent.

If the deposits are made on your own notes?—Certainly.

Do you require a notice?—The notes are drawn thirty days after sight, but our rule is invariably to pay on demand, deducting the thirty days' interest.

Do you ever lend money on mortgage?—No, that is not our system; country bankers are sometimes obliged to take mortgages, but we never do if we can avoid it.

What do you do with the notes of other country banks paid into your house?—We send them to those other banks for payment.

What is the proportion between the amount of your notes in circulation and the amount of deposits, and the proportion between the amount of your notes in circulation and the amount of Bank of England paper which you retain, in order to answer your notes in Bank of England notes?—We generally find that if we have £20,000 in circulation, £1,000 is ample in the country to answer any demand in Bank of England paper; if a neighbouring bank should fail, or any extraordinary circumstance arise, we immediately increase our deposit of Bank of England paper; the communication with London is now so immediate and rapid, that any very large amount of Bank of England paper is found, by experience, to be unnecessary; certainly short of the amount which it would have been thought prudent to have kept thirty years ago. Our deposits fluctuate

even more than the amount of our circulation; we had very
few deposits in 1816 and 1817, for the last twelve months the
deposits have increased; I think the amount of our deposits
bear about the proportion of one-third of the circulation.

In what way do you invest that part of your deposit which is
with the London banker?—We keep all our deposit and a vast
proportion of our circulation in Government security in London, in funded and unfunded property, so that it may be
convertible at an hour's notice; we also keep a deposit of a
certain sum with our London banker, without interest, as a
compensation for doing our business.

Do your London Bankers allow you any interest upon the
sums above the deposit?—Yes; our Bankers allow us 3%, but
I believe some others give 4%.

Supposing the Bank Restriction Act removed, and then your
country banks were subject to pay their notes in cash, on
demand, they being allowed to continue to issue one and two
pound notes as at present, do you think there would be, in the
part of the country with which you are connected, such a
decided preference for cash, as compared with country bank
paper, as to lead to a great demand for the conversion of that
paper into coin?—I should think not; and I should be very
sorry indeed, as it would be very inconvenient to us to carry on
our business, if it were possible to change all the one and two
pound notes into coin.

You think that the parties would remain in general very well
satisfied with country bank paper as a circulating medium?—
Yes, provided the value is kept equal to the standard, I think
they would; having known the convenience of paper, they
would not change it for coin. In the latter end of the year 1816
and beginning of 1817 we had a circulation of coin for some
months; it cost us in that period nearly one hundred pounds to
transmit the surplus quantity of coin to London, of which four
fifths in value, at least, consisted of gold; we could not get rid
of it in the country, our customers preferring our notes.

Did you make any objection to deliver coin to any person who brought the notes?—We wished them to take coin, but they preferred notes and we were obliged to transmit the coin to London; some who had hoarded guineas, brought them in, and requested as a favour that we would give them our notes for them.

Were the guineas that were then in circulation, and which you offered to give in exchange for your notes, perfectly new ones, and such as no doubt could attach to as to their being of full weight?—Many of them were full weight, some of them were not.

Were the guineas such as you might have compelled the party to take as a legal tender?—Many of them, but not all.

Did you find any demand for those that were of full weight? —Not the least. In the Spring of 1817, I brought with me to town near 1,000 guineas, from one of our banks; On taking them to our London Banker, they requested as a favour, I would not leave them there; they had lately sent so many to the Bank of England that they did not like to trouble them any more; besides, the bank only took those which were quite full weight.

Supposing that instead of country banks being subject to pay their notes in cash, they were subjected to pay their notes only in Bank of England notes, the Bank of England note alone being convertible into cash at the will of the holder; do you think there would be, for the purpose of internal circulation in those parts of the country with which you are connected, any demand for coin?—In my opinion, the circulation of the country will not at all require coin, except silver for small payments; I think gold coin would certainly not be required, and I illustrate that by our experience in 1816, as before described.

Had you any sovereigns in the country in 1816?—We had very few.

Supposing that a positive obligation were imposed upon the Bank to resume cash payments at the expiration of two years from the present period, and that subsequently to the resumption of cash payments by the Bank, country banks should be allowed to issue their notes in the same way that they are allowed at present, namely, one and two pound notes convertible into Bank of England paper; should you have any apprehension with respect to the effect of such an obligation on the Bank, with reference to those banking establishments with which you are connected?—I should not.

Do you consider that the amount of country bank paper in circulation necessarily fluctuates with the amount of Bank of England paper?—I think it does; it is extremely difficult to answer that question correctly; I have taken a great deal of pains upon it; I think in 1816 it will be found that the Bank of England circulation was higher or as high as it ever had been, and that arose in my opinion from the then discredit of country banks; we all at that time, instead of keeping a deposit of Bank of England of one in twenty, kept three or four in twenty, for the whole country was in a state of agitation and alarm; we heard of country banks failing every day, and that threw the rest into disrepute; but the circulation of the country bank paper is in my judgment governed in a great measure by the issues of the Bank of England, in quiet and ordinary times.

Do you think that if the Bank were, in the course of twelve months, to make a reduction in their issues to the extent of three millions below their present amount, that after a given time, that would necessarily lead to a corresponding reduction in the amount of country bank paper?—I think so.

Is the circulation of Somerset confined to country bank paper generally?—Almost entirely.

There are no bills of exchange circulated?—Very few in comparison to Lancashire and Worcestershire; I do a good deal of business in Worcestershire, and take many bills there of ten or fifteen pounds, which perform the office of circulating medium; in Somersetshire the circulation is almost entirely in cash notes.

Have you calculated the amount of country paper in circulation in Somersetshire?—Yes, I have frequently calculated the amount in that county, excluding Bristol and Bath, where there is a good deal of local circulation; I think the County of Somerset may have about £250,000 in circulation, independently of those two places.

What amount had it at the time the country bank paper was at the highest amount, and what amount when at the lowest?— I think it was down in 1816 to about £130,000; the highest at any one period, for twenty years, I should think was £350,000.

Is not country bank paper preferred to Bank of England paper in the County of Somerset?—Yes, in general, for obvious reasons; the forgeries of the Bank of England have been very great for the last few years.

Do not you think habit occasions a preference?—Yes: more particularly if the public know the parties and their property.

Would not persons who have been in the habit of receiving paper, continue to do so in preference to coin, if they were satisfied of the solvency of the country banker?—Certainly, I am of that opinion.

Has not the principle on which country bank paper has been issued in this country for several years past, in your opinion, led to and produced a rise in the prices of commodities?—I should think, from what I have heard and seen of many Banks, it must have had that effect, for they have been very improvidently managed; they lent their property on very inadequate security, and we have seen the unfortunate result in many instances.

Does not an excess in the issue of paper currency, supposing it to exist, meaning always, a currency incovertible into gold or silver coin, lead into the very nature of things to an absorption of that excess in the prices of commodities?—I think it does.

When you state that you conceive the payment of country Bank paper in notes of the Bank of England, will be perfectly satisfactory are you at all acquainted with the plan for the resumption of cash payments, commonly called Mr. Ricardo's? —Certainly I am.

With reference to the payment of country paper in notes of the Bank of England, and of the resumption of payments by the

Bank, do you think this plan will afford a facility both to country bankers and to the Bank of England?—I think it would.

What are the inconveniences which you consider would arise from this change in the mode of paying the notes of the Bank of England?—I am not aware of any inconvenience which can arise; I think it would be attended with very considerable convenience to pay the larger sums in bullion; it appears to me to be a very great improvement on a 'well regulated' paper currency; and it has always struck me, that at the resumption of cash payments by the Bank, the above would be by far the best plan I ever heard of; I think it would do away with a great part of that which many dread, a great and general demand for guineas; and after a year or two, seeing how the plan answered, the circulation of coin might be introduced, if found necessary.

Are you engaged in other business except that of a country banker?—Yes; I am a manufacturer of Salt: the house with which I am connected is the largest payer of duty in England, we pay £1,000 a day duty; the amount of our duty last year was near one-fifth of the whole duty on Salt.

How are the payments made?—Devonshire, Somersetshire, Gloucestershire, and other parts, are supplied from our works, and the payments are made in bills of exchange and cash notes, and the amount of currency which passes through our hands is of course very considerable; our remittances to London last year were upwards of £12,000,000.

Are your one pound notes payable in London?—Yes; we have found very great inconvenience from local circulation, that is notes not payable in London, notwithstanding the bankers in our County, with a view to facilitate their business, have for the last seven years fixed on some centrical point where, on a certain day, they meet to exchange their notes, upon the principles of the clearing-house in London, by which means the circulation is economised; this mode of exchange is also adopted in Bristol.

Have you any suggestion to offer to the Committee to give greater security to the circulation of country bank paper?— If any thing should be done, of which I have many doubts, in my opinion no method is so proper as assimilating them to the Bank of England, by lending a proportion of their capital to the government at a certain interest. The mode which has been suggested of making them lodge security in some proportion to the amount of their circulation appears to me liable to many objections, as nothing is more uncertain than the amount of circulation; it varies at different periods of the year, and frequently a sudden demand is made for it; in one day, within a month from this period, we issued at one of our banks, on a large fair day, near £10,000 in cash notes, nearly the whole of which were given in exchange for other country bank and Bank of England notes.

Should you see any objection to a further assimilation to the Bank of England, by allowing a number of partners exceeding six to be associated in country banks?—I think it would be injurious to the existing establishments.

In what mode would it be injurious?—By lessening the business of the established country banks.

Would it be likely to diminish their business by the circumstance of the public being disposed to place a higher confidence in banks such as have been described?—Probably it would: ours, which has existed for nearly fifty years, might have its circulation diminished by a company setting up in opposition to it; but I think business done by a company would not be transacted so much to the satisfaction of individuals as it is when done by a few persons . . . Evidence of Vincent Stuckey. *Secret Committee on the Resumption of Cash Payments* (1819), 243–8

25 Thomas Joplin Reform of the Banking System

Joplin (1790–1847), a banker of Newcastle-upon-Tyne, was an enthusiastic supporter of joint stock banking and his contribution to English banking theory has been somewhat neglected. He was associated with the Provincial Bank of

Ireland from 1824, and in 1833 founded the National Provincial Bank with his cousin George Fife Angus.

Banks are by far the most important of all our commercial establishments. They are the fountains of our currency, the depositories of our capital, and at once the wheels and pillars of our trade. Business to any great extent could not be carried on without them. All who have cash transactions of any kind are more or less dependent upon them. The landed proprietor finds them a convenient place of deposit for the ready money he possesses, or a useful resource in case of need. The capitalist, when he deems them safe, can lodge his money with them, receive interest for it, and have it ready when the chances of trade or changes of property may throw a desirable purchase in his way. Merchants and traders of every denomination are enabled through them to send money to, and receive it from the most distant places, to raise money when in want of it upon the Bills which they receive from their customers, to have those Bills presented for payment through a channel which in general secures their being duly honoured, and to deposit in them those sums which any particular occasion, or the current demands of their business require. Their Promissory Notes, also, furnish the country with a useful and convenient circulating medium, and are in the hands of every one.

They are, therefore, intimately connected with every class of society. Every person who has anything to do either with capital or money is interested in their stability. But the capitalist, merchant, manufacturer and tradesman, and all who have large payments to make and receive, are continually under the necessity of trusting them in amounts, the loss of which might prove their utter ruin. They have besides daily to confide in them for the negotiation of Bills and advances of capital, which, in commercial transactions, are continually required.

On this account, a very deep interest is felt in the welfare of Banks. Nothing can in any way affect them without exciting the immediate attention of the public, and (if it involve their credit) without producing the greatest possible agitation and alarm. Thus when the slightest apprehension is entertained respecting their solvency, however groundless it may sometimes prove, a run upon them immediately takes place. That is, hundreds of people immediately crowd the doors of the Banks, to demand payment of the Notes they hold, or to withdraw that money out of their hands, which they have deposited with them. This puts a stop to their usual banking operations. People in trade cannot receive that accommodation upon which they have relied, upon which the regularity of their payments, and, consequently, upon which their credit, depends; and no person can take their Bills upon London, for the purpose of remitting money to meet their engagements at a distant (the only mode by which they can make such remittances), without placing their money in a state of peril, which they cannot ascertain to be groundless, until the run upon them is over. All is, therefore, confusion; and the whole community is thrown into a state of apprehension and alarm, which may be better conceived than described.

Upon such occasions the greatest exertions are always made to allay the fears and restore the confidence of the public; and very great risks are sometimes run in doing so. It is not unusual for the friends of a Bank so situated, to issue out Bills or Notices, pledging themselves to the public, to take its Notes in payment, to any amount. By this measure, should the Bank happen to fail, many of them would necessarily be ruined. Within these few years, pledges of this kind were repeatedly issued in favour of the Durham, Stockton and Sunderland Banks, all of whom ultimately failed. As, however, these pledges were not attended with any serious consequences, to those who issued them, it is probable that the Banks did not stop payment immediately when they were issued, or otherwise they must have overlooked the obligation contracted, and, from inadvertency, not have called upon the parties to redeem the pledge they had given.

We may, however, form some idea of the inconveniences in which the mercantile world are involved, when people are found

P

wandering so far out of the track of ordinary prudence as to guarantee the security of establishments with whose affairs they have no intimate acquaintance, and whose solvency would involve them in certain destruction.

Nothing, in fact, can affect the credit of the Banks without being immediately felt in a corresponding degree by the public; and the actual stoppage of an extensive Banking concern deranges the whole frame of mercantile affairs, and carries confusion, misery and ruin, into every department of society.

Great, however, as the inconveniences are which the discredit of Banks, and consequent runs upon them occasion; and great as are the calamities by which their failures are uniformly attended, they have been, both in this country and Ireland, of very common occurrence.

By an account printed in the appendix to the Lords' Report upon the Bank resuming Cash Payments, it appears, that in seven years, viz from 1810 to 1816 inclusive, no fewer than one hundred and forty-seven commissions of bankruptcy had been issued against Country Banks alone, and in thirty years nearly three hundred; an average of failures, proportioned to the total number of these establishments, in all probability far exceeding that of any other regular business.

Sometimes, as if epidemically, the Banks of a whole district fail together, as was the case a year to two ago,* in the south of Ireland. That part of the country was, in consequence, involved in the greatest distress; its trade was materially injured and a shock given to its prosperity, from which it is said not yet to have recovered. The same event happened also in the counties of Northumberland and Durham a few years back, when the Durham, Sunderland and Stockton Banks failed within a short time of each other. This district, however, was better able to endure it, though the inconveniences generally felt were great and the sufferers numerous. Even in this town, to which the evil but partially extended, the want of confidence

---

* This was written in the latter part of the year 1821.

and the general state of alarm which it produced, must be fresh in the recollection of every one.

Now, while England and Ireland are continually subject to disasters of this kind, it seems an extraordinary fact, that Scotland is totally free from them; the Scotch Banks rarely, if ever, either failing or losing money.

No one, I dare say, will from this imagine that there is anything different in the nature of their money transactions, or that trade is subject to fewer vicissitudes in Scotland than with us. I believe that trade is pretty much the same in both nations, or if there is any difference, that the merchants of Scotland are the more speculative and less stable of the two. But the true cause of the difference is to be found in the nature of their respective Banking Establishments; the Scotch Banks being Joint Stock Companies, while the English Banks are private partnerships.

The Scotch Banks consist of a great number of Proprietors or Stock Holders who contribute, some to the extent of one hundred pounds, some of a thousand, and some of many thousands. By these means they form a joint capital, establish a Bank and entrust the management of it to a Committee chosen from their body, called a Court of Directors. The English Banks, on the contrary, never consist of more than six partners, though often fewer, and are for the most part, managed by one, or at the furthest, by two of them.

To the uniform success of Joint Stock Banking Companies, history affords but one exception, viz.:—The case of the Douglass, Herron & Co. (or Ayr) Bank, some account of which is given by Smith, page 58, Vol. 2d. of his Wealth of Nations. If, however, we examine the circumstances which produced that failure, we shall find it attributable to causes which are not likely to again occur and that, as an exception, it merely establishes the rule . . .

. . . From the great credit enjoyed by the Scotch Banks, they are enabled to transact business to a much greater extent, and on very different principles than with us. From this source still more important, though less obvious benefits arise, and these it may not be improper for us in the first place to consider.

The original and proper business of a Banker is to trade in capital. He ought to be that medium between the borrower and lender in the money market, which a merchant is in other commodities. It is the business of a merchant or trader to buy of the producer on the one hand and to sell to the consumer or retailer on the other. He acquires a knowledge of both parties and they of him, and for his credit, capital, labour and knowledge, he charges a profit upon the commodity which, through his agency, is transferred from the party who has it to sell, to the party wanting to purchase it. Now, what a merchant is in other commodities, the Scotch Banks are in money. They borrow of those who have it to lend, and lend to those who want to borrow it, acquire a knowledge of both parties and charge a profit of one per cent. upon the transaction. Any person opening an account with them receives four per cent.[1] upon the balance in their hands. He may pay money to the credit of his account when he chooses, and he receives interest for it from the day it is deposited: he may draw his money out of the Bank when and in such sums as he thinks proper, and only loses interest upon the sum drawn, from the day of receiving it. On the contrary, any person giving proper securities, may open an account with them, and draw to the extent of the security given, for which they will charge him five per cent. upon the fluctuating balance he owes. Consequently, a person who has money to lend is saved all the trouble, not unattended with risk, of mortgages and may have his money, or any part of it, at any time, should a desirable purchase fall in his way; whereas with a mortgage he cannot draw his money when he wants it— must take it altogether when he does draw it—or, if the borrower chooses, must take it whether he wants it or not. Their object, however, in borrowing, being to lend, the facilities given to borrowers, are equally great. In the first place, they will dis-

[1] Since the above was written, they have reduced the rate of interest to 2½% and have raised it again to 4%.

count bills and other mercantile securities, that are perfectly regular and good, at any time, and to any amount. Thus merchants can calculate with certainty upon being accommodated in the course of regular transactions to any extent, which is of infinite service to them, as it would be better for a merchant not to have such assistance at all, than to have any uncertainty respecting it. In the next place, they grant Cash Accounts, that is, any person in business by giving two sufficient securities may open an account with them, and overdraw them to the extent of the security given, for which, as before stated, he is charged five per cent. upon the balance he owes. Very great advances, not to mercantile men only, but to all classes of persons, are made in this way; and in the last place, they make advances upon real property, some of them to a very considerable extent. The plan they pursue, I believe, is for the proprietor to pledge his estate, or other property, with the Bank for a given amount, open an account with it, and draw as his occasions may require, to the amount prescribed. Thus, when any persons wish to borrow, the facilities held out to borrowers induce them equally with the lenders to make application to the Bank.

As individuals often call in the money they have lent out on mortgage when they can find better employment for it, or when the death of the party produces a division of property, by which a great expense to the mortgagee is incurred in procuring a fresh mortgage, Banks are therefore more to be depended upon, and borrowers being just as much wanted by them as lenders, and the money which they lend being rarely, or in fact, never called in again until it is the pleasure of the borrower to pay it off, people in want of money, will prefer dealing with the Banks at even a higher percentage, while lenders, on their part, prefer dealing with them at a percentage something less than individuals would give. Thus in consequence of the security of their property, and the readiness with which they can at all times obtain it when wanted, a difference of one per cent. is not found to be a sufficient inducement for the borrowers and lenders to pass by the Banks and to transact their business direct with each other. If they did, the gain would, of course, have to be divided between them, and a half per cent. would be no compensation to either party for the additional inconvenience, risk and trouble in which they would be involved. Whereas the Bank being open and ready at all times to meet the wants of each party, unless among particular friends, neither party ever thinks of making further enquiries upon the subject, but transacts the business with the Banks as a matter of course. They are, therefore, at once, the great depositories of the money capital of the country* and the source from whence the supplies of it are drawn.

Although considerable advances are made by the Scotch Banks upon real property, it is rather a ground of complaint, that they have been too much in the habit of speculating in the funds, when it might have been more to the advantage of their country that they should have lent out their capital at home; and while lending their money at home appears to be preferable for a Public Bank to gambling in the funds, it seems also to be the duty of such an establishment to lend its money at home whenever it can do so with safety.

The failures which continually take place amongst the English, particularly the Country Banks and the consequent discredit in which they are held, of course almost totally preclude them from trading in capital in the manner pursued by the Banks of Scotland. The London Bankers are the only Bankers it is generally understood, who at all do so, and they are not considered good mortgagees. Their strictness in requiring powers of sale etc. to be granted to them, which their limited credit renders necessary, in order to be able to call in their money at the shortest notice, should the state of their credit at any time require it, places the mortgagor in a state of disagreeable depen-

---

* There are thirty-two Banking Companies in Scotland and it is computed by the Bankers themselves, that the money deposited with them, by the Public, is considerably above 20 millions.

dence. The business of an English Country Bank is, however, principally confined to lending out that capital which it raises by the circulation of its Notes and the comparatively small sums deposited with it, mostly without interest (its customers seldom depositing more money with it, than their current occasions require) and to buying and selling Bills upon London. The advances of capital which it makes are, of necessity, principally confined to the discounting of such short-dated Bills of Exchange, as through its London agents, can be turned at any time into cash; as it is always liable to be called upon to pay off its Notes, and all the money in its hands, at the shortest notice, it should always be prepared to do so; and the most prudently managed and best English Banks are those which confine themselves most strictly to the limits which their uncertain credit prescribes to them.

Credit is, in fact, the proper capital of a Bank, without which it is impossible for it to be carried on with any great advantage to the country. For want of this the business of English Banks, extensive as it may appear, is quite inconsiderable compared with that of the Banks of Scotland, and far short of what it would be with a different system.

Thus then, it appears to be the result of experience, that while our Banks are often destructive, at all times dangerous, and at the very best totally inadequate, from want of stability and credit, to perform their proper functions, the Scotch Banks never fail, nor is any danger ever apprehended from them, and that, in consequence, Banking is carried on in that kingdom to an extent unknown and, of course, with advantages totally unfelt in our own.

We have stated that the superiority in the success, as well as in the stability and credit of the Scotch Banks, arise from their being public, and not private concerns, which is also proved by our own experience. We have but one Public Bank, the Bank of England, and it has uniformly done well since its first establishment. The same may also be inferred of the Bank of

Ireland, the only Public Bank in that country; lately, when applying for a renewal of its charter, it appeared that besides its annual dividends, it had made and saved half a million of money; a sum much greater than the Stock-holders had any conception of. This at once proves that successful management is not at all peculiar to Scotland, or any nation, but is inherent in the system itself.

The cause of this difference proceeds from the charters of the Bank of England and Ireland which prevent, in their respective countries, more than six persons from forming a Banking Company while in Scotland there is no such monopoly and Banks can be established on the proper principles and as many people become partners in them as choose.

From the limited number of partners in our Banks, their management has frequently fallen into hands totally incompetent to such a trust. There is, perhaps, nothing in the theory of Banking very complicated. But to manage a Bank well requires a degree of firmness and judgment which every individual does not possess. If a Banker be too safe and injudiciously cautious in his transactions, he is apt to ruin his business for want of liberality; if too confident, to ruin himself for want of prudence; while he must possess firmness sufficient to enable him to refuse the most pressing solicitation of even his friends, when necessary to do so. This knowledge, discrimination and firmness, not only require natural talent in the person possessing them, but previous practice and experience in the business of the world. Whereas persons are often placed in the management of English Provincial Banks, by some connection or other chance, which usually determines the lot of individuals in the common affairs of life. Or, if they are chosen expressly for their presumed fitness for the trust, their fitness will then depend upon whether the partners who chose them, are themselves sufficiently competent to form such a choice; independent of which, however, the energy and vigilance of every individual is at times apt to slumber, and we occasionally find the ablest men get very far wrong.

Now, the true reason of the success of Public Banks may be ascribed to their never being managed by any single person, but by a Court of Directors, periodically chosen by the holders of stock;* and their fitness for the trust does not depend upon the opinion of an individual or two, but of hundreds, founded upon the clear evidence which their successful management of their own affairs has afforded. No man is ever chosen as the Director of a Joint Stock Company, where the choice is unbiassed by influence, who has not given sufficient proof in the eyes of the world of his ability for the management, and has not justly inspired his fellow proprietors with that confidence which they repose in him.

The principal causes which produce the ruin of Private Banks may be stated to be, first, a confusion in their accounts, arising from a bad or relaxed and careless management, so very frequently exhibited in common affairs; but which, in banking, must ever be fatal; secondly, speculations with the capital in the Bank; and thirdly, and most frequently, accommodating great houses, either from motives of private friendship, or the temptation of extra Banking profits, until they are so involved that they must stand or fall with them. The two great failures which have happened in this part of the country were Surtees, Burdon & Co. and the Durham Bank. The first was produced by entering into private speculations with the capital in its hands, and the last by accommodating a great mining company. But with Public Banks these causes, by which failures are generally produced, cannot exist. In the first place, the vigilant check necessarily kept upon the Accountant, and those who have the charge of the books, which must at all times show, without trouble to the Directors, the state of the Company's affairs, prevents the possibility of their getting back or into

* Since this Pamphlet was written, two Joint Stock Companies, being establishments on a limited scale, have suffered loss by a departure from this principle, the Directors having placed, in each case, so unbounded a confidence in the managing officer, as to tempt him to abuse it, and apply the funds of the Company to his own use.

confusion. In the next place, the Directors could not appropriate the money of the Bank to views of private speculation, if they were wishful to do so as they are a check upon each other. If they were respectable men, they would not attempt it and if they were not, they would not be there; besides, there is no instance recorded of such a thing. In the third place, they have too little personal interest in the Bank to be tempted by extra profit out of the path of safety, in accommodating great houses; or if they were influenced by private friendship to do so, it could never be the case with them all; and they would be also in that respect a check upon each other.

Independent of the general Court of Directors, there is also a Managing Director, Cashier, Secretary and Accountant or sometimes Cashier and Accountant alone, according to the business done, either the Cashier or Secretary in the latter cases acting as Managing Director and taking all the practical management; and if the Directors are careful to choose men fit for these stations and see that they do their duty, the Company will generally succeed.

The Directors having in general, business of their own to attend to, cannot give their whole attention to the Bank affairs. Their part is more to deliberate, judge and determine, than to contrive. Consequently the Managing Director or he who is at the head of the executive department, sits with and joins the Directors in their deliberations, and proposes to them such views and opinions as his practical knowledge and undivided attention to the affairs of the Bank suggest to him. These they take into consideration and approve, alter or otherwise direct, as they may think proper. The energetic and profitable management of such a business, therefore, greatly depends upon the ability of its officers, who are expected to submit a variety of views and propositions to the Directors, of which there is no fear that they adopt any which are too speculative. The errors of Public Banks are generally on the side of safety. But when the practical management is not in the hands of men possessed in some degree of ready apprehension, practical energy and talent for business, it is consistent, I understand, with experience, that the business is apt to become less profitable.

The business, however, of such a Bank, though it may not be pursued with energy, is seldom neglected. When the Directors can give no attention to the concern, they resign or when it is their turn to go out, are not re-elected. On the other hand, they are not likely to get wrong in taking up sanguine views, by which individuals often mislead themselves. They are responsible in the estimation of the Stock-holders for all that is done and individually have but little to gain by success; whereas, if their management produced any considerable loss to the Company, they would be turned out of office and stand committed with the public in a manner that would necessarily produce feelings of the most painful nature.

As, therefore, it thus appears, that the causes which operate in producing the failure of Private Banks are totally prevented by the constitution of Public Companies, we cease to wonder at the uniform success by which the latter are attended. But the risk incurred by Bankers is not, perhaps, so great as we are apt to imagine. With loans on property or on the personal securities required to establish a cash account, there is no risk at all. Property is not taken, if not sufficient to cover the loan upon it and the securities accepted when a cash account is opened, are each of them required to be sufficiently able to fulfil the obligation of the bond they enter into. Should anything happen to either of them, another name must be immediately substituted. Independent therefore of the party with whom the account is opened, there are always two perfectly good and sufficient sureties, to make up any deficiency, even to the full amount of the debt, should it be called for.

The great risk incurred by a Bank, is in the Discounting of Bills of Exchange, though it is, at the same time, its most desirable business, from being the principal means by which it keeps its Notes in circulation. But with this class of business also, the risk, under proper management, is much less than is supposed. It is said that the Bank of England, in ordinary times, does not calculate upon a greater loss than one pound in three hundred thousand. Leith is a very speculating town and its Merchants are subject, in consequence, to considerable vicissitudes. Yet the Branch of the Commercial Bank there, during the first four years of its establishment, did not lose one pound out of many millions of discounts, although, in consequence of having entirely new connections to form, it rejected no business that it could with any degree of prudence accept. The experience of those also, who live in country towns, where the losses which the Banks sustain are generally known, will point out to them, if they have made the observation, that it is only very rarely that a well managed Bank suffers any loss at all.

The Scotch Banks, in fact, in the arrangements which they make with their agents established in distant towns, assume that there is no risk whatever and lay it down, as a rule, that if they incur any loss, they are to suffer it themselves. The Directors in general select for Agents, tried men of business, who have proved, by the manner of conducting their own affairs, their capability of successfully transacting whatever may be confided to them. Securities are required of them, in a town of any business to the extent, I understand, of not less than ten thousand pounds and they receive a fixed salary of (say) from two to four hundred per annum, according to the size of the place, and business done in it. It is, I believe, generally calculated by the Agent, that if he can make out a case of very unforeseen loss, it will be partly allowed him; but the assumed principle is, that there need be none at all. It is a most curious circumstance, however, and completely proves the insecurity of private management in Bank affairs, that the Banks lose more money through their Agents than in any other way.

The distance of the town, where the Agent is established, from the Bank, renders it impossible that any proper judgment can be formed by the Directors, of the stability of the persons with whom the Agent does business. The great sum, however, required as security, the business character he possesses and the risk he himself runs, naturally remove all suspicion as to the prudence of his transactions. Should his affairs become involved, he is, perhaps, sufficiently clever to hide it for a considerable time. This he probably does with the hope of recovering himself, until the failure, perhaps of some house he has imprudently accommodated or his deficiency is too great for further concealment, when his own ruin, the loss of the friends who are security for him and the loss of the Bank besides, to perhaps three times the amount, prove his unfitness for the trust that has been reposed in him.

This does not infrequently happen, and no greater proof of the insecurity of private management could well be afforded. If Agents, without the temptation of profit, and under the control of their Banks, cannot keep right, how much more likely are Private Banks to get wrong, without any such control and with all the usual temptations to influence them? Thomas Joplin. *An Essay on the General Principles and Present Practice of Banking in England and Scotland . . .* (1827), 1–25

_____

26 George Carr Glyn   Defence of the London Private Bankers

G. C. Glyn (1797–1873) was a second generation London private banker of considerable influence; he joined the family firm of Vere, Glyn and Hallifax as a partner in 1819. An opponent of the establishment of joint stock banks in London, Glyn was an able defender of the special relationship built up between the Bank of England and the private bankers of the capital.

_____

Can you give the Committee any idea of what proportion the advances a private Banker makes to his customer, bears to the gross amount of his deposits?—Our object is to employ as much money as we can amongst our customers.

Is it not generally a small proportion that you employ in that way, as compared with the gross amount of deposits?— No, a much larger proportion is employed in bills of exchange and notes than in public securities.

Can you state what proportion they bear to the total amount of deposits?—These advances to customers fluctuate so much at different times, that it is impossible to say; they are a small proportion, compared with the total amount, but they are large in themselves; and supposing we were deprived of the deposits we now have, it would not be prudent to continue the same amount of advances on promissory notes that we do now.

You are speaking of loans to your customers for short periods? —Yes.

Do not you consider that a private London Banker, who is a Banker for commercial houses in the City, is very differently situated from a Banker at the West end of the town, who has the accounts of country gentlemen and individuals out of trade? —I should conceive it is a totally different sort of business; and I should say that our reserved deposit was necessarily a much larger one than the deposit at the West end of the town Banker.

You cannot rely upon the use of money deposited with you to the same extent that the Bankers at the West end of the town may?—Certainly not . . .

Does it occur to you that the interests of the Public require any important change in the laws which regulate Banking at present?—I speak of London more particularly, where I do not think they require any great alteration; my conviction is, I mention it reluctantly, because this is a point upon which I may be thought to have an interest, but it seems to me that the business of London with the Bank of England, as the Bank of issue, and with private Bankers, as the channels through which the necessary accomodation are given to the different commercial interests, is as good a system as can be devised; instances occur every day in which it would be impossible for the first mercantile houses in London to deal with the Bank of England, or with a Joint-Stock Company; they come often to ask for loans, for the purpose of executing orders received from abroad, for the export of bullion and other commodities, they communicate confidentially with their private Banker, but they could not follow this course or make these communications to the

directors of a Joint-Stock Bank, some of whom might probably
be their rivals in trade and in these operations; and again,
among the second class of traders, we are obliged to proceed
often upon the knowledge we have acquired of their business
and character, a system upon which a Joint-Stock Company
could not act; I consider also that if these modes of accomodation were withdrawn, the distress among many of the traders in
London would be extreme, and the impediments to business
insuperable.

Do not you think there is a great evil in the change itself, in a
matter so sensitive as the public credit, unless there be a strong
reason for the change?—I consider it a very great evil, and
have no doubt that at the present moment the expectation of
some change likely to take place in the system of Banking is
inducing many of the large dealers in London to withhold from
extensive transactions.

Do you conceive it to be important to have the question set
at rest as early as possible?—I think it very important, and
believe I am expressing the opinion of a very large portion of
the traders of the city . . .

You stated that the establishment of Joint-Stock Banks in
London, governed by bodies of directors, would not be capable
of giving so much useful and discriminating assistance to traders,
as private Bankers can give; would you apply that observation
to the country as well as to London?—No, I think there is a
great distinction between the country and London business;
in a country town, with a limited population, the Directors are
as well able to judge of their customers as a private Banker can
be; but in London I think it is almost impossible for the Directors,
who would be coming in and going out by rotation, to make
themselves acquainted with the character and circumstances
of individuals, in the same way as private Bankers could and do.

Might not the Directors both in the country and in London
be retained for a longer period?—I only instance the fact as it
occurs generally.

Do the Joint-Stock Bank Directors retain their situation a

shorter period than the Directors of the Bank of England?—There is only one that I am particularly acquainted with; in that, the Directors change a certain number every year.

Do they come in again by rotation?—I do not know.

Supposing the Directors to retain their places for as long a period in London as in the country, would you see any distinction between London and the country?—I should draw this distinction generally, that you cannot get a Director to do that for his proprietors, which a private Banker would do for himself; but I think that in a country town, individuals are so well known to each other, that there is no necessity for that acquired knowledge, which there is here.

Would not you think that the circumstances of individuals in London not being so well known, would give to a Joint-Stock Bank, governed by a great number of Directors, possessing each of them their knowledge of individuals, an advantage which the Country Banker would not possess?—It is the duty of a private Banker to become acquainted with his customers; his business depends upon it, and his advances must be governed by this knowledge; if you can persuade the Directors of a Joint-Stock Bank to take the same interest for their proprietors which an individual does for himself, then, perhaps, much of the difficulty might be removed. Evidence of George Carr Glyn. *Select Committee on the Bank of England Charter* (1832)

PART FOUR

The Development of Joint Stock Deposit Banking

THOMAS JOPLIN in 1822 wrote anonymously *An Essay . . . on Banking* in which he showed that the Bank of England's monopoly of joint stock banking applied only to the issue of notes and did not inhibit the formation of joint stock deposit banks. Joplin thought that banking in England would have greater stability if it was based on corporate banks, as in Scotland, which would not only increase the capital base of the banks but would also give the additional advantage of allowing their affairs to be open to the public scrutiny of their shareholders. In the first edition of the *Essay* he suggested that a joint stock bank should be established upon Tyneside, his locality; the *Essay* was extended and reprinted by Joplin several times and the 1824 edition contained a plan to establish a joint stock in London. The government, in particular Lord Liverpool, was in favour of the establishment of joint stock banks but the planned legislation foundered on the opposition of the private country bankers. The crisis of 1825 revealed the basic weakness of the country banks and the government reacted quickly, passing in 1826 an Act (7 Geo. IV, c.46) which permitted joint stock banks of issue to be formed in England and Wales outside a 65 mile radius of London (27).

Though the banks which were founded under the 1826 Act were commonly known as joint stock banks, before the law they were large co-partnerships without limited liability. They tended to be small parochial concerns, in many ways similar to the private banks that the government intended them to replace. This localised nature was one of the main characteristics of joint stock banking during the first half of the nineteenth century. The immediate growth in the numbers of joint stock banks after 1826 was slow and hesitant in the face of the opposition of both the private country bankers and the Bank of England which was establishing provincial branches. The hostility of the private bankers to the legislation of 1826 was expressed in pamphlets (28), through memorials to the government, and by the *Circular to Bankers* which began publication in 1827. Joplin thought that the reason for the slow development of joint stock banking was the lack of the privilege of limited liability (29) but Gilbart explained that the bank shareholder was well protected against the liability for its debts both under the terms of the 1826 Act and by the deed of settlement, the legal instrument which constituted a bank (30). Whereas Gilbart was clear on the liability of the shareholder, he remained confused over the question of whether a joint stock bank could be set up in London. Joplin had already revealed 'the flaw in the Bank's monopoly' and was later to state the importance of a London base for a new joint stock bank (31). The development of joint stock banking was also hindered by the clauses in the 1826 Act which did not permit a joint stock bank either to draw bills under £50 on London or for less than six months' sight, precisely the character of financial paper that was most wanted in the provinces. Between 1826 and 1832 twenty-six joint stock banks were formed successfully in the provinces, mainly in the north and east, and including the conversion of the remarkable Stuckey's private bank.

The evidence given before the 1831–2 Committee on the renewal of the Bank of England's charter was wide ranging and reflected the antagonism between the three interested groups, the Bank of England, the private country bankers, and the new joint stock banks. Its report failed to make any definite recommendations because of the lack of unanimity and it was left to Lord Althorp, the Chancellor, to discuss the renewal of the charter with the Bank's directors. The government favoured a precise legal code for the joint stock banks which would establish them as corporation, allow the non-issuing banks limited liability, and Althorp was inclined to allow the establishment of joint stock banks in London. The Bank of England opposed any further erosion of its monopoly and the country bankers were also hostile to such suggestions which resulted in Althorp being forced to shelve the planned legislation. The Bank's charter was simply renewed but the Act of renewal allowed joint stock banks outside of the London region to draw bills of less than £50 on London and a declaratory clause was inserted which stated that joint stock banks of deposit could be formed within the London area (32). In addition the Usury laws were waived with respect to three month bills which not only allowed the Bank of England to raise its discount rate above five per cent, but also encouraged banks to invest their funds in commercial bills as opposed to government securities. A boom in the formation of joint stock banks followed the Bank Charter Act of 1833 both in the provinces and in London which reached a peak in 1835–6.

W. R. Douglas, a Scottish merchant in London, before the passage of the 1833 Act had begun to form a bank 'on the Scotch system' for the metropolis. A promotional syndicate of Scottish Lords and gentlemen was active by August 1833 and it twice petitioned Parliament. The pressure from this group was probably responsible for the inclusion of the declaratory clause in the Bank Charter Act of 1833 and in 1834 the syndicate formed the London and Westminster Bank, the first London joint stock deposit bank. This bank proposed to pay interest on its deposits, contrary to the practice of the existing London private banks and the Bank of England, but at the same time was to charge for its services; the aim of the bank's promoters was to attract the custom of the growing middle classes. Two more London joint stock banks were formed before 1836, the London Joint Stock Bank and the London and County Bank, on the model of the London and Westminster; by 1857 a further seven metropolitan banks had been established (33). The provisions of the 1826 Act did not apply to the London joint stock banks of the 1830s which meant, for instance, that they could not sue or be sued in the name of an officer. When the London and Westminster petitioned the House of Commons for these powers, the necessary bill was opposed successfully by the Bank of England which had refused already the London and Westminster a drawing account. The London joint stock banks could not accept bills at less than six months, a restriction which the Bank of England insisted should continue with respect to the London banks on the renewal of its charter in 1833. In 1836 the Bank of England announced that it would not discount bills bearing the endorsement of a note issuing joint stock bank or bills payable at the London and Westminster (34). The new London banks were also opposed by the London private bankers who refused the London and Westminster admission to the Clearing House (35). The London joint stock banks prospered in spite of these restrictions; the deposits of the London and Westminster in 1836 were £643,332 and by 1846 had reached £3,280,864.

The general economic prosperity of the first half of the 1830s provided a favourable environment for the development of joint stock banks of which 114 were in existence in 1837. Joplin was one of the promoters of the National Provincial Bank of England and although he was in favour of a London base for the bank (31), the profits from issuing notes kept the National Provincial from establishing a London branch until 1866. The National Provincial began with a large branch network, acquired by taking over existing private banks (36), a precedent for the scale of banking in the second half of the nineteenth century, however most of the provincial joint stock banks established in the 1830s were small scale and local institutions (37). Many of the provincial banks within a few years of their formation ceased issuing notes and became deposit banks. They offered interest on all balances kept with them, competed ruthlessly on the rates of interest that they offered, kept no reserves except till money, and relied on rediscounting to maintain their liquidity (38). Their habit of investing in bills of exchange and their dependence on rediscounting increased the importance of the role of the London bill broker and widened the London money market.

Rediscounting combined with mismanagement lead to excesses and failures of which the most spectacular examples were the insolvencies of the Northern and Central Bank of England, the North of England Banking Company, and the Norwich and Norfolk Banking Company. Rediscounting was necessary for the banking system to operate efficiently nationally since, without banks with wide branch networks, the practice allowed funds to move from surplus to deficit areas via the London money market. Rediscounting in the 1830s came to be used for accommodation purposes rather than for sound trading to such an extent that it undermined the stability of the banking system. The abuse of rediscounting was a result of poor management and the 1826 Act allowed great liberality, controlling neither the constitution nor the conduct of the joint stock banks.

By the spring of 1836 the position and affairs of many of the new joint stock banks was giving rise to anxiety which lead to William Clay in the House of Commons to move for a select committee to investigate their conduct. Clay was in favour of limited liability, fully subscribed capitals, and complete publicity of the banks' affairs; this he thought would give rise to a sound banking system. The select committee which sat until 1838 examined in detail the constitution and business of the new banks and found in many cases the existence of management poor in quality and banks with inadequate capitals. The first report of the committee showed the inadequacy of the 1826 Act and suggested that banks should be regulated more closely (39). The evidence collected by the 1840–1 select committee was equally adverse; few of the creations of the 1835–6 boom came up to the rigorous standards of the National Provincial which employed inspectors to check on the manage-

ment of its branches (36). The situation revealed by the committees of 1836–8 and 1840–1 put a damper on the creation
of further banks and paved the way for new legislation. Between
1838 and 1843 banking law was amended in a minor way; in
1838 banks were allowed to be sued by or sue their shareholders
(1 & 2 Vict. c.96) and in 1840 this provision was extended to
include criminal cases (3 & 4 Vict. c.111) Clergymen were
allowed legally to be bank shareholders in 1841 (4 & 5 Vict.
c.14). Full repeal came in 1844 with the Bank Charter Act and
the Joint Stock Bank Act (7 & 8 Vict. c.113).

The Bank Charter Act was an attempt to centralise the note
issue in the hands of the Bank of England and consequently it
stipulated that there were to be no further banks of issue formed,
while the note circulation of the existing banks was to be
restricted. In future banks would forfeit their issuing powers if
they went bankrupt, ceased banking business, were converted
to a joint stock bank, or if they opened a London branch. There
were publicity provisions which required a weekly account of
the note issue of a bank, an annual return of a bank's proprietors,
and which allowed a bank's books to be inspected. An attempt
was made to check branch expansion by requiring a £30
licence for each new branch opened after 1844. The London
joint stock banks did benefit as the Act lifted the restriction on
their right to draw, accept, or endorse any bills other than those
payable on demand. Peel was also responsible for the introduction of the Joint Stock Bank Act under which all future joint
stock banks were to obtain a charter before their establishment
and were required to have a minimum nominal capital of
£100,000 divided into shares whose lowest denomination was
to be £100. In order to form a bank, a deed of partnership had
to be constituted by the holders of at least half of the bank's
shares on which ten per cent of the capital had been subscribed.
The deed, together with a petition for a charter then had to be
submitted to the Board of Trade for scrutiny. If a bank was
successful in obtaining a charter, it could commence business
once 50 per cent of its capital was subscribed. The restrictions

on the London joint stock banks were entirely removed by the Act which allowed them to sue and be sued in the name of an officer. The Joint Stock Bank Act did not incorporate Clay's suggestion of granting limited liability nor did it stipulate that all of a bank's capital had to be subscribed but the banking code of 1844 did extend the provisions regarding the publicity to be given to bank's affairs. This system of banking regulation was extended to Scotland and Ireland in 1846 (9 & 10 Vict. c.75). The Act's major effect as a result of its onerous conditions was to greatly reduce the number of banking promotions; between 1844 and 1857 when the Act was repealed only twelve new banks were formed. The 1844 code did not raise the standard of banking; four of the twelve banks formed under the Act failed or went into liquidation during the Act's duration, the most important failure being the Royal British Bank in 1856 (40). The excesses of the Royal British Bank and the London and Eastern Bank, which failed in 1857, persuaded Lowe in 1857 to repeal the 1844 Act and place banks on the same legal basis as other corporate companies, though this was not achieved fully until the consolidation of company law in 1862.

While there were the same number of joint stock banks in existence in 1860 as there had been in 1840, there were considerable changes in the size and importance of the joint stock banks during this period. The deposits of the banks rose, for example the deposits the London Joint Stock banks had increased from £4 million to £40 million in 1857, and in 1855 the London joint stock banks began to open branches. The growth in deposit banking was not simply a result of the 1844 restrictions on the note issue but was also stimulated by the increasing use of the cheque. In 1853 a penny uniform stamp duty on cheques replaced the previous regressive scale and the process of cheque clearing was simplified and cheapened during the 1850s through the enlargement of the London Clearing House. Since the 1830s the London joint stock banks had continued to press to be admitted to the clearing. In June 1853 it was decided that settlements between joint stock and private banks could be made by Bank of England cheques rather than notes and finally in 1854 the London joint stock banks were admitted to the Clearing House. A country clearing system was established by the London Clearing House in 1858, following the threat of independent action by the country bankers, and in 1864 the Bank of England joined the system. The increase in the number of London joint stock banks resulted in open competition for deposits through the rate of interest offered. The banks were limited in setting their deposit rate by the return they obtained from utilising such funds so that by the mid-1850s the general practice was to offer 1 per cent below Bank Rate on deposits, Bank Rate being a general indicator of the level of the money market rate. This structure of interest rates was shaken in 1857 when Bank Rate rose to 10 per cent during the crisis. The London and Westminster refused to raise its deposit rate above 8 per cent and the other London banks followed a similar policy (41). There was a tacit agreement from the early 1860s between the London banks that there should be a ceiling on deposit rates during a crisis period. In the provinces deposit rates did not have such a direct relationship with Bank rate, being generally fixed at $2\frac{1}{2}$ per cent, and this remained the practice until after World War I (42).

Company Law was radically altered in 1855–6 with introduction of the limited liability and the simplification of the process of company registration. The reform was extended to include the banks by a series of acts passed in 1857 (20 & 21 Vict. c.49) and 1858 (21 & 22 Vict. c.91) but certain features of the 1844 banking code, such as the £100 minimum share value, were retained, and banks were not placed on an equal legal footing with other companies until the consolidation of company law in 1862 (25 & 26 Vict. c.89) (43). The repeal of the 1844 banking code together with an upturn in economic activity in 1862 lead to a rapid increase in the number of banks and associated financial institutions; between 1863 and 1866, 876 companies were publicly promoted of which 108 were either banks, discount, or finance companies (44). In the boom of the early 1870s, there was a further flurry of bank formations and altogether between 1860 and 1874, 24 new domestic joint stock banks were successfully established. The new banks took up limited liability from their inception but the banks formed prior to 1858 remained on the whole unlimited. Many bankers saw an advantage in being unlimited as it provided apparently an additional element of security for their depositors. This belief in unlimited liability was overthrown in 1878 by the failure of the City of Glasgow Bank, an unlimited concern (45). Its shareholders were twice asked for capital to meet the bank's debts; the first call was for £500 per £100 stock held and it fell on 1,800 separate individuals, resulting in the bankruptcy of a third of the proprietors. A second call of £2,250 per £100 held was made and was met by 269 shareholders. The severity of the failure of the City of Glasgow Bank produced considerable disquiet and unease amongst bank shareholders generally and resulted in the general adoption of limited liability by joint stock banks. The legal difficulties which this entailed were overcome by an Act passed in 1879 (42 & 43 Vict. c.76) (46) which embodied the principle of reserved liability. The London joint stock banks registered under the Act in 1882.

Since 1826 there had been a tendency towards increasing concentration in banking; between 1825 and 1843 there were 122 amalgamations of which 93 involved the absorption of private banks by joint stock. There was a lull after 1844 but with the expansion in the number of joint stock banks in the 1860s and 1870s there was an increase in the incidence of amalgamations. The 1860s were marked by joint stock banks taking over the more important private concerns; in 1864 the London and Westminster acquired Messrs Jones Loyd & Co and the Bank of Manchester bought Messrs Heywood, Kennard. After 1870 the process of consolidation changed in character with an increase in the number of amalgamations between joint stock banks which gave rise first to important regional banks and then banks with a national network of branches. By

1904 there were 14 London joint stock banks, 39 provincial joint stock banks, and 12 national joint stock banks and the latter had the largest number of branches, 2,721, and control over the greater volume of deposits, £362·4 million. At this time there were 35 provincial private banks of which 18 were note issuing. Amalgamations continued and resulted in the emergence of the 'big five' joint stock banks by 1918 which led to an informal agreement with the government that there should be no further mergers involving major banks (47).

Bank branches by the 1880s were being opened in the suburbs and rural areas with the banks acquiring the accounts of small tradesmen and shopkeepers. This geographical and social extension of the banking habit increased further the use of the cheque, while a similar economy of notes and coins was arising through development of savings banks and postal orders (48). During the nineteenth century the English joint stock banks seldom became involved in the provision of long term finance to industry. This was due to both the lack of demand for such funds because of the long established tradition amongst industrialists of self-finance and to the liquidity risks that such loans involved. When industrial banking did occur, it often played a part in bank failures as for instance with the closure of the Royal British Bank in 1856 which lost £100,000 in a loan to the Cefn Iron and Coal Works. After 1860 one change did occur in banking practice, prompted by the decline in the use of the inland bill of exchange, the London joint stock banks began to accept foreign bills of exchange (49). English joint stock banking during the nineteenth century was concerned predominantly with the amassing of deposits which were lent in various ways, but usually on a short term basis.

————

27 The Banking Co-partnerships Act, 1826

————

Whereas an Act was passed in the Thirty-ninth and Fortieth Years of the Reign of His late Majesty King George the Third, intituled *An Act for establishing an agreement with the Governor and Company of the Bank of England, for advancing the sum of Three Millions towards the Supply for the Service of the Year One Thousand Eight Hundred*: And whereas it was, to prevent Doubts as to the Privilege of the said Governor and Company, enacted and declared in the said recited Act, that no other Bank should be erected, established, or allowed by Parliament; and that it should not be lawful for any Body Politic or Corporate whatsoever, erected or to be erected, or for any other Persons united or to be united in Covenants and Partnerships, exceeding the Number of Six Persons, in that Part of *Great Britain* called *England*, to borrow, owe or take up any Sum or Sums of Money of their Bills or Notes payable on Demand, or at any less Time than Six Months from the borrowing thereof, during the continuance of the said Privilege to the said Governor and Company, who were thereby declared to be and remain a Corporation, with the Privilege of exclusive Banking, as before recited; but subject nevertheless to Redemption on the Terms and conditions in the Said Act specified: And whereas the Governor and Company of the Bank of England have consented to relinquish so much of their exclusive Privilege as prohibits any Body Politic or Corporate, or any Number of Persons exceeding Six, in *England*, acting in Copartnership, from borrowing, owing or taking up any Sum or Sums of Money on their Bills or Notes payable on Demand, or at any less time than Six months from the borrowing thereof; provided that such Body Politic or Corporate, or Persons united in Covenants or Partnerships, exceeding the Number of Six Persons in each Copartnership, shall have the whole of their Banking Establishments and carry on their Business as Bankers at any Place or Places in *England* exceeding the Distance of Sixty-five Miles from *London*, and that all the Individuals composing such Corporations or Copartnerships, carrying on such business, shall be liable to and responsible for the due Payment of all Bills and Notes issued by such Corporations or Copartnerships respectively: be it further enacted by the King's Most Excellent

Majesty, by and with the advice and consent of the Lords Spiritual and Temporal, and Commons, in this present Parliament assembled, and by the Authority of the same, that from and after the passing of this Act it shall and may be lawful for any Bodies Politic or Corporate erected for the Purposes of Banking, or for any Number of Persons united in Covenants or Copartnerships, although such persons so united or carrying on business together shall consist of more than Six in Number, to carry on the Trade or Business of Bankers in *England*, in like Manner as Copartnerships of Bankers consisting of not more than Six Persons in Number may lawfully do; and for such Bodies Politic or Corporate or such Persons so united as aforesaid, to make and issue their Bills or Notes at any Place or Places in *England* exceeding the Distance of Sixty-Five Miles from *London*, payable on Demand, or otherwise at some Place or Places specified upon such Bills or Notes, exceeding the Distance of Sixty-Five Miles from *London*, and not elsewhere, and to borrow, owe, or take up any Sum or Sums of Money on their Bills or Notes so made and issued at any such Place or Places as aforesaid: Provided always, that such Corporations or Persons carrying on such Trade or Business of Bankers in Copartnership shall not have any House of Business or Establishments as Bankers in *London*, or at any Place or Places not exceeding the Distance of Sixty-Five Miles from *London*; and that every Member of such Corporation or Copartnership shall be liable and be responsible for the due Payment of Bills and Notes which shall be borrowed, owed, or taken up by the Corporation or Copartnership of which such Person shall be a Member, such Person being a Member at the Period of the Date of the Bills or Notes, or becoming or being a Member before or at the Time of the Bills or Notes being payable, or being such Member at the Time of the borrowing, owing or taking up of any Sum or Sums of Money upon any Bills or Notes by the Corporation or Copartnership, or while any Sum of Money on any Bills or Notes is owing or unpaid, or at the Time the same became due from the Corporation or Copartnership; any Agreement, Covenant, or Contract to the contrary notwithstanding.

II. Provided always, and be it further enacted, That nothing in this Act be contained shall extend to be construed to extend to enable or authorize any such Corporation or Copartnership exceeding the Number of Six Persons, so carrying on the Trade or Business of Bankers as aforesaid, either by any Member of or Person belonging to any such Corporation or Copartnership, or by any Agent or Agents, or any other Person or Persons on behalf of any such Corporation or Copartnership to issue or re-issue in *London*, or at any Place or Places not exceeding the Distance of Sixty-Five Miles from *London*, any Bill or Note of such Corporation or Copartnership, which shall be payable to Bearer on Demand, or any Bank Post Bill; nor to draw upon any Partner or Agent, or other Person or Persons who may be resident in *London*, or at any Place or Places not exceeding the Distance of Sixty-Five Miles from *London*, any Bill of Exchange which shall be payable on Demand, or which shall be for a less Amount than Fifty Pounds: Provided also, that it shall be lawful notwithstanding anything herein or in the said recited Act contained, for any such Corporation or Copartnership to draw any Bill of Exchange for any Sum of Money amounting to the Sum of Fifty Pounds or upwards payable, either in London or elsewhere, at any period after date or after sight.

III. Provided also, and be it further enacted, That nothing in this Act contained shall extend or be construed to extend to enable or authorize any such Corporation or Copartnership exceeding the Number of Six Persons, so carrying on the Trade or Business of Bankers in London as aforesaid, or any Member, Agent, or Agent of any such Corporation or Copartnership, to borrow, owe, or take up in *London*, or at any Place or Places not exceeding the Distance of Sixty-Five Miles from *London*, any Sum or Sums of Money on any Bill or Promissory Note of any such Corporation or Copartnership payable on Demand, or at any less Time than Six Months from the borrowing thereof, nor to make or issue any Bill or Bills of Exchange or Promissory

Note or Notes of such Corporation or Copartnership contrary to the Provisions of the said recited Act of the Thirty-Ninth and Fortieth Year of King George the Third, save as provided by this Act in that Behalf: Provided also, That nothing herein contained shall extend to be construed to extend to prevent any such Corporation or Copartnership, by any Agent or Person authorized by them, from discounting in London or elsewhere, any Bill or Bills of Exchange not drawn by or upon any Person on their Behalf.

IV. And be it further enacted, That before any such Corporation or Copartnership exceeding the Number of Six Persons, in *England* shall begin to issue any Bills or Notes, or borrow, owe, or take up any Money, on their Bills or Notes, an Account or Return shall be made out, according to the form contained in the Schedule, marked (A) to this Act annexed, wherein shall be set forth the true Names, Title, or Firm of such intended or existing Corporation or Copartnership, and also the Names and Places of Abode of all the Members of such Corporation or of all Partners concerned or engaged in such Copartnership as the same respectively shall appear on the books of such Corporation or Copartnership and the Name or Firm of every Bank or Banks established or to be established by such Corporation or Copartnership, and also the Names and Places of Abode of Two or more Persons, being Members of such Corporation or Copartnership, and being resident in *England*, who shall have been appointed Public Officers of such Corporation or Copartnership together with the Title or Office or other Description of every such Public Officer respectively, in the name of any One of whom such Corporation shall sue or be sued as hereinafter provided, and also the Name of every Town and Place where any of the Bills or Notes of such Corporation or Copartnership shall be issued by any such Corporation, or by their Agent or Agents; and every such Account or Return shall be delivered to the Commissioners of Stamps, at the Stamp Office in *London*, who shall cause the same to be filed and kept in the said Stamp Office and an Entry and Registry thereof to be made in a Book or Books to be there kept for that Purpose by some Person or Persons to be appointed by the said Commissioners in that Behalf, and Book or Books any Person or Persons shall from time to time have liberty to search and inspect on Payment of the Sum of One Shilling for every Search.

V. And be it further enacted, That such Account or Return shall be made out by the Secretary or other Person, being One of the Public Officers appointed as aforesaid, and shall be verified by the Oath of such Secretary or other Public Officer, taken before any Justice of the Peace, and which Oath any Justice of the Peace is hereby authorized and empowered to administer; and that such Account or Return shall, between the 28th of *February* and the 25th day of *March* in every year, after such Corporation or Copartnership shall be formed, be in like Manner delivered by such Secretary or other Public Officer as aforesaid to the Commissioners of Stamps, to be filed and kept in the Manner and for the Purpose as hereinbefore mentioned.

VI. And be it further enacted, That a copy of any such Account or Return so filed or kept and registered at the Stamp Office, as by this Act is directed, and which Copy shall be certified to be a true copy under the Hand or Hands of One or more of the Commissioners of Stamps for the Time being, upon Proof made that such Certificate has been signed with the Handwriting of the Person or Persons making the same, and whom it shall not be necessary to prove to be a Commission or Commissioners, shall in all Proceedings, Civil or Criminal, and in all Cases whatsoever, be received in evidence as Proof of the Appointment and Authority of the Public Officers named in such Account or Return, and also of the Fact that all Person named therein as Member of such Corporation or Copartnership were Members thereof at the date of such Account or Return.

VII. And be it further enacted, That the said Commissioners of Stamps for the time being shall, and they are hereby required, upon application made to them by any Person or Persons requiring a Copy certified according to this Act, to any such

Account or Return as aforesaid, in order that the same be
produced in Evidence or any other Purpose, to deliver to the
Person or Persons so applying for the same such certified Copy,
he, she, or they paying for the same a Sum of Ten Shillings and
no more.

VIII. Provided also, and be it further enacted, That the Secretary or other Officer of every such Corporation or Copartnership shall, and he is hereby required, from Time to Time, as
often as occasion shall render it necessary make out upon Oath,
in Manner hereinbefore directed, and cause to be delivered to
the Commissioners of Stamps as aforesaid, a further Account
or Return according to the Form contained in the Schedule
marked (B) to this Act annexed, of the Name or Names of any
Person or Persons who shall have been nominated or appointed
a new or additional Public Officer or Public Officers of such
Corporation or Copartnership, and also of the Name or Names
of any Person or Persons who shall have ceased to be Members of
such Corporation or Copartnership, and also of the Name or
Names of any Person or Persons who shall have become a
Member or Members of such Corporation or Copartnership,
either in addition to or in the Place or Stead of any former
Member or Members thereof, and of the Name or Names of
any new or additional Town or Towns, Place or Places, where
such Bills or Notes are or are intended to be issued and where
the same are to be made payable; and such further Accounts
or Returns shall from Time to Time be filed and kept and
entered and registered at the Stamp Office in *London*, in like
Manner as hereinbefore required with respect to the original
or annual Account or Return hereinbefore directed to be made.

IX. And be it further enacted, That all Actions and Suits, and
also all Petitions to found any Commission of Bankruptcy against
any Person or Persons, who may be at any Time indebted to
any such Copartnership carrying on Business under the
Provisions of this Act, and all Proceedings at Law or in Equity
to be commenced or instituted for or on behalf of any such
Copartnership against any Person or Persons, Bodies Politic or

Corporate, or others, whether Members of such Copartnerships or otherwise, for recovering any debts or enforcing any claims or Demands due to such Copartnerships, for for any other Matter relating to the concerns of such Copartnership, shall and lawfully may, from and after the passing of this Act, be commenced or instituted and prosecuted in the Name of any One of the Public Offices nominated as aforesaid for the Time being of such Copartnership, as the nominal Plaintiff or Petitioner for and on behalf of such Copartnership; and that all Actions or Suits, and Proceedings at Law or in Equity, to be commenced or instituted by any Person or Persons, Bodies Politic, or Corporate, or others whether Members of such Copartnership or otherwise, against such Copartnership, shall and lawfully may be commenced, instituted and prosecuted against any one or more of the Public Officers nominated as aforesaid for the Time being of such Copartnership, as the nominal Defendant for and on behalf of such Copartnership; and that all Indictments, Informations and Prosecutions by or on behalf of such Copartnerships, for any Stealing or Embesslement of any Money, Goods, Effects, Bills, Notes, Securities, or other Property of or belonging to such Copartnership, or for any Fraud, Forgery, Crime or Offence committed against or with Intent to injure or defraud such Copartnership, shall and Lawfully may be had, preferred, and carried on in the Name of any One of the Public Officers nominated as aforesaid for the Time being of such Copartnership; and that in all Indictments and Informations to be had or preferred by or on behalf of such Copartnership against any Person or Persons may whomsoever, notwithstanding such Person or Persons may happen to be a Member or Members of such Copartnership, it shall be lawful or sufficient to state the Money, Goods, Effects, Bills, Notes Securities or other Property of any One of the Public Officers nominated as aforesaid for the Time being of such Copartnership; and that any Forgery, Fraud, Crime or other Offence committed against or with Intent to injure or defraud any such Copartnership shall and lawfully may, any

R

such Indictment or Indictments notwithstanding as aforesaid, be laid or stated to have been committed against or with Intent to injure or defraud any one of the Public Officers nominated as aforesaid for the time being of such Copartnership; any Offender or Offenders may thereupon be lawfully convicted for any such Forgery, Fraud, Crime or Offence; and that in all other Allegations, Indictments, Informations or other Proceedings of any kind whatsoever, in which it otherwise might or would have been necessary to state the Names of the Persons composing such Copartnership, it shall and may be lawful and sufficient to state the Name of any One of the Public Officers nominated as aforesaid for the Time being of such Copartnership; and the Death, Resignation, Removal or any Act of such Public Officer, shall not abate or prejudice any such Action, Suit, Indictment, Information, Prosecution, or other Proceeding commenced against or by or on behalf of such Copartnership, but the same may be continued, prosecuted, and carried on in the Names of any other Public Officers of such Copartnership for the Time being.

X. And be it further enacted, That no Person or Persons, or Body or Bodies Politic or Corporate, having or claiming to have any Demand upon or against any such Corporation or Copartnership, shall bring more than One Action or Suit, in case the Merits shall have been tried in such Action or Suit, in respect of such Demand; and the Proceedings in any Action or Suit, by or against any one of the Public Officers nominated as aforesaid for the Time being of any such Copartnership, may be pleaded in bar of any other Action or Actions, Suit or Suits, for the same Demand, by or against any other of the Public Officers of such Copartnership.

XI. And be it further enacted, That all and every Decree or Decrees, Order or Orders, made or pronounced in any Suit or Proceeding in any Court of Equity against any Public Officer of any such Copartnership carrying on Business under the Provisions of this Act, shall have the like effect and Operation upon and against the Property and Funds of such Copartnership and upon and against the Persons and Property of every or any Member or Members thereof, as if every or any such Members of such Copartnership were Parties before the Court to and in any such Suit or Proceeding; and that it shall and may be lawful for any Court in which such Order or Decree shall have been made, to cause such Order or Decree to be enforced against every or any Members of such Copartnership in like Manner as if every member of such Copartnership were Parties before such Court to and in such Suit or Proceeding, and although such Members are not before the Court.

XII. And be it further enacted, That all and every Judgement and Judgements, Decree or Decrees, which shall at any Time after the passing of this Act be had to recovered or entered up as aforesaid, in any Action, Suit, or Proceedings in Law or Equity against any Public Officer of any such Copartnership, shall have the like Effect and Operation upon and against the Property of such Copartnership, and upon and against the Property of every such Member thereof as aforesaid, as if such Judgement or Judgements had been recovered or obtained against such Copartnership; and that the Bankruptcy, Insolvency, or stopping Payment of any such Public Officer for the Time being of such Copartnership, in his individual Character or Capacity, shall not be nor construed to be the Bankruptcy, Insolvency or stopping Payment of such Copartnership; and that such Copartnership and every Member thereof, and the Capital Stock and Effects of such Copartnership, and the Effects of every Member of such Copartnership, shall in all cases, notwithstanding the Bankruptcy, Insolvency or stopping Payment of any such Public Officer, be attached and attachable, and be in all respects liable to the lawful Claims and Demands of the Creditor and Creditors of such Copartnership, or of any Member or Members thereof, as if no such Bankruptcy, Insolvency, or stopping Payment of such Public Officer of such Copartnership had happened or taken place.

XIII. And be it further enacted, Execution upon any Judgement in any Action obtained against any Public Officer for the time being of any such Corporation or Copartnership carrying on the Business of Banking under the Provisions of this Act, whether as Plaintiff or Defendant, may be issued against any Member or Members for the Time being of such Corporation or Copartnership; and that in case of any such Execution against any Member or Members for the Time being of such Corporation or Copartnership shall be ineffectual for obtaining Payment and Satisfaction of the Amount of such Judgement, it shall be lawful for the Party or Parties so having obtained Judgement against such Public Officer for the Time being, to issue execution against any Person or Persons who was or were a Member or Members of such Corporation or Copartnership at the Time when the Contract or Contracts or Engagement or Engagements in which such Judgement may have been obtained was or were entered into, or became a Member at any Time before such Contracts or Engagements were executed, or was a Member at the Time of the Judgement obtained; Provided always, that no such Execution as last mentioned shall be issued without Leave first granted, on Motion in open Court, by the Court in which such Judgement shall ove been obtained, and when Motion shall be made on Notice to the Person or Persons sought to be charged, nor after the Expiration of Three Years next after any such Person or Persons shall have ceased to be a Member or Members of such Corporation or Copartnership.

XIV. Provided always and be it further enacted, That every such Public Officer in whose Name any such Suit or Action shall have been commenced, prosecuted, or defended, and every Person or Persons against whom Execution upon any Judgement obtained or entered up as aforesaid in any such Action shall be issued as aforesaid, shall always be reimbursed and fully indemnified for all Loss, Damages, Costs, and Charges, without Deduction, which any such Officer or Person may have incurred by reason of such Execution, out of the Funds of such Copartnership, or any Failure thereof, by Contribution from the other Members of such Copartnership, as in the ordinary Cases of Copartnership.

XV. And to prevent any Doubts that might arise whether the said Governor and Company, under any by virtue of their Charter, and the several Acts of Parliament which have been made and passed in relation to the Affairs of the said Governor and Company, can lawfully carry on the Trade or Business of Banking, otherwise than under the immediate Order, Management, and Direction of the Court of Directors of the said Governor and Company; be it further enacted, That it shall and may be lawful for the said Governor and Company to authorise and empower any Committee or Committees, Agent or Agents, to carry on the Trade and Business of Banking, for and on behalf of the said Governor and Company, at any Place or Places in that Part of the United Kingdom called *England*, and for that purpose to invest such Committee or Committees, Agent or Agents, with such Powers of Management and Superintendance, and other Authority to appoint Cashiers and other Officers and Servants as may be necessary or convenient for carrying on such Trade and Business as aforesaid; and for the same Purpose to issue to such Committee or Committees, Agent or Agents, Cashier or Cashiers, or other Officer or Officers, Servant or Servants, Cash, Bills of Exchange, Bank Post Bills, Bank Notes, Promissory Notes and other Securities for Payment of Money: Provided always, that all such Acts of the said Governor and Company shall be done and exercised in such Manners as may be appointed by any Bye Laws, Constitutions, Orders, Rules, and Directions from Time to Time hereafter to be made by the General Court of the said Governor and Company in that Behalf, such Bye Laws not being repugnant to the Laws of the Part of the United Kingdom called *England*; and in all Cases where such Bye Laws, Constitutions, Orders, Rules, or Directions of the said General Court shall be wanting, in such Manner as the Governor, Deputy-Governor and Directors, or the Major Part of them assembled, whereof the said Governor or Deputy-Governor is always to be One, shall or may direct, such Directions not being repugnant to the Laws of that part of the United Kingdom called

England, anything in the said Charter or Acts of Parliament, or other Law, Usage, Matter or Thing to the contrary thereof notwithstanding: Provided always, that in any Place, where Trade and Business of Banking shall be carried on for and on behalf of the said Governor and Company of the Bank of England, any Promissory Note issued on their Account in such Place shall be made payable in Coin in such Place as well as in *London.*

XVI. And be it further enacted, That if any Corporation or Copartnership carrying on the Trade or Business of Bankers under the Authority of this Act be desirous of issuing and re-issuing Notes in the Nature of Bank Notes, payable to the Bearer on Demand, without the same being stamped as by Law is required, it shall be lawful for them so to do on giving Security by Bond to His Majesty, His Heirs, and Successors, in which Bond Two of the Directors, Members, or Partners of such Corporation or Copartnership shall be the Obligators, together with the Cashier or Cashiers, or Accountant or Accountants employed by such Corporation or Copartnership, as the said Commissioners of Stamps shall require and such Bonds shall be taken as such reasonable Sums as the Duties may amount unto in the Period of One Year, with condition to deliver to the said Commissioner of Stamps, within Fourteen Days after the *Fifth* day of January, the *Fifth* day of April, the *Fifth* day of *July,* and the *Tenth* day of October in every Year, whilst the present Stamp Duties shall remain in force, a just and true Account, verified upon the Oaths or Affirmations of Two Directors, Members or Partners of such Corporation or Co- partnership, and of the said Cashier or Cashiers, Accountant or Accountants, or such of them as the said Commissioner of Stamps shall require, such Oaths or Affirmations to be taken before any Justice of the Peace as hereby authorised and empowered to administer, of the Amount or Value of all their Promissory Notes in Circulation on some given Day in every Week, for the Space of One Quarter of a Year prior to the Quarter Day immediately preceding the Delivery on such

Account, together with the Average Amount or Value thereof according to such Account; and also to pay, or cause to be paid into the Hands of the Receivers General all Stamp Duties in *Great Britain*, as a Composition for the Duties which would otherwise have been payable for such Promissory Notes issued within the Space of One Year, the Sum of Seven Shillings for every One hundred Pounds, and also for the Fractional Part of One Hundred Pounds, of the said Average Amount or Value of such Notes in Circulation, according to the true Intent and Meaning of this Act; and on the due Performance thereof such Bond shall be void; and it shall be lawful for the said Commissioners to fix the Time or Times of making such Payment, and to specify the same in the Condition to every such Bond; and every such Bond may be required to be renewed from Time to Time, at the Discretion of the said Commissioners or the major Part of them, and as often as the same shall be forfeited, or Party or Parties to the same, or any of them, shall die, become bankrupt or insolvent, or reside in Parts beyond the Seas.

XVII. Provide always, and be it further enacted, That no such Corporation or Copartnership shall be obliged to take out more than Four Licences for the issuing of any Promissory Notes for Money payable to the Bearer on Demand, allowed by Law to be re-issued in all for any Number of Towns or Places in *England*; and in case any such Corporation or Copartnership shall issue such Promissory Notes as aforesaid, by themselves or their Agents, at more than Four different Towns or Places in *England*, then after taking out Three distinct Licences for Three of such Towns or places, such Corporation or Copartnership shall be entitled to have all the rest of such Towns or Places included in the Fourth Licence.

XVIII. And be it further enacted, That if any such Corporation or Copartnership exceeding the Number of Six Persons in *England* shall begin to issue any Bills or Notes, or to borrow, owe, or take up any Money on their Bills or Notes, without having caused such account to Return as aforesaid to be made out and delivered in the Manner and Form directed by this

Act, or so neglect or omit to cause such Account to be renewed Yearly and every Year, between the days of Times hereinbefore appointed for that Purpose, such Corporation or Copartnership so offending shall, for each and every Week they so neglect to make such Account or Return, forfeit the Sum of Five Hundred Pounds; and if any Secretary or other Officer of such Corporation or Copartnership shall make out or sign any false Account or Return, or Any Account or Return which shall not truly set forth all the several Particulars by this Act required to be contained or inserted in such Account or Return, the Corporation or Copartnership which such Secretary or other Officer so offending shall belong shall for every such Offence forfeit the sum of Five Hundred Pounds, and the said Secretary or other Officer making out or signing any such Account or Return as aforesaid, shall knowingly and willingly make a false Oath of or concerning any of the Matters to be therein specified and set forth, every such Secretary or other Officer so offending and being thereof lawfully convicted, shall be subject and liable to such Pain and Penalties as by any Law now in force Persons convicted of wilful and corrupt Perjury are subject and liable. XIX. And be it further enacted, That if any such Corporation or Copartnership exceeding the Number of Six Persons, so carrying on the Trade or Business of Bankers aforesaid, shall, either by any Member of or Person belonging to any such Corporation or Copartnership issue or re-issue in *London*, or at any Place or Places not exceeding the Distance of Sixty-Five Miles from *London*, any Bill or Note of such Corporation or Copartnership which shall be payable on Demand; or shall draw upon any Partner or Agent, or other Person or Persons, who may be resident in *London*, or at any Place or Places not exceeding the Distance of Sixty-Five Miles from London, any Bill of Exchange which shall be payable on Demand, or which shall be for a less Amount than Fifty Pounds; or if any such Corporation or Copartnership exceeding the Number of Six Persons, so carrying on the Trade or Business of Bankers in *England* as aforesaid, or any Member, Agent or Agents of any such Corporation or Copartnership, shall borrow, owe, or take up in *London*, or at any Place or Places not exceeding the Distance of Sixty-five Miles from *London*, any Sum or Sums of Money on any Bill or Promissory Note or Note of such Corporation or Copartnership payable on Demand, or at any less Time than Six Months from the borrowing thereof, or shall make or issue any Bill or Bills of Exchange or Promissory Notes of such Corporation or Copartnership contrary to the Provisions of the said recited Act of the Thirty-Ninth and Fortieth Years of King George the Third, save as provided by this Act, such Corporation or Copartnership so offending, or on whose Account or Behalf any such Offence as aforesaid shall be committed, shall for every Offence forfeit the Sum of Fifty Pounds.

XX. Provided also, and be it further enacted, That nothing in this Act contained shall extend or be construed to extend or to prejudice, alter, or affect any of the Rights, Powers, or Privileges of the said Governor and Company of the Bank of England; except as the said exclusive privilege of the Governor and Company is by this Act specially altered and varied.

XXI. And be it further enacted, That all pecuniary Penalties and Forfeitures imposed by this Act shall and may be sued for and recovered in His Majesty's Court of Exchequer at Westminster, in the same Manner as Penalties incurred under any Act or Acts relating to Stamp Duties may be sued for and recovered in such Court.

XXII. And be it further enacted, That this Act may be altered amended or repealed by any Acts to be passed in this present Session of Parliament.

SCHEDULES REFERRED TO BY THIS ACT

Schedule A

Return or Account to be entered at the Stamp Office in London, in pursuance of the Act passed in the Seventh Year of the Reign of King George the Fourth intituled (*Here insert the title of this Act*).

Firm or Name of the Banking Corporation or Copartnership, viz; (*Set forth the Firm or Name*)

Names and Places of Abode of all the Parties concerned or engaged in such Corporation or Copartnership, viz. (*Set forth all the names and Places of Abode*).

Names and Places of the Bank or Banks established by such Corporation or Copartnership, viz. (*Set forth all the Names and Places*).

Names and Description of the Public Officers of the said Banking Corporation or Copartnership, viz. (*Set forth all the Names and Descriptions*).

Names of the several Towns and Places where Bills or Notes of the said Banking Corporation of Copartnership are to be issued by the said Corporation or Copartnership, or their Agent or Agents, viz. (*Set forth the Names of the Towns and Places.*)

A.B. of — — Secretary (*or other Officer, describing the Office*) of the above Corporation or Copartnership maketh Oath and saith, That the above doth contain the Name, Style, and Firm of the above Corporation or Copartnership, and the Names and Places of Abode of the Several Members thereof, and all the Banks established by the said Corporation or Copartnership, and the Names, Title, Descriptions of the Public Officers of the said Corporation or Copartnership, and the Names of the Towns and Places where the Notes of the said Corporation or Copartnership are to be issued, as the same respectively appear in the Books of the said Corporation or Copartnership, and to the best of the Information, Knowledge, and Belief of this Deponent. Sworn by me — — Day of — — at — — in the County of — —

C.D., Justice of the Peace in and for the said County

Schedule B

Return or Account to be entered at the Stamp Office in London, on behalf of an Act passed in the Seventh Year of the Reign of

King George the Fourth, intituled (*Insert the Title of this Act*), viz.

Names of any and every new or additional Public Officer of the said Corporation or Copartnership, viz.

A.B. in the Room of C.D. deceased or removed (as the case may be). (*Set forth every name*).

Names of any and every Person who may have ceased to be a Member of such Corporation or Copartnership. (*Set forth every Name*).

Names of any additional towns or Places where Bills or Notes are to be issued, and where the same are to be payable.

A.B. of — — Secretary (*or other Officer*) of the above named Corporation or Copartnership maketh Oath and Saith, That the above doth contain the Name and Place of Abode of any and every Person who hath become or been appointed a Public Officer of the above Corporation or Copartnership, and also the Name and Place of Abode of any and every Person who hath ceased to be a Member of the said Corporation or Copartnership and of any and every Person who hath become a Member of the said Corporation or Copartnership and of any and every Person who hath become a Member of the said Copartnership since the Registry of the said Corporation or Copartnership on the — — day of — — 1st, as the same respectively appear on the Books of the said Corporation or Copartnership and to the best of the information, Knowledge, and Belief of this Deponent. Sworn before me, — — The day of — — at — — in the County of — —

C.D., Justice of the Peace in and for the said County. 7 Geo. IV, c.46.

28 R. Conway   Hostility to Corporate Banking

Conway was a London private banker and the pamphlet, of which the following is an extract, was written at the height of the 1820s boom. In it Conway opposed a Loan company which was attempting to obtain a charter from Parliament.

Of the view of a Loan Banking Company, notwithstanding

the high estimation in which the private characters of its members may stand in public, the British Public, I am persuaded, and more particularly its enlightened Representatives, cannot be mistaken. No one, however dim his mental eye may be, save actual idiotism, but will clearly see and distinctly too, that the grand and primary object of an establishment of this nature is, the attainment of an exorbitant rate of interest on their capital; or, in other words, self-aggrandisement.

Of an Establishment of the nature of that under present notice, considered in a moral point of view, too much cannot be said or written against its incorporation.

And for that express and undisguised purpose, the attention of the Legislature, and all those who are more immediately concerned in the guidance of public morals, this Treatise is more particularly and earnestly claimed.

That there are too many doors of this description already open to the unwary, the inexperienced, and the thoughtless, is a fact lamentably too obvious—Every concern professing to lend money on mortage, life interest, reversions, or indeed on any description of property whatever, even on the basis of the present legally restricted rate of interest, are only so many receptables inviting immorality and dissipation.

What then, I would ask, can the character of that Company or Money Lenders be, who step forward for the avowed purpose of encouraging what is here most deprecated. And what then can be said of a Company that will unblushingly ask, and as unfeelingly take from the already embarrassed tradesman, from Six to Seven per cent upon Loans above the present rate of Interest. That such a Company is actuated by principles of public good, cannot be said. Is it the poor and the needy that are the objects of their solicitude? Certainly not, for the poor they invite into poverty still greater, and the needy into positive ruin. Is it in contravention to the rate of interest exacted by any other Establishment? Certainly not.

That self-interest and self-aggrandisement, be the only aim of so formidable a Company, such as a Loan Banking Company would inevitably be, is a matter of serious enquiry, for the more legitimate arbiters of the merits and demerits of an association of the nature and characters here described.

Wealth creates power, and power creates influence, and when united in opposition to the public weal, becomes dangerous. I say this, fearlessly, in reference to the Equitable Loan Banking Company about to be established by legislative enactment: the interests of this Company are in direct opposition to the best interests of the Community; and when its baneful influence becomes extended over the empire, it will ingulph within its ruinous vortex, the best interests of the United Kingdom, and her dependent Colonies. It would involve its property in perplexities as numerous as inexplicable; and the danger that would ensue from a sudden change of property should be, and ought to be fearfully apprehended; which at times, even in private bargains and sales, have been surrounded with innumerable difficulties, real as well as mental; and, in some instances, insurmountable.

That a seriously destructive change of property would result from the measures of such a Company, and sanctioned by an Act of Parliament, is abundantly evident from the nature of that property itself which this Company propose taking into pledge: besides the ordinary description of property, such as Apparel and Trinkets, namely, British and Foreign produce; such as Baltic, West Indian, and Colonial produce, Hops, Raw Silk, Timber, Wool, and Wine, at a rate of interest, not less than Ten per Cent—that the prudent man will borrow money at so extravagant a rate of interest is not likely,—the wealthy importer, certainly not at all, nor the merchant in moderate circumstances, but rarely; but as much cannot be said of the needy importer, or the less substantial consignee: the contemplated consequences to such and their connexions is certain ruin! Here is a scope for the wild, the extravagant, and the thoughtless—Here is a facility of raising the wind, the whirlwind of destruction. R. Conway. *A treatise on the Impolicy of a Loan Banking Establishment* (1825), 3–6

29 T. Joplin   Banking and Limited Liability

Thomas Joplin (1790–1847), born in Newcastle, the son of a sculptor, was the propagandist for joint stock banking in England. His *Essay on Banking* (1822) contained a proposal for the formation of a joint stock bank on Tyneside while the 1826 edition of the *Essay* includes the prospectus for a London joint stock bank. These initial proposals met with no success and in 1824 Joplin became concerned with the formation of the Provincial Bank of Ireland; he was involved with the management of this bank until 1828. Joplin then became part of a group which in 1833 formed the National Provincial Bank of England. During the late 1830s Joplin, with the Committee of the Joint Stock Banks Association, set up a newspaper to protect the joint stock banking interest. After some differences of opinion with the board of the National Provincial, Joplin left the bank, dying abroad in 1847.

The Law, which, by confining the number of partner in Banks to six, prevented the establishment of Joint Stock Banking Companies, was considered the source of these evils, and the remedy proposed was an alteration of that Law. It was in consequence so far altered as to permit the establishment of Banking Companies at the distance of sixty-five miles from London.

The Act of the 7th of Geo. IV. Chap. 46, by which this alteration is effected, is extremely simple in principle. After authorising the formation of Banking Companies, consisting of an unlimited number of Partners, at any distance, not being less than sixty miles from London, it provides that the names of all the partners in each, shall be registered at the Stamp Office; that the company shall sue and be sued by a public officer; that each partner shall be liable for the engagements of the Company to the whole extent of his fortune; and that after obtaining judgement against the proper officer of the Company, the property of any shareholder may be taken into execution.

The severity of the law in this latter respect, and the great respectability and personal influence of the private Bankers throughout the country, prevented the public for some time from availing themselves of it. But a few Banks, after great efforts having been established, and proving pre-eminently successful, others followed with like results, until they have at length become general throughout the country, many private Bankers having been induced to coalesce with, and other to convert themselves into these companies. T. Joplin. *An Examination of the Report of the Joint Stock Bank Committee* (2nd edition 1837), 2–3

30 J. W. Gilbart   Joint Stock Banks

James William Gilbart (1794–1863), a practical banker, had an important influence on the development of joint stock banking in England. He received his early training as a banker with the London private bank of Everett, Walker & Co, and in 1827 was made manager of the Kilkenny and Waterford branches of the Provincial Bank of Ireland, the bank which Joplin had played a part in founding. Gilbart wrote *Practical Treatise on Banking* while at Kilkenny and the work was subsequently to go through many editions. He was also involved in adult education being a member of two London debating societies and the founder of one at Waterford, and it was this side of Gilbart's activities which later resulted in him being made a Fellow of the Royal Society in 1846, his nomination sponsored by G. R. Porter and T. Tooke. In 1833 Gilbart was appointed the general manager of the newly formed London and Westminster Bank and he held this post until 1859 when he became a director. Gilbart became very quickly an important figure in the joint stock banking world; in 1838 he and Vincent Stuckey were the official spokesmen for the Association of Joint Stock Banks. Gilbart wrote on many subjects, his two outstanding books on banking being *A Practical Treatise of Banking* and *History and Principles of Banking*.

As some persons abstain from becoming partners in joint stock banks, from an apprehension of the danger which they incur in consequence of the whole of their property being answerable for the debts of the bank, I shall quote those sections of the act (7 Geo. IV. c.46) which have reference to this subject . . .

From the above extracts it appears that no legal proceedings can be taken in the first instance against an individual shareholder, but must be directed against the public officer, whose name is registered at the Stamp Office. That not more than one action can be brought for one demand.—That after a shareholder has transferred his share, he is not liable for any debts which the bank may subsequently contract; nor for the debts contracted at the time he made the transfer, unless the execution issued against the funds of the bank, and against the existing shareholders, should be 'ineffectual for obtaining payment and satisfaction of the amount;' and in this case the proceeding must first be by motion in open court.—And that three years after the transfer, the party is released from all responsibility, though the funds of the bank should be annihilated, and every shareholder become bankrupt.

This responsibility, which even legally considered is very trifling, may be still farther limited by the deed of settlement. When a Joint Stock Bank is formed, a deed of partnership is prepared, and is signed by every shareholder. This instrument is called a deed of settlement. The shareholders have no power to limit their responsibility in reference to their creditors, but they may do so in reference to each other; and may guarantee one another against any claims that may be advanced against any one of their number: this is actually done. The deed of settlement provides that no shareholder shall be answerable for the debts of the bank to a greater extent than the proportionate amount of his share; and that the moment he has transferred his shares to another party, he is wholly free from any claims or responsibility whatever. The act of parliament says to every shareholder, 'you are responsible to the whole extent of your property for all the debts of the bank.' The deed of settlement says to him, 'if any claims be made upon you, while a shareholder, by the creditors of the bank, we, the other shareholders, engage to pay our proportion of the debt; and if you have ceased to be a shareholder, we indemnify you against any claim whatever.' It is obvious then, that while the other shareholders continue in a state of solvency, no individual shareholder runs any risk. This may be illustrated by supposing an extreme case. I will suppose that I am holder of five shares in a banking company, whose stock is divided into ten thousand shares; and that all the money paid up, whatever it may be, is lost, and the bank is 20,000 in debt. The proportion of this debt which I ought to pay is 10. The creditor sues the public officer of the bank, and obtains judgement against him; and considering me to be a rich man, he singles me out as the shareholder against whom he will first issue execution. The sheriff's officers seize my goods and chattels, or whatever property I have, to the extent of the £20,000. This is the law, and I have no redress. But in the deed of settlement it is covenanted and agreed that no shareholder shall be answerable for the debts of the company, to a greater extent than the proportionate amount of his shares; and all the shareholders guarantee every one of their number against any claim beyond this proportion. Now then, though I have no redress against the creditor, I have a redress against the other shareholders and I will sue them upon the deed of settlement. As soon as I have obtained judgement, I will issue execution against their property, until I have re-paid myself the whole £20,000, excepting the £10 which is my proportion of the loss. I have here supposed the case to proceed to extremities; but it is highly improbable that the affairs of any bank would be allowed to proceed to this extremity. As soon as the state of its affairs were known, a meeting of the proprietors would take place; they would pay down the £2 per share which they had lost; the deed of settlement would be put into the fire; and there would be an end of the company.

It appears then that the enactment which renders the whole

s

of the property of every shareholder answerable for the debts of the bank, is very just and satisfactory. It is satisfactory to the public, inasmuch as it gives them the most ample guarantee for the payment of the debts of the bank, whether those debts arise from notes or deposits. It is satisfactory to the shareholders; for although each shareholder may consider the whole of his property liable for all claims upon the bank, yet he knows that by the deed of settlement the property of all the other shareholders is answerable to him for all claims, beyond the proportionate amount of his shares: and hence the guarantee to him is just as ample as the guarantee to the public.

So far from militating against the interest of the shareholders, this enactment has the effect of increasing their profits, inasmuch as it enables them to carry on business with a less amount of capital—and hence to make a larger dividend. I will suppose that a banking company employs a capital of £200,000, upon which there is an annual profit of £16,000 or 8 per cent, and all the shareholders are responsible to the full extent of their property. Let a law be passed abolishing this responsibility. The public will now look with greater scrutiny into the affairs of the bank; they will calculate whether this capital be sufficient to sustain any heavy loss, and what risk they may run in receiving their notes or making deposits. To secure public confidence the directors will find it necessary to make a further call upon the proprietors for £200,000. But as this surplus capital cannot be employed in the business, it must be invested in government securities, which at utmost will yield but 4 per cent. Now the shareholders instead of having a profit of £16,000 upon a capital of £200,000, will have a profit of £24,000 upon a capital of £400,000. Instead of receiving 8 per cent, on their capital, they will divide but 6 per cent. It is obviously not for the advantage of a bank to call up a larger portion of its capital, than what is necessary for carrying on its operations. All the surplus capital must be employed in a manner less productive, and the average profit will be diminished. And besides, when a bank has immense sums invested in the public securities, there is danger that the director will attempt to make these sums more productive by gambling in the funds; whereby the capital of the bank—the sole security to the public—may be placed in jeopardy.

To many persons it appears surprising that no joint stock bank has yet been formed on a large scale, with branches in all the provincial towns, but that the Bank of England is allowed to take possession of all the main posts without opposition. Such a bank would have an advantage over the country private banks, inasmuch as the notes issued at one branch would be paid from courtesy at every other branch. Thus the notes of this bank would have a more extended circulation than those of any provincial bank. It might also have an advantage over the branches of the Bank of England, by allowing interest on deposits, and opening cash accounts, on the system of the Scotch banks. The business of remitting money to and from London might be transacted through a London banker till the year 1833, when London might be made the head quarters; and in the mean time the various branches might be governed by a board of directors meeting in London. The act merely requires that the 'copartnership shall not have any house of business, or establishment as bankers in London, or at any place or places not exceeding sixty-five miles from London.' The residence of a board of directors in London, for the purpose of governing banks situated sixty-five miles distant, would be no infringement of the act. Indeed the Provincial Bank of Ireland is governed in this way, and has its establishment in St. Helen's Place. It appears then that a provincial bank for England and Wales might easily be formed under the existing law.

But though this limitation in regard to distance does not prohibit the formation of joint stock banks, there are other enactments which operate as serious obstacles. In the first place, the new joint stock bank could not issue any notes under £5 while the Bank of England and the country bankers are permitted to issue the small notes until the year 1829. The new bank would thus be cut off from one source of profit, and would have to incur the risk and experience of obtaining their gold from London. How then could they sustain a competition with other banks? But there is also another restriction. The bank could not draw on London any bills under the value of £50. The majority of bills wanted in the country are under this amount; yet such bills the joint stock bank could not supply. The effect of these two restrictions in preventing the formation of new banks is felt most severely in those parts of England which are situated on the borders of Scotland . . .

According to a Parliamentary return, the following joint stock banks have been established under the act:—

Title	Head Office	No. of Partners	Branches
1. Bristol Old Bank	Bristol	8	none
2. Stuckey's Banking Co	,,	10	8
3. Lancaster Banking Co.	Lancaster	77	none
4. Norfolk & Norwich Joint Stock Co.	Norwich	120	2
5. Huddersfield Banking Co.	Huddersfield	351	none

No's 2, 4, and 5, issue their notes without stamp, in consequence of a composition. J. W. Gilbart. *A Practical Treatise on Banking* . . . (1828), 54, 56–61

31 T. Joplin London as the Centre of the Banking System

The comparatively limited progress then, we must remark, which Joint Stock Banks have hitherto made in this country, cannot be attributed to the indifference of the Public regarding them. We may hear them everywhere adverted to as desirable and important objects; and where-ever they have been set on fort, they have been subscribed to with an avidity, which is not likely to be diminished by the great success which has uniformly attended them. But the Public, though by no means timid in such undertakings, generally hang back until parties of wealth and influence take the lead. With respect to Banking Companies in particular, they naturally wish, and in the first instance expect to see, people of considerable respectability at the head of them; and such people in provincial places, from personal and other motives, are slow in coming forward. In general they do not possess that information of the nature and details of the business, which is requisite to its commencement and conduct, and this want of knowledge is not only an impediment in itself, but productive also of another, in augmenting their apprehension of the responsibility involved. The leading people, moreover, in second rate market towns, moving in the same little sphere of Society, are mostly intimate or connected with the existing Bankers, and therefore, feel a delicacy in proposing any measure that may be injurious to them.

It is thus that we are often forced into the right method of accomplishing an object, by the difficulties and ill success of attempting it in a wrong one. From the comparatively slow advance already made in the establishment of Joint Stock Banks, more especially in those districts where they are most wanted, it is obvious that little is to be expected from the local efforts of individuals in originating their formation; and we naturally turn to Scotland, from whence the system is borrowed, to ascertain by what omission or misdirection we have failed in our endeavours to adopt it. Now it is true that the best Banks in Scotland are metropolitan institutions, but that the local Joint Stock Banks which may be found in the principal towns, owe to these institutions their origin and progress. In Ireland, likewise, it was not until the Provincial Bank of Ireland, which is a London Company, had established its Branches, that local companies started into existence. It is idle, therefore, to look for any extensive improvement from solitary and unattested attempts that have already been made. An impulse must be given from some great central seat of intelligence and wealth;

and London is evidently the spot best calculated for the purpose.

It is not, however, in the paucity alone of the present Joint Stock Banks that a reason exists for the comprehensive measure we are contemplating. Were they to become ever so general, they are of too feeble a character to accomplish the great objects of their design. A large majority of them have a cash capital varying only from twenty to fifty thousand pounds. Such banks, being unable to pay the expense of a proper system of checks, and possessing a more confined knowledge of the business of Banking, are at once more liable to loss and less competent to bear it. With such small capitals, it is clear, they could never conduct their operations on a broad scale of public accommodation. With resources so limited, they must, like private Banks, keep their funds within reach; and in agricultural districts, where the accommodation required is of a permanent description, they could never afford it on the principle, or to the extent, that is necessary. For the same reason, they would be unable to prevent the capricious contractions of their circulation. As we have before observed, they ought not for this purpose, to be deterred from lending money, on any good security that the Public may have to offer, when a sufficient demand for it does not exist in the ordinary channels—a useful liberality of which such Banks are incapable. Neither, again, does their insulated position bring within their scope the information necessary to govern them in checking an improper expansion of their issues, when the demand for money beyond the supply has a tendency unduly to enlarge them, and renders a judicious control over their operations, one of the most delicate and important functions of their office.

In short, though these banks may do very well, as in Scotland, if the system be upheld by more powerful establishments, yet, without that support, they would however numerous, be unproductive of the benefits desired. The radical principle of their weakness is, that the capital they possess wants the power of consolidation. With a large establishment, a much smaller amount of capital is requisite than with a number of small ones.

The British Linen Company of Scotland has about twenty-five establishments; and if its capital were equally divided amongst them, the portion to each would be 20,000—a sum totally inadequate to sustain the credit of the least of them. Yet united, its capital is fully sufficient for all the business it can obtain. Thus, also, it is with the Joint Stock Banks constituted here. United, their capitals would be ample; but as at present constructed, they are wholly unequal to the duties, which it is the interest of the Public that they should be able to perform.

In whatever light, therefore, we consider the subject—whether we direct our views to the means of stimulating the formation of local Banks and supporting those already in operation; or of giving accommodation to the Public on a better system of dealing; or of supplying the largest amount of credit to the business of Banking, with the smallest amount of capital, as in Scotland—in whatever light, we repeat, the subject is considered, a Metropolitan Institution is obviously the *desideratum* to be sought.

We may also mention, that such an Institution is necessary as a stay to the existing Country Banks, which will never be wholly superceded, and which therefore, it is desirable to protect. A great source of difficulty, arises from their being driven to London for assistance. If they could obtain it on the spot, as they could with a Branch of the Metropolitan Establishment in their neighbourhood, it would enable them to do business more safely and extensively than they do because, on an emergency, they would have assistance at hand, which would never be refused or niggardly afforded. Such an Establishment, in fact, would have the same interest in supporting a private Bank, that the Scotch Banks have in supporting each other. T. Joplin. *The Advantages of the Proposed National Bank of England, Both to the Public and Its Proprietory* (1833), 13–16

32 The Bank Charter Act, 1833

II. And be it further enacted, That during the Continuance of the said Privileges [given to the Governor and Company of the Bank of England] no Body Politic or Corporate, and no Society or Company, or Persons united or to be united in Covenants or Partnerships, exceeding Six Persons shall make or issue in *London*, or within Sixty-five miles thereof, any Bill of Exchange or Promissory Note, or Engagement for the Payment of Money on Demand, or upon which any Person holding the same may obtain Payment on Demand: Provided always, that nothing herein or in the said recited Act of the Seventh Year of the Reign of his late Majesty King George the Fourth contained shall be construed to prevent any Body Politic or Corporate, or any Society or Company, or Incorporated Company or Corporation, or Copartnership, carrying on or transacting Banking Business at any greater Distance than Sixty-five miles from *London*, and not having any House of Business or Establishment as Bankers in *London*, or within Sixty-Five Miles therefore (except as herein-after mentioned), to make and issue their Bills and Notes, payable on Demand or otherwise, at the Place at which the same shall be issued, being more than Sixty-five Miles from *London*, and also in *London* and to have an Agent or Agents in *London*, or at any other Place at which such Bills or Notes shall be made payable for the Purpose of Payment only, but no such Bill or Note shall be for any Sum less than Five Pounds, or be re-issued in *London* or within Sixty-five Miles thereof.

III. 'And whereas the intention of this Act is, that the Governor and Company of the Bank of England should, during the Period stated in this Act (subject nevertheless to such Redemption as is described in this Act), continue to hold and enjoy all the exclusive Privileges of Banking given by the said recited Act of the Thirty-ninth and Fortieth Years of the Reign of His Majesty King George the Third aforesaid, as regulated by the said recited Act of the Seventh Year of His late Majesty King

George the Fourth, or any prior or subsequent Act or Acts of Parliament, but no other or further exclusive Privilege of Banking: And whereas Doubts have arisen as to the Construction of the said Acts, and as to the Extent of such exclusive Privilege; and it is expedient that all such Doubts should be removed, be it therefore declared and enacted, That any Body Politic or Corporate, or Society, or Company, or Partnership, although consisting of more than Six Persons, may carry on the Trade or Business of Banking in *London*, or within Sixty-five Miles thereof, provided that such Body Politic or Corporate, or Society, or Company, or Partnership do not borrow, owe, or take up in England any Sum or Sums of Money on their Bills or Notes payable on Demand, or at any less Time than Six Months from the Borrowing thereof, during the Continuance of the Privileges granted by this Act to the said Governor and Company of the Bank of England. 3 & 4. Will. IV. c.98, Ss.2, 3

---

33 D. Salomons   The London and Westminster Bank
Sir David Salomons (1797–1873), financier and banker, was for many years the most influential director of the London and Westminster Bank. He joined the committee which was forming the bank in December 1833, and subsequently took a very active part in its affairs. Salomons wrote a number of pamphlets on banking and currency, the corn laws, and railways, but most of his writing was concerned with Jewish disabilities. Salomons played an important part in Jewish emancipation being the first Jew to be elected an MP in 1851 and in 1855 was the first Jewish Lord Mayor of London. He was made a baronet in 1869.

The London and Westminster was the earliest [London] joint stock bank, I believe?—Yes; it was established in 1834; sanctioned, it may be said, by a clause in the Bank Charter Act of 1833, which authorised more than six persons to carry on the business of banking, provided certain business of borrowing and owing, or taking up money, described in the Act, was not practised; which we always understood and believed to refer to issuing notes, but which was afterwards held by law, to be that we could not accept bills of exchange, and for ten years we were unable to accept bills of exchange, till by a clause in the Act of 7th and 8th Victoria we were expressly permitted to do so.

The formation of the London and Westminster Bank has been followed by the formation of several other banks?—Yes; the London and Westminster was established in March 1834; the London and County in 1836; the Union in February 1839; the Commercial in 1840; the Royal British, in November 1849; the City, in August 1855; the Western Bank of London and the Unity Bank, in May 1856. Perhaps I may state to the Committee, that the banks, beginning with the Royal British, were established under an Act of Parliament of the 7th and 8th Victoria, under letters patent and a charter; the London and County, the Union, and the Commercial were established before 1844 . . .

Is there any important difference between the nature of your business and the business of the ordinary private bankers?—None whatever—we profess as to our general business to follow the rules which are supposed to be followed by private bankers, with this exception, that we have introduced the principle of taking money on deposit at interest for fixed periods, payable according to agreement, either on demand or at some day's notice.

Was that a high rate of interest originally?—We fixed, when we first started, for sums under £1,000, 2 per cent interest, leaving larger sums to be settled at the time when the parties deposited their capital; but we have been obliged by alterations in the rate of money and other circumstances, competition amongst other things, to raise our rates nearer to the Bank rate.

What is the maximum rate of interest which you have ever allowed?—We make a distinction between two classes of depositors, those who deposit sums under £500 and those who leave sums above £500. As to those above £500 we have regulated ourselves for the last three or four years by Bank rate, keeping at about 1 per cent under the Bank rate, and for sums below £500, keeping it 2 per cent under the Bank rate . . .

The amount of the deposits held by the banks may be collected, may it not, from published statement; circulars to the proprietors?—I have a statement of it here, which I can put in; I beg to state that with respect to the banks other than my own, I collect the information from their published reports; I have no other authority.

I suppose a considerable part of your deposits are the deposits of country banks.—No, I should say not a considerable part. Some of depositors are our customers, having current accounts with us. Others are merely depositors with us; but a very large mass of the deposits which we hold are the deposits of the general public; persons who leave their money for a short time, and take it away again.

Have you any deposits which are of a permanent character? —I should say not.

Have you any deposits from small depositors?—A very large amount.

Do you consider that these deposits have been withdrawn by you from other banks, or that the institution of joint stock banks has given rise to a new class of deposits?—I should say that almost the whole of our business describes the augmented capital and resources of the country; that, taking the whole of our customers together, there is a very inconsiderable part which represents persons who have left other bankers; that almost the whole of our business describes new business, persons probably who had not bankers before; and new connexions, persons who have gone into business within the last 24 years. A very inconsiderable portion, indeed, is the transfer of accounts from private bankers to the joint-stock banks. I speak as to my knowledge of my own bank; I cannot answer concerning any other with the same certainty . . .

Will you be kind enough to tell us what is the mode in which you employ the deposits entrusted to you?—Taking them altogether, including those on which no interest is allowed

Amount of Deposits of the undermentioned Banks on 31st December in each Year, except in the cases of Union Bank and Commercial Bank, which are on 30th June

Year	London & Westminster £	London Joint Stock £	Union £	Commercial £	London & County £	City £	Bank of London £	Unity £
1834	180,380							
1835	266,884							
1836	643,332							
1837	793,148	594,101						
1838	1,387,855	1,145,421			186,477			
1839	1,266,845	1,035,088			351,275			
1840	1,361,545	1,170,893	377,755		437,995			
1841	1,499,328	1,403,188	503,550	168,977	581,279			
1842	2,087,757	1,771,739	745,988	246,824	858,802			
1843	2,219,624	2,046,285	956,467	216,948	996,082			
1844	2,676,741	2,245,330	1,591,200	239,622	1,231,412			
1845	3,590,014	2,460,475	2,012,548	500,728	1,489,738			
1846	3,280,864	2,446,017	2,170,310	440,721	1,588,585			
1847	2,733,753	1,971,912	2,510,064	409,925	1,225,120			
1848	3,089,659	2,328,056	2,644,728	406,217	1,354,730			
1849	3,686,623	2,792,507	2,835,617	541,804	1,675,494			
1850	3,969,648	2,949,869	2,963,583	612,596	2,030,238			
1851	4,677,278	3,157,575	3,094,316	764,541	2,465,768			
1852	5,581,706	3,591,506	4,268,438	964,177	3,281,603			
1853	6,259,540	5,010,623	4,878,731	1,246,824	3,417,130			
1854	7,177,244	6,161,154	7,031,477	1,265,903	3,779,944			
1855	8,744,095	6,241,594	8,363,460	1,317,554	4,443,359	944,475		
1856	11,438,461	7,224,527	9,045,606	1,536,361	3,543,824	1,388,933		
1857	13,889,021	10,737,580	10,874,640	936,724	3,533,425	1,388,933	1,114,846	117,380

(because the current accounts do not receive interest), the first demand upon our deposits is for our customer, in the discount of bills or any other advances that they may require temporarily; all the surplus is employed in the discount of commercial bills, or lent upon Government securities.

Are those loans and those discounts of commercial bills through the medium of bill-brokers?—Yes.

You make loans on Government securities?—We make loans on Government securities to brokers also.

Do you employ any part of your deposits in loans for a longer period, such as in railway debentures, or anything of that sort? —We should not call those loans; we occasionally invest a portion of our deposits in railway debentures, but those we limit to the shortest possible dates, generally to a year or 18 months. Evidence of D. Salomons. *Select Committee on the Bank Acts* (1858), 1126–7, 1130–2, 1134–8, 1140–3

_____

34 J. W. Gilbart   The Bank of England and the Joint Stock Banks

_____

During the last autumn [1836] were there many periods when there was a considerable difficulty in getting good bills discounted?—Yes.

During how great a portion of the last autumn has there been a difficulty of that kind?—I could not speak exactly to the portion; it has taken place at particular seasons when there has been a difficulty in getting first-rate bills done except at an advanced rate of interest; but if the bills were good, and it was known that the Bank of England would take them again, then they would pass, but the Bank of England would never take any bill indorsed by a joint stock bank of issue, consequently many of those bills could not be done except at an advanced rate of discount.

Do you mean to say, that with respect to bills unexceptionally good in themselves, with respect to which a bill-broker would have no hesitation, that even those bills were difficult of discount

if it was known that they had the indorsement of any joint
stock bank of issue?—Yes, it is known to be the rule that the
Bank of England will not discount bills which have the indorsement of any joint stock bank of issue, and instances have
occurred of the acceptances of the first bankers in London
being refused on that account . . .

And you stated that it was the practice of the Bank of England
not to take bills of joint stock banks of issue; what do you consider to be the reason of that?—It arises from their hostility to
joint stock banks of issue.

What do you understand by their hostility to joint stock
banks of issue?—They look upon them as rival establishments,
and they adopt that as one mode of restraining their operations.
Evidence of J. W. Gilbart. *Select Committee on Joint Stock Banks*
(1837), 2006–8, 2029–30

35 The London Clearing House and the Joint Stock Banks

In February 1834, J. W. Gilbart, on behalf of the London
and Westminster Bank wrote to ask permission to send a clerk
to the Clearing House. This request met with the following
reply and it was not until 1854 that the London joint stock
banks were admitted to the clearing.

To J. W. Gilbart, Esq.
SIR: I have laid before the committee of bankers your letter
of the 18th instant requesting permission on the part of the
directors of the London and Westminster Bank to send a clerk
to the Clearing House in the ordinary way, and in reply I am
desired to acquaint you that the committee decline complying
with such request under the consideration that the Clearing
House is intended exclusively for the accommodation of private
bankers. R. M. Holland. 'The London Bankers Clearing
House' in H. Withers *et al, The English Banking System*
(Washington, 1910), National Monetary Commission, Senate
Document No 492

36 Daniel Robertson   The National Provincial Bank of England

Daniel Robertson (d 1864), a Scot, was trained as a lawyer but became a banker, first with the Commercial Bank of Scotland and then the Glasgow Union Bank. In 1835 Robertson was appointed as the general manager of the newly founded National Provincial Bank and his policy was responsible for the bank's success. On his retirement in 1863 Robertson was made a director of the Bank.

Where is the business of the National Provincial Bank of England carried on?—In the country, beyond 65 miles; it has a board of control and correspondence in London.

Is there a Board of Directors?—Yes.

From the records of the Stamp Office, it appears that you have places of business at Aberystwyth, Birmingham, Brecon, Llandovery, Hay, Bath, Shepton Mallet, Boston, Castle Carey, Somerton, Biddeford, Southmolton, Torrington, Bury St. Edmunds, Cheltenham, Cardiff, Bridge End, Dursley, Gloucester, Hereford, Honiton, Stowmarket, Ipswich, Woodbridge, Lichfield, Rugby, Tiverton, Wisbeach, Whittlesea, Chatteris, Long Sutton, Worcester, Sudbury, Wootton-under-Edge, Yarmouth, Bristol, Norwich, Leicester and Dolgelly; what sort of management have you at those places of business?—We have a local board of directors, manager and accountant.

Is there a local board of directors at each of these places?— At some of them we have not; we have a difficulty sometimes in procuring a proper person to fill that office, and where a branch is chiefly one of deposit only, a local board is not so much necessary . . .

What description of persons do you select as local directors? —We select gentlemen of local influence, unconnected with business.

On what grounds do you select gentlemen unconnected with business?—Because, where they engaged in business, persons in the same line of trade would not open accounts with us, as their transaction would be overlooked, and their connexions known to their rivals . . .

What control is exercised by the manager over the accounts of the local directors?—Local directors cannot transact any business without the concurrence of the manager. The duties imposed upon them are to see that the manager and accountant faithfully perform their respective duties, to examine the cash on hand weekly, and also into the accuracy of the weekly returns before transmission to London, to review the whole affairs of the branch once a week, and in particular to consider the different loans, with a view of limiting or extending the same as circumstances require. In short, to exercise a general superintendence over every department of the branch, and to report from time to time as may be necessary to the London board.

Is the manager a check upon the local directors, or the contrary?—The one is a check upon the other.

Is their joint assent required with respect to the discount of bills of the making an advance?—Yes. In all cases where there is a difference of opinion they report to the London board . . .

In the event of their assent, have they an unrestricted power of making advances, giving accommodation?—They have a discretionary power as to making advances to a certain extent, but for any considerable or special advances they report to and receive instructions from the London directors.

In the places you have not designated as places where you have a local direction, what system of management have you adopted?—We have a manager, who gives security to a considerable amount, and an accountant; and we have also returns, which they send in weekly, from which we can easily know whether the branch is prudently managed or not . . .

What notes do you issue?—£5, £10, and at some places £20 notes; we have also issued at one place a few £50 notes.

Are all those dated at the places of issue?—Yes.

Have you as many different plates as you have places of

issue?—We have five plates, one for each of our London agents.

Are those notes issued at those different branches all dated at the place; where they are issued?—Yes.

Are they all made payable there?—Yes, and in London.

Have you any agencies or sub-branches?—We have a great number.

Where are they?—The Bath bank has three sub-agencies, Shepton Mallet, Castle Carey and Somerton; Biddeford has two, Southmolton and Torrington, Brecon has two, Llandovery and Hay; Cardiff has two, Bridgend and Cowbridge; Dolgelly has two, Machynlleth and Bala; Honiton has Exmouth; Ipswich has Stowmarket and Woodbridge; Pwllheli, Tremadoc; Wisbeach has Whittlesea, Chatteris, Long Sutton and Holbeach; Worcester and Ledbury, Bromyard and Yarmouth; Lowestoft and Halesworth.

Does your bank contemplate the extension of the number of those branches and sub-branches?—Yes, we do.

You have no defined limits within which you restrict the establishment of those branches?—We have not.

What notes do you issue at those sub-branches?—We issue notes of the principal branch.

Those notes are not dated at the sub-branch where they are issued, neither are they made payable there?—No.

Practically, are they paid there?—They are invariably paid there.

Have you any rule with respect of the proportion of cash you keep at any bank or branch or sub-branch as compared with the amount of the liabilities of that branch?—We have no fixed rule. At branches which are remotely situated we keep a greater supply of specie, for instance, at Cardiff and Aberystwyth, and all our branches in North and South Wales.

When you require cash at any particular branch, what steps do you take to supply that branch with cash?—If there is an extra supply at any branch near it, we order that to be transmitted to the other, and if not we remit from London.

How do you procure it in London?—From our agents.

T

In what way?—By an order on our account.

Who are your agents?—Messrs. Ladbrookes & Co., Spooners & Co., the London and Westminster Bank, Barnetts, Hoare & Co., Hanbury Taylor and Lloyd.

They procure them from the bank?—We do not know where they procure them; that is their business, as they must pay us money which we keep in their hands when we want it.

Do you keep a balance in the hands of each of those agents?—We keep a sum of money to meet our drafts and notes.

Do they advance you money?—No, we always keep them in funds.

In what way do you keep them in funds?—They are chiefly kept in funds by remittances from and payments made in London on account of our branches. When these are inadequate, we discount; but it will be observed from our returns, that it is necessary for us to do this to a very limited extent.

Do you discount with your agents?—We do, and with other parties.

It is by discounting bills sent up from your branches in the country you provide funds when they are required?—Yes, or by the lodgement of other securities.

Do you retain a sum in cash at your principal bank in London?—We keep no money there, nor do any act of banking whatever.

Where do you keep a sum of money to answer immediate demands?—In Exchequer bills we have £30,000; we also have, as already stated, always a balance at our different bankers to meet our drafts and notes.

If any considerable demand were to arise for money, in what manner would you provide for that?—In the first place, we have £30,000 in Exchequer Bills, which would be immediately available, and we have bills of exchange to a considerable amount, which we could readily discount . . .

What has been your dividend?—Five per cent.

Do you contemplate no difficulty from the very great extent of your branches, their number, and their distance from

London?—No; we have no difficulty whatever in the management of them.

Suppose great commercial difficulties should arise, do you consider that the danger and risk of the establishment would be very much augmented by the number of its branches?—I can scarcely anticipate that there would be a run on all the branches at the same moment; it might be on one district.

Supposing a run on one or two or three of them, so as to affect the credit of the bank itself, do you not think there would be a tendency to alarm in respect of the other branches?—There might be; but before such alarm extended to our other branches we should be prepared to meet a run.

Do you think in the event of there being any alarm, extending over between 40 and 50 branches, the means of supplying resources to those branches would be very available?—I should think that we could in the course of a post provide them with the necessary supplies to meet any run upon them, and more time than this would be allowed to us, as when a crisis of this kind takes place there is always some indication of its approach...

You have issued 7,000 £20 shares at a premium?—7,355; 9,000 were applied for.

How many shares have you yet unissued?—I do not know that the directors have fixed the number of £20 shares. They made this issue from there being a strong desire in the country for shares of a smaller denomination than the original shares of the company.

Is there no amount of shares fixed by your deed of settlement? —Ten thousand £100 shares are fixed by the original deed of settlement, but the directors have the power of creating an additional 10,000 for the country, with the view of securing local influence, should it appear to them desirable to do so.

How many of those have been issued?—Ten thousand.

Then they have still the power of issuing 10,000 £100 shares? —Yes.

Under what deed is that power given?—Under the original deed.

Can they issue as many £20 shares as they think fit in their discretion?—Yes.

By the power of the original deed?—Not by the original deed. Two general meetings of the proprietors, lately held, gave the necessary powers to the directors to issue those £20 shares.

The proprietors conferred upon them the unlimited discretion of issuing those £20 shares?—Yes.

What is the net sum received for premium on shares?—I have already said it is upwards of £20,000. The net sum I cannot state without reference to our books.

Do you keep a separate account of that money?—Yes, we do.

Has any portion of it been applied to dividends?—Not a sixpence, and we do not intend to do it.

Has there been any resolution of the proprietors, declaring what is to be done with the money so obtained?—No; it is understood that it is to be kept as a reserved fund, the £100 shareholders and the £20 shareholders equally participating in it . . .

You state yourself to have been connected some years with Scotch banking; of course you must have had in your mind the subject of joint stock banking; have you any suggestions to make to the Committee with a view to improving the existing law of England?—I am not prepared to speak as to any alteration in the existing law. The system of banking in England is certainly different from that in Scotland; I do not think it is conducted on such safe principles; I consider the system of overdrafts in England unsafe, and what we would not allow in Scotland.

In Scotland you would not permit the account to be overdrawn without collateral security?—We would not . . .

Do you think the limited liability affords any security against a temporary stoppage?—I am not aware that it could.

Do you think, in cases of difficulty, it would be easy to call up money?—More easy, I should say, where there is a large nominal capital. Under our own deed we could procure additional capital in the course of a month.

From your experience of banking affairs, if there were a call on the shareholders in a time of difficulty in the money market, would it produce a supply of money?—To a certain extent it would, although of course, it would not be so readily answered as if made at a more favourable period . . .

You state that you have inspectors?—We have two.

How often do they visit the numerous branches in your districts?—Once at least in twelve months, and sometimes oftener; they are sent down occasionally.

Do you send them down occasionally, in addition to their annual visits?—We do.

What species of inspection takes place when they visit a branch?—In the first place, they count the cash in the possession of the manager; they then balance the books, and thoroughly examine all the bills, vouchers and other property of the bank in the manager's possession, and in particular they institute the most rigid inquiry as to the responsibility of parties receiving advances at the branch.

Do they report to you?—They do.

Do all your agents at the branches give security?—They do.

To what extent?—From £3,000 to £5,000, none less than £3,000.

Have they any limit as to their power of discounting?— They have a discretionary power.

Have they any general rule laid down limiting that discretion, or is it left absolutely to the agents at the branches?—It is left to their discretion, with certain rules for their government in the exercise of it. In making large advances they generally consult the London board.

Is there a limitation in amount?—No, we do not limit them in discounting bills, but if a cash credit is applied for, they report to the London office, and the London directors reject or comply with the application, as they see fit.

The question respects the discount of Bills?—They have discretionary power in that respect.

Every transaction entered into at your branches you are

responsible for?—Certainly. Evidence of D. Robertson. *Select Committee on Joint Stock Banks* (1836), 2810–13, 2815–16, 2818–20, 2821–2, 2824–48, 2867, 2871–4, 2881–92, 2905–6, 2925–7, 2931–40

37 'The Circular to Bankers'   New Banks in 1836

The Circular to Bankers was founded in 1827 by the Committee of Country Bankers and it was edited for 20 years by Henry Burgess. The journal generally reflected the views of the private country bankers being opposed to the gold standard and any expansion of the powers of the Bank of England. It was also hostile to the new joint stock banks.

Sirs,

We propose to give, as nearly as we can, something like a sketch of the number of the existing Joint-Stock Banks in Lancashire and Yorkshire, pretty accurately according to the order of their establishment. Formerly the opening of a bank was a sort of epoch in the commercial history of a county, but at the present day so rapidly do they multiply that we cannot be by any means certain that some new ones have not been formed since the time to which our information reaches. We will number the Mother Banks and state as correctly as we can the number of branches where they have been formed, belonging to each.

1. The Lancaster Banking Company at Lancaster was the first Joint Stock Bank formed in the two great manufacturing and commercial counties of York and Lancaster. At the time of its formation there was no bank at Lancaster; the number of its branch offices is not, we believe fewer than five; in all   6 *banks*

2. The Bank of Manchester, which has, we believe only two branches   ...... 3 *banks*

3. The Bank of Liverpool, without a branch ...... 1 *bank*

4. The Huddersfield Banking Company, with one branch   ...... 2 *banks*

5. The Sheffield Banking Company, without any
branches   ...... 1 *bank*

6. The Manchester and Liverpool District Bank,
which has about sixteen branches   ......17 *banks*

7. The Bradford Banking Company, without any
branch   ...... 1 *bank*

8. The Commercial Bank of Liverpool, with no
branches   ...... 1 *bank*

9. The York Banking Company, with about five
branches   ...... 6 *banks*

10. The Hull Banking Company, with six or seven
branches   7 to 8 *banks*

11. The Halifax Banking Company, with no branch   1 *bank*

12. The Mirfield and Huddersfield Banking Company
with two branches   ...... 3 *banks*

13. The Bradford Union Bank, with no branches ... 1 *bank*

14. The Leeds Banking Company, with one branch   2 *banks*

15. The Wakefield Banking Company, with one
branch   ...... 2 *banks*

16. The Barnsley Banking Company, with no branches 1 *bank*

17. The Saddleworth Banking Company, with two
branches   ...... 3 *banks*

18. The Northern and Central Bank of England, with
about forty-four branches   ......45 *banks*

19. The Commercial Bank of England, with about
thirty branches   ......31 *banks*

20. The York Union Banking Company, with about
eight branches   ...... 9 *banks*

21. The Liverpool Union Bank, without a branch .. 1 *bank*

22. The Mirfield Banking Company, with one branch 2 *banks*

23. The Yorkshire District Bank, with perhaps
twenty-five branches, all in the county of
Yorkshire   ......26 *banks*

24. The Leeds and West Riding Banking Company.. 1 *bank*

25. The Traders Bank of Liverpool   ...... 1 *bank*

26. The Liverpool United Trades Bank   ...... 1 *bank*

27. The Royal Bank of Liverpool   ...... 1 *bank*
28. The Union Bank of Manchester   ...... 1 *bank*
29. The Manchester and Salford Bank   ...... 1 *bank*
30. The South Lancashire Banking Company, which we believe is intended to have several branches.
31. The Liverpool and South Wales Banking Company, with headquarters in Liverpool; also intended to have many branches.
32. Ashton, Stayley-Bridge, Hyde, &c. Banking Company   ...... 1 *bank*
33. Bury and Heywood Banking Company   ...... 1 *bank*

We have been requested by correspondents to give a sketch of the new banks in these two important counties, and we offer this—not by any means as a perfect one, either in regard to the priority of formation, or the precise name of all, or the exact number of branches—but as the best which we have at present the means of giving. At all events the number of new banks is not smaller than we have stated, without including two or three now projected, as for example the Imperial Bank of Liverpool, the Imperial Bank of Manchester, the Liverpool and Isle of Man Bank, the Manchester, Liverpool and Birmingham Banking Company.

In answer therefore to the question, how many new banks have been formed in Lancashire and Yorkshire within the last six or seven years, we may safely state that there have not been fewer than thirty principal or mother banks, and not a smaller number of new banks altogether than 150 or 160. The above gives 33 and 180, and though the whole of the principal banks are situated in those two counties, some of the branches from them are in other counties.

This increase in the number of banks among the most enter-prising, industrious, and wealthy population of the British dominions, may serve as an indication of the extension of the same system in other parts of the country. In the district of which Birmingham, for example, is the great centre of traffic and operations, the increase of Banks has been as great, in proportion to the business to be transacted in it, as it has been in Yorkshire and Lancashire; and we believe the disposition to speculate in new banks was never more active than it is at the present moment. An attempt is being made to form a County or District Bank with a central office in Birmingham; another Joint-Stock Bank has been formed at Coventry, which will we understand, open in the present month. *The Circular to Bankers* (May 1836), 330–1

38 Rediscounting by Joint Stock Banks

The following extract is from an anonymous pamphlet, the main aim of which was to encourage subscribers for the shares of the London and Westminster Bank. While a 'puff', the pamphlet is written in moderate language and reveals that the writer was well informed of banking practice.

This is the common and every-day vice also of the Joint Stock Banking Companies which have been lately established in many provincial towns. The practice seems to be, to establish a Bank upon a nominal capital of £500,000 or a million upon which a deposit of some £50,000 or £100,000 only (as a guarantee capital) is called up. Upon the strength, or rather weakness, of these inefficient means, the new Bank, by virtue of deposits entrusted to it, or notes issued, advances, by way of loans or discounts, say £400,000 or £500,000, which is of itself engagement quite sufficient in proportion to the paid-up capital; but, in fact too many of these institutions go far beyond this, because, whenever the bills offered to them exceed the amount of their available capital, of the deposits in hand, and of the notes issued, they still go on discounting all that is offered, relieving themselves by re-discounting the excess in London, and thus running into liabilities upon a scale more imprudent than any now practised by the Private Bankers, who, in consequence of severe and repeated losses, and moreover aware of the existing distrust, have certainly gained some useful experience. *Hints by Way of Encouraging the formation of a Joint-Stock Banking Company in London* (1834), 11–2

39 The Regulation of Joint Stock Banks

The following is an extract from the first report of the Secret Committee on Joint Stock Banks set up in 1836 as a result of the speech of William Clay in the House of Commons.

Your Committee will now call the attention of the House to some few facts which illustrate the present system.

Subject to the local restrictions imposed for the protection of the privilege of the Bank of England, it is open to any number of persons to form a Company for Joint Stock Banking, whether for the purpose of deposit, or of issue, or both.

1. The Law imposes on the Joint Stock Banks no preliminary obligation beyond the payment of a license duty, and the registration of the names of the Shareholders at the Stamp Office.

2. The Law does not require that the Deed of Settlement shall be considered or revised by any competent authority whatever, and no precaution is taken to enforce the insertion in such Deeds of clauses the most obvious and necessary.

3. The Law does not impose any restrictions upon the amount of nominal capital. This will be found to vary from £5,000,000 to £100,000, and in one instance an unlimited power is reserved of issuing shares to any extent.

4. The Law does not impose any obligation that the whole or any certain amount of shares shall be subscribed for before banking operations commence. In many instances Banks commence their business before one-half of the shares are subscribed for, and 10,000, 20,000, and 30,000 shares are reserved to be issued at the discretion of the Directors.

5. The Law does not enforce any rule with respect to the nominal amount of shares. These will be found to vary from £1,000 to £5. The effects of this variation are strongly stated in the Evidence.

6. The Law does not enforce any rule with respect to the amount of Capital paid up before the commencement of business. This will be found to vary from £105 to £5.

7. The Law does not provide for any publication of the liabilities and assets of these Banks, nor does it enforce the communication of any balance sheet to the Proprietors at large.

8. The Law does not impose any restrictions by which care shall be taken that dividends are paid out of banking profits only, and that bad or doubtful debts are first written off.

9. The Law does not prohibit purchases, sales and speculative traffic on the part of these Companies in their own stock, nor advances to be made on the credit of their own shares.

10. The Law does not provide that the Guarantee Fund shall be kept apart and invested in Government or other securities.

11. The Law does not limit the number of branches or the distance of such branches from the Central Bank.

12. The Law is not sufficiently stringent to insure to the Public that the names registered at the Stamp Office are the names of persons *bona fide* Proprietors, who have signed the Deed of Settlement, and who are responsible to the Public.

13. The provisions of the Law appear inadequate, or at least are disregarded, so far as they impose upon Banks the obligation of making their notes payable at the places of issue.

All these separate questions appear to Your Committee deserving of the most serious consideration, with a view to the future stability of the Banks throughout the United Kingdom, the maintenance of Commercial Credit, and the preservation of the Currency in a sound state. *First Report of the Secret Committee on Joint Stock Banks* (1836), viii–ix

---

40 'The Economist' The Failure of the Royal British Bank, 1856

The Royal British Bank, which was formed in 1849, was the most important bank to be founded under the onerous conditions of the 1844 Joint Stock Banking Act. Its failure in 1856 through mismanagement was to be one of the worst scandals of the 1857 crisis period.

The failure of a modern joint stock bank in the metropolis at a time when the condition of the trade of the country is so prosperous, and when there have been no general causes in any way to account for it,—when, on the contrary, banking has proved so profitable a business that unheard of dividends have been paid for two years past, and in consequence a number of new banks have been established, has taken the public very much by surprise, and has very naturally created a doubt as to the stability of others. The Royal British Bank has—however, been so exceptional in its character, business and resources, ever since its commencement, that it has rather been a matter of surprise to those who have closely watched its annual balance sheets, that it could ever have enjoyed the credit it did, or been so far trusted by the public as it was, than that it should be found in difficulties. The career of this bank is an extraordinary example of the little trouble the public take to think for themselves, and of the incautious manner in which they trust their money . . .

Not that it is the amount of capital alone which ought to give credit to a bank; on the contrary, as in most cases, the deposits far exceed the capital, it is more essential that they should be safely invested. But there is one fact which, so far as the Royal British is concerned, is conclusive as to abuse which must have existed in the management of their deposits. When the run commenced upon the Bank a few days before it suspended, the deposits amounted to more than £800,000; after paying about £200,000 the doors were closed:—It is fair therefore to infer that the whole or the greater part of the balance of the securities representing the remaining £600,000 were of a character not convertible, and upon which money could not be obtained: a sad look out for the creditors . . .

The rule laid down by the Duke of Wellington when he impressed upon his officers who had small savings to invest, that 'a high rate of interest meant a bad security' (that is comparatively with the ordinary current rate)—is one which, if the depositors of the Royal British Bank had observed, they would have avoided their present losses. Depositors were tempted by interest at a rate of four and five per cent., at a time when the Bank rate was much lower, and when other bankers could not find suitable banking securities to yield so much by one per cent. and more than this bank gave to their customers . . .

How few have the courage to meet a loss? As far as facts at present appear, one of the chief causes of the ruin of this bank was its difficulties to admit a loss of some £10,000 advanced to iron and coal works in Wales. Taking this transaction in the light least discreditable to the directors, they, finding themselves involved to the extent of £10,000, in an attempt to extricate themselves are said to have worked the mines until the loss now will be short of £200,000. When private traders cannot succeed, we may be sure that a bank will never make a concern pay. But this again is only the repetition of the same error which has ruined many banks before. *The Economist* (1856), 1034–5

41 D. Salomons London Deposit Rates and Bank Rate

When the Bank rate rose as high as 10 per cent., [1857] what was the rate of interest which you allowed?—Eight per cent. on sums above £500. I must offer some explanation to the Committee with regard to that. Not expecting the rate of interest to be raised so very high, there was a sort of tacit understanding on the part of the London and Westminster Bank (we had nothing in writing which would compel us) to give within 1 per cent of the rate; but one of the banks, the Union, and I think another bank, had something more than an implied contract, they had a prospectus which compelled them to give within 1 per cent of the Bank rate of discount. Without our having any printed engagement, we had fallen very much into that course of business; but when the Bank rates were advancing, we had a meeting with the various joint-stock banks of London; I think it was at the time when the Bank discount was 8 per cent.; and it was proposed that we should not advance beyond 7 per cent whatever might be the future rise of discount by the Bank of

England. We could not agree upon that; consequently, when the Bank rose from 8 per cent to 9, we rose ours to 8, but we never exceeded it; 8 per cent therefore was the utmost limit that we paid for sums above £500, and 7 per cent for amounts below £500 . . .

When you say that you have come to some fresh arrangement with regard to your allowance of interest upon deposits, do you speak of yourselves as the London and Westminster Bank, or of some of the other banks in combination with yourselves?— I think all the banks have come to an understanding that it is not desirable, either for their proprietors or for the public, to follow closely at all times the alterations of the Bank. I believe it is understood amongst them all that they do not intend following that course in future.

Is that from a feeling, that it is rather dangerous under particular circumstances?—I cannot admit as to its being dangerous, but there can be no doubt of this, that there is notion in the public mind which we ought not to contend against, that when you offer a high rate of interest for money, you rather do it because you want the person's money, than because you are obeying the market rate; and I think it is desirable that we should show that if persons wish to employ their money, and want an excessive rate, they may take it away and employ it themselves.

You think that there is now a general understanding amongst the banks which you have mentioned, to act upon a different principle from that on which they acted during last October and November?—I think I may say that I know that to be the case.

Was not it the fact that this system of giving so high a rate of interest upon money at call, commenced very much with the establishment of some banks during the last year or two, which, instead of demanding 10 days' or a month's notice, were willing to allow interest upon only three days' notice; did not that system begin about two years ago?—I do not think it began with the new banks; I think it began with one of the older banks; I know that, as regards my own bank, that we were forced into it; I forgot to say that, with regard to ourselves in taking money on deposit, the parties must leave the money a month, or they lose interest. We do not take money from any depositor at interest unless upon the understanding and condition that it remains a month with us; he may withdraw it within the month, but then he forfeits interest; it will not carry interest unless it is with us a month, and then it is removable on demand without notice.

Is it or is it not a fact that some of the banks pay interest upon their current accounts?—Yes, I think most of the new banks do so; and the Union Bank of London does it.

At a smaller rate than upon their deposits, I presume?— I think at a smaller rate, but I believe it is a fixed rate on the minimum balance for some period, either six months or one month. I do not exactly know the period. Evidence of D. Salomons. *Select Committee on the Bank Acts* (1858), 1134, 1164–9

42 R. B. Wade   Provincial Deposit Rates

R. B. Wade was a director of the National Provincial Bank of England from 1855 to 1897 and in 1875 gave evidence on the bank's behalf.

What rate of interest did you allow the public on their deposit receipts, say for 1874?—In London we always give 1 per cent. under Bank rate, in the country our rates vary according to the district in which the branch is situated. At the present moment, I suppose if I said that the rates were $2\frac{1}{2}$ and 3 per cent., it would practically cover the mass of our deposits.

Do you give a higher rate for your deposits in the provinces than you do in London?—As a rule we do.

On current accounts you allow nothing I think?—Only in certain cases. Mr. Atkinson [the manager of the National Provincial] has stated, that in certain districts it is the custom to allow something. We have to deal with all these matters according to the custom of the part of the country in which the branch is situated. It varies in every part of England, and we have of course to accommodate ourselves to the wishes of the public wherever we may find ourselves.

You have no uniform rate?—We have no uniform rate.

How are the rates regulated; are they regulated from the central office, or do you allow your agents in various parts of England to fix what shall be the rates upon deposits?—They are regulated from the central office. Evidence of R. B. Wade. *Select Committee on Banks of Issue* (1875), 1917–21

43 Joint Stock Banks and the Companies Act of 1862

The Joint Stock Banking Act of 1844 was progressively repealed by Acts in 1857 (20 & 21 Vict. c.49) and in 1858 (21 & 22 Vict. c.91) and by the latter act, banks could be formed with limited liability. Company law was consolidated in 1862 and by the Act of 1862 (25 & 26 Vict. c.89) banks were placed on the same footing as any other trading company; the final vestige of the 1844 code, the £100 minimum share denomination for banks, was repealed by the provisions of the 1862 act.

4. No Company, Association, or Partnership consisting of more than Ten persons shall be formed, after the Commencement of this Act, for the purpose of carrying on the Business of Banking, unless it is registered as a Company under this Act, or is formed in pursuance of some other Act of Parliament, or of Letters Patent; and no Company, Association, or Partnership consisting of more than Twenty Persons shall be formed, after the commencement of this Act, for the Purpose of carrying on any other business that has for its object the Acquisition of Gain by the Company, Association, or Partnership, or by the individual Members thereof, unless it is registered as a Company under this Act, or is formed in pursuance of some other Act of Parliament, or of Letters Patent, or is a Company engaged in working Mines within and subject to the Jurisdiction of the Stannaries...

44. Every Limited Banking Company and every Insurance Company, and Deposit, Provident, or Benefit Society under this Act shall, before it commences business, and also on the First *Monday* in *February* and the First *Monday* in *August* in every Year during which it carries on Business, make a Statement in the Form marked D, in the First Schedule hereto, or as near thereto as Circumstances will admit, and a Copy of such Statement shall be put up in a conspicuous Place in the registered Office of the Company, and in every Branch Office or Place where the Business of the Company is carried on, and if Default is made in compliance with the Provisions of this Section the Company shall be liable to a Penalty not exceeding Five Pounds for every Day during which such Default continues, and every Director and Manager of the Company who shall knowingly and wilfully authorize or permit such Default shall incur the like Penalty.

Every Member and every Creditor of the Company mentioned in this Section shall be entitled to a Copy of the above-mentioned Statement on Payment of a Sum not exceeding Sixpence . . .

56. The Board of Trade may appoint One or more competent Inspectors to examine into the Affairs of any Company under this Act, and to report thereon, in such Manner as the Board may direct, upon the Applications; (that is to say),

(1) In the Case of a Banking Company that has a Capital divided into Shares, upon the Application of Members holding not less than One Third Part of the whole Shares of the Company for the Time being issued: . . .

175. The Expression 'Joint Stock Companies Acts' as used in this Act shall mean 'The Joint Stock Companies Act, 1856', 'The Joint Stock Companies Acts, 1856, 1857', 'The Joint Stock Banking Companies Act, 1857', and 'The Act to enable Joint Stock Banking Companies to be formed on the Principle of Limited Liability', or any One or more of such Acts, as the Case may require; but shall not include the Act passed in the Eighth Year of the Reign of Her present Majesty, Chapter

U

One hundred and ten, and intituled *An Act for the Registration, Incorporation, and Regulation of Joint Stock Companies* . . .

182. No Banking Company claiming to issue Notes in the United Kingdom shall be entitled to Limited Liability in respect of such Issue, but shall continue subject to Unlimited Liability in respect thereof, and if necessary, the Assets shall be marshalled for the Benefit of the general Creditors, and the Members shall be liable for the whole Amount of the Issue, in addition to the Sum for which they would be liable as Members of a Limited Company . . .

188. Every Banking Company existing at the Date of the passing of this Act which registers itself as a Limited Company shall, at least Thirty Days previous to obtaining a Certificate of Registration with Limited Liability, give Notice that it is intended so to register the same to every person and Partnership Firm who have a Banking Account with the Company, and such Notice shall be given either by delivering the same to such Person or Firm, or leaving the same or putting the same into the Post addressed to him or them at such Address as shall have been last communicated or otherwise become known as his or their address to or by the Company; and in case the Company omits to give any such Notice as is herein-before required to be given, then as between the Company and the Person or Persons only who are for the Time being interested in the Account in respect of which such Notice ought to have been given, and so far as respects such Account and all Variations thereof down to the Time at which such Notice shall be given, but not further or otherwise, the Certificate of Registration with Limited Liability shall have no operation . . .

FORM D.

The Capital of this Company is — —, divided into Shares of — — each.

The Number of shares issued is — —

Calls to the Amount of — — Pounds per Share have been made, under which the Sum of — — Pounds has been received.

The Liabilities of the Company on the First Day of January (*or* July) were,—

Debts owing to sundry Persons by the Company:

On Judgment, £

On Speciality, £

On Notes or Bills, £

On Simple Contracts, £

On estimated Liabilities, £

The Assets of the Company on that Day were,—

Government Securities (*stating them*), £

Bills of Exchange and Promissory Notes, £

Cash at the Bankers, £

Other Securities, £

If the Company has no Capital divided into Shares the Portion the Statement relating to Capital and Shares must be omitted ...

25 & 26 Vict. c.89, ss.4, 44, 56, 175, 182, 188

44 'The Banker's Magazine' New Banks in the 1860s

It is generally understood that Joint-Stock Bank enterprise will be further promoted both in London and the provinces. The 'limited Liability' principle is likely to take root firmly in the country as well as in the metropolis. The symptoms of success associated with the Alliance, the Imperial, and the Metropolitan and Provincial, have encouraged the formation of the London and Middlesex Bank, which is to absorb the business of the Unity without adopting its liabilities, and it is said the subscription list for the shares is already nearly filled. There was a talk of a bank for London and Southwark, but this it is feared will not be carried out, and some of the new banks may probably enter into competition for a branch in that locality. Through this means, banking accommodation, if it be essential, will be applied to that district, and no new establishment will be required. The Union Bank of Ireland it is understood is making progress, the directors being engaged in devising plans for general operations in the sister island. No doubt a field is here furnished which can, without the least injury to the other banks, be cultivated with success. So long a period has elapsed since banking institutions have been extended throughout Ireland that a new establishment must attract customers and connexions which will ensure a fair amount of self-support. Banks for some of the colonies, and also for distant countries, are likewise in course of organisation, and if the existing plethora shall continue will be brought forward for public support. Indeed, although a temporary lull has been experienced for the last few weeks, the satisfactory statements exhibited at the ordinary half-yearly meetings, with the reports of the success of the new establishments, has quite revived the dormant energies of promoters and encouraged them to fresh and vigorous operations. Still whatever may be the appearance of prosperity *in futuro*, those who engage in the formation of banks must not treat it as a light or easy task, only to be accomplished for immediate reward. *The Bankers' Magazine*, XXII (1862), 476

45 'The Bankers' Magazine' The Failure of the City of Glasgow Bank

It is a long while since we have had to chronicle any event so serious to the banking world as the failure of the City of Glasgow Bank, which took place on Tuesday, October 2nd. A rumour that the bank was in difficulties, which had been in circulation some days previously, had been vigorously denied, and public confidence in the concern had never been shaken. Many of those engaged in banking had, however, long felt doubts about the class of business which had been carried on. The fact that the acceptances of the bank which had been so long and so largely in circulation were often drawn by connec-tions of the directors, had excited so much suspicion that by more than one of the leading banks of the country these bills

were never taken at all, and by many were taken only with caution. But to the general public these doubts did not suggest
themselves, and the business of the bank was conducted as usual
to the close of the very day on which the transactions of the bank
came to a close. Several circumstances conduced to this. In
the first place the high credit in which the Scotch banks have
always stood was extended to the City of Glasgow Bank almost
as a matter of course. In the next, the half-yearly balance-sheets
showed large and continually increasing totals, and that the
profits made were large and apparently substantial, and no
suspicion existed as to the manner in which these statements had
been falsified. Our August number contains the thirty-ninth
annual report of the directors, made at the annual meeting of
July 3rd. On this occasion a dividend at the rate of 12 per cent
was declared, and, as far as the report shows, everything appeared
to have been in the most perfect order. Though the bank was
very closely identified with the prosperity of Glasgow, the
operations of the company were far from being confined to that
city alone, and 133 branches in different parts of Scotland bore
witness to the energy with which the business had been
extended . . .

This is not the first time that the City of Glasgow Bank has had
to close its doors. In the panic of 1857, on November 11th, the
day after the Western Bank of Scotland had been compelled
to suspend payment, the City of Glasgow Bank had to announce
that it also was unable to meet its liabilities. In December of
the same year, however, it was able to resume operations, and
soon recovered its former position, and even gained a greater
amount of confidence from the public than it had obtained
before. There is, however, a very great difference now in the
position of the bank, and in that of business generally, if we
compare what has occurred in 1878 with what took place in
1857. Then several large and leading merchant houses had
failed . . .

But in 1878 the position of affairs was a very different one.
There certainly has long existed, and there still exists, a very

severe commercial depression; one of the most protracted, the most trying, which the business community has ever experienced. The severity of this trial has been enhanced by the fact that it is not confined to Great Britain alone. The whole of the Continent of Europe has been more or less suffering from the same cause, and America has not long emerged from a similar period of difficulty. Still, though this long-continued drain on the business resources of the country is still going on, there was no particular pressure laid upon the City of Glasgow Bank, under the force of which it had to yield. Externally the business seemed to prosper. The dividends declared had been 10 per cent. in 1874, 11 per cent., in 1875, the same rate in 1876, 12 per cent. in 1877 (we quote from information supplied by the bank itself), and the same rate for the present year as in 1877. The value of the shares of the bank was well supported in the outer market, though the announcement that the bank held more than £150,000 nominal of its own stock may partly account for the high price at which it was maintained, which was 235½ for the £100 paid on the very day preceding the stoppage. The number of shareholders of the bank was returned as follows to the 'Banking Almanac':—

City of Glasgow Bank	Number of Shareholders
1874	1,212
1875	1,273
1876	1,264
1877	1,249

There appears to have been 1,343 names on the list at the time of the suspension, and since the number of shareholders appears to have been diminishing for the three years preceding the failure, we think it probable that the discrepancy between the numbers in 1878 and at the present time may arise from the names of trustees and executors being enumerated separately in the larger figures, while the others refer to the number of holdings on the roll.

Immediately after the stoppage, Messrs. McGrigor and

Anderson were chosen investigators. A meeting of the shareholders was summoned for the 22nd October, the earliest date at which by the statutory regulations it could be held. The report of the investigators now issued shows that the worst opinions which had been formed of the position of the business fell short of actual facts. The causes which have led to the downfall of this once flourishing concern appear, however, to have been, broadly speaking, very much the same as those which have led to the failure of so many other banks before, namely, the trusting of enormous sums to a few borrowers. This, even when the firms concerned are of first-rate standing, is a very dangerous course for any bank to take; but when, as in this instance, the houses trusted were engaged in carrying on a speculative and risky trade, the downfall of the establishment which assisted them was only a question of time. In one case, at least, the advances were made on the security land in New Zealand, and although in this case the assets held may probably turn out better than those taken in some instances, yet to make very heavy advances on fixed securities of this nature can never be a desirable thing for a bank. A bank should never, to any large amount, make such advances as do not turn into cash without long delay. The City of Glasgow Bank have not only made very heavy advances of this description, and locked up its money thus in securities of an inconvertible nature, but it had also given acceptances to a very large amount. The report of the investigators will be found at another page of this Journal. It gives the acceptances at £2,742,106, whereas they only figured in the balance-sheet as £1,488,245, the statement in that account having been falsified. Here again there was another great source of danger to the bank. We know that there are some who consider that it is a legitimate thing for a bank to accept bills largely against produce, and that when sufficient securities are held against liabilities of this nature, no very great amount of risk is incurred. To a moderate extent this may be the case. But we can never think it consistent with the prudent conduct of business for a bank, unless it holds very large sums indeed in reserve, at call and at short notices, to pledge itself as the City of Glasgow Bank appears to have done to an extent nearly double of its capital and its reserve. For the securities held by a bank against acceptances are not, it must be remembered, securities which mature at a given date like bills, they are securities which it takes time to turn into cash, securities which are more or less at the command of the market, not securities which are readily available at a moment's notice.

The report of the investigators shows the utterly rotten state into which the business has been brought by the criminal folly of the directors. The other Scotch banks have done their utmost to prevent the shock to credit from extending. They resolved at once to accept the notes of the bank which had failed exactly as if the event had not occurred, and by this prudent conduct they stayed the first risings of a storm of panic, the results of which might have been very disastrous. The question of the best mode of dealing with the deposits in order to diminish the great inconvenience and loss which the stoppage entailed on so many persons was a more serious one, and further time for deliberations was required ... *The Bankers' Magazine* XXXVIII. (1878), 917–21

46 The Companies Act, 1879   Reserved Liability

The failure of the City of Glasgow Bank was the greatest shock to the English banking system since the crisis of 1825. The severity of this failure of an unlimited bank lead to a trend amongst banks established before 1858 to adopt limited liability. Pressure from the banking community was responsible for the provisions of the Companies Act of 1879 which enabled banks to re-register with capital structures incorporating reserved liability.

Be it enacted by the Queen's most Excellent Majesty, by and with the advice and consent of the Lords Spiritual and Temporal, and Commons, in this present Parliament assembled, and by the authority of the same, as follows:

1. This Act to be cited as the Companies Act, 1879.

2. This Act shall not apply to the Bank of England.

3. This Act shall, so far as is consistent with the tenor thereof, be construed as one with the Companies Acts, 1862, 1867, and 1877, and Those Acts together with this Act may be referred to as the Companies Acts, 1862 to 1879.

4. Subject as in this Act mentioned, any company registered before or after the passing of this Act as an unlimited company may register under the Companies Acts, 1862 to 1879, as a limited company, or any company already registered as a limited company may re-register under the provisions of this Act.

The registration of an unlimited company as a limited company in pursuance of this Act shall not affect or prejudice any debts, liabilities, obligations, or contracts incurred or entered into by, to, with, or on behalf of such company prior to registration, and such debts, liabilities, contracts, and obligations may be enforced in manner provided by Part VII. of the Companies Act, 1862, in the case of a company registering in pursuance of that Part.

5. An unlimited company may, by the resolution passed by the members when assenting to registration as a limited company under the Companies Acts, 1862 to 1879, and for the purpose of such registration or otherwise, increase the nominal amount of its capital by increasing the nominal amount of each of its shares.

Provided always, that no part of such increased capital shall be capable of being called up, except in the event of and for the purpose of the company being wound up.

And, in cases where no such increase of nominal capital may be resolved upon, an unlimited company may, by such resolution as aforesaid, provide that a portion of its uncalled capital shall not be capable of being called up, except in the event of and for the purposes of the company being wound up.

A limited company may by a special resolution declare that any portion of its capital which has not been already called up shall not be capable of being called up, except in the event of and for the purpose of the company being wound up; and thereupon such portion of capital shall not be capable of being called up, except in the event of and for the purposes of the company being wound up.

6. Section one hundred and eighty-two of the Companies Act, 1862, is hereby repealed, and in place thereof it is enacted as follows:— A bank of issue registered as a limited company, either before or after the passing of this Act, shall not be entitled to limited liability in respect of its notes; and members thereof shall continue liable in respect of its notes in the same manner as if it had been registered as an unlimited company; but in case the general assets of the company are, in the event of the company being wound up, insufficient to satisfy the claims of both the note-holders and the general creditors, then the members, after satisfying the remaining demands of the note-holders, shall be liable to contribute towards payments of the debts of the general creditors a sum equal to the amount received by the note-holders out of the general assets of the company.

For the purposes of this section the expression 'the general assets of the company' means the funds available for payment of the general creditor as well as the note-holder.

It shall be lawful for any bank of issue registered as a limited company to make a statement on its notes to the effect that the limited liability does not extend to its notes, and that the members of the company continue liable in respect of its notes in the same manner as if it had been registered as an unlimited company.

7. (1) Once at least in every year the accounts of every banking company registered after the passing of this Act as a limited company shall be examined by an auditor or auditors, who shall be elected annually by the company in general meeting.

(2) A director or officer of the company shall not be capable of being elected auditor of such company.

(3) An auditor on quitting office shall be re-eligible.

(4) If any casual vacancy occurs in the office of any auditor the surviving auditor or auditors (if any) may act, but if there is no surviving auditor, the directors shall forthwith call an extraordinary general meeting for the purpose of supplying the vacancy or vacancies in the auditorship.

(5) Every auditor shall have a list delivered to him of all books kept by the company, and shall at all reasonable times have access to the books and accounts of the company; and any auditor may, in relation to such books and accounts, examine the directors or any other officer of the company: provided that if a banking company has branch banks beyond the limits of Europe, it shall be sufficient if the auditor is allowed access to such copies of and extracts from the books and accounts of any such branch as may have been transmitted to the head office of the banking company in the United Kingdom.

(6) The auditor or auditors shall make a report to the members on the accounts examined by him or them, and on every balance sheet laid before the company in general meeting during his or their tenure of office; and in every such report shall state whether, in his or their opinion, the balance sheet referred to in the report is a full and fair balance sheet properly drawn up, so as to exhibit a true and correct view of the state of the company's affairs, as shown by the books of the company; and such report shall be read before the company in general meeting.

(7) The remuneration of the auditors shall be fixed by the general meeting appointing such auditor or auditors, and shall be paid by the company.

8. Every balance sheet submitted to the annual or other meeting of the members of every banking company registered after the passing of this Act as a limited company shall be signed by the auditor or auditors, and by the secretary or manager (if any), and by the directors of the company, or three of such directors at the least.

9. On the registration, in pursuance of this Act, of a company which has been already registered, the registrar shall make

provision for closing the former registration of the company, and may dispense with the delivery to him of copies of any documents with copies of which he was furnished on the occasion of the original registration of the company; but, save as aforesaid, the registration of such a company shall take place in the same manner and have the same effect as if it were the first registration of that company under the Companies Acts, 1862 to 1879, and as if the provisions of the Acts under which the company was previously registered and regulated had been contained in different Acts of Parliament from those under which the company is registered as a limited company.

10. A company authorised to register under this Act may register thereunder and avail itself of the privileges conferred by this Act, notwithstanding any provisions contained in any Act of Parliament, royal charter, deed of settlement, contract of copartnery, cost book, regulations, letters patent, or other instrument constituting or regulating the company. 42 & 43 Vict. c.76

---

47 Treasury Committee Bank Amalgamations

The following is an extract from the Treasury departmental committee's report on bank amalgamations made in 1918. The Committee was alarmed by the possibility of the creation of a money trust through further bank amalgamations and recommended legislation to protect the public interest. The consequent bill was dropped and replaced by a private understanding between government and the banks which allowed the continued absorption of small banks but did not permit the merging of any of the 'big five'.

---

3. Bank absorptions and amalgamations are, of course, no new phenomenon in this country. About 300 instances have occurred in the past, more than half of which have taken place in the last 50 years. In one or two cases arrangements made provisionally for amalgamation have been defeated by the opposition of local customers of the bank which it was proposed to absorb; but, on the whole, banking policy has gradually but steadily pursued

the path of consolidation and absorption, and, until recently, the amalgamation effected have, generally speaking, been carried through without stirring up serious opposition or arousing public interest. As a result, the number of private banks has fallen from 37 to 6 since 1891, and the number of English joint stock banks from 106 to 34 during the same period.

4. Several recent amalgamations, however, have undoubtedly provoked an unusual amount of interest, and have been seriously criticised in certain quarters. This change in public opinion appears to be due mainly to the fact that amalgamations have changed their type and consist no longer in the absorption of a local bank by a larger and more widely spread joint stock bank, but the union of two joint stock banks, both already possessing large funds and branches spread over a wide area. These two types of amalgamation differ very materially from one another, and arguments used to justify the former type do not necessarily apply to the latter.

THE OLD TYPE OF AMALGAMATION—ABSORPTION OF LOCAL BANKS BY A LARGER AND MORE WIDELY-SPREAD JOINT STOCK BANK

5. As modern amalgamations are mainly of the new type, it is unnecessary for us to elaborate the various arguments used in connection with amalgamations of the older type. Very briefly, what the arguments amount to is that both the local (or more or less local) bank and the larger widely-spread bank secure to their customers certain advantages of a different kind, but that, like other institutions, each has also the defects of its qualities. Some districts—notably Lancashire and Yorkshire— have clung to their local banks. But in most instances amalgamation schemes have been carried out without serious difficulty, and if material hardship had resulted to the trade generally in the districts affected, there would no doubt have been greater local opposition to subsequent absorption schemes, and new local banks would even have been opened.

6. As regards the new type of amalgamation, the main arguments laid before us in support of the policy of amalgamation
are as follows:—

(a) *The convenience and gain to Trade secured by an extension of
Bank areas.*—Just as the large banks of the past secured certain
advantages to trade by collecting deposits from parts of the
country where they were not required, and placing them at
the disposal of other parts which stood in need of advances, so
it is claimed that this process can be carried still further with
advantage by amalgamating large banks with one another.

This is no doubt true, though, of course, the degree to which
an extension of area is in fact secured by amalgamating banks
differs considerably in each case. The following table is an
analysis of two recent amalgamations and one proposed
amalgamation in this respect:—

TABLE I – NUMBERS IN 1918 (IN ROUND FIGURES)

		London Branches	Provincial Branches (excluding sub-branches and including only one Branch in each place)	Foreign Agencies Held
a	National Provincial	26	251	31
	Union of London & Smith's	31	78	150
b	London County & Westminster	110	180	400
	Parr's	35	160	35
c	London City & Midland	107	419	850
	London Joint Stock	41	109	70

Note: In London an amalgamation can secure no material extension of area, and usually means a net reduction in the number of competing banks in the City, as all other important competitors are already represented there and cannot therefore, as is sometimes the case in other districts, add a new element of competition to counterbalance the amalgamation. Should no new such element arise, there will be a similar net reduction in the number of competing banks in nearly all the most important towns outside London at which the second of the two banks was represented in cases (a) and (c) above, as the first bank in each case secured the following number of new places out of the total number taken over, viz., (a) 51 (out of 78), (b) 152 (out of 160), (c) 54 (out of 109). In cases (a) and (c) very few of the new places secured were in towns of importance. The 55 overlapping places in case (c) include such towns as Barnsley, Barrow, Darlington, Doncaster, Gateshead, Grimsby, Hull, Leeds, Middlesbrough, Newcastle, Portsmouth, Sheffield, West Hartlepool, and York; and in case (a) the 27 overlapping places included Bath, Birmingham, Bournemouth, Bradford, Brighton, Bristol, Derby, Doncaster, Exeter, Grimsby, Huddersfield, Hull, Leeds, Lincoln, Nottingham, Plymouth, Sheffield, Southampton and York.

It should be added that, in case (c), in addition to the branches shown above, the Joint Stock Bank have 106 sub-branches in small places where they have no branch, and that in only about nine of those places are the City and Midland represented. Similarly, the Union of London and Smith's had a number of sub-branches in small places, at most of which the National Provincial were not represented.

There must come a point when the policy of substituting one large bank for two will usually mean a very small extension of area, if any, and some reduction of competition. That point has already been reached in London, and is being approached in a few of the largest towns where most of the important competing banks are already established.

It should be added that if both the amalgamating units have, before amalgamation, lent up to their full resources, home trade *as a whole* cannot gain any increase in accommodation as a result of the amalgamation. Except at the expense of smaller traders, large trade combines could not obtain larger advances in all from the combined resources of the amalgamation than they could have obtained from the separate banks before.

(b) *The argument from size*: Numerous representations have reached us to the effect that large banks are better for traders, and particularly for large traders, than small banks because, with their large resources, they can safely make individual advances on a more generous scale. And it is argued that banks must grow now to keep pace with the growth in size of business houses generally, and to enable them to deal with the demands of after-the-war trade both at home and abroad.

This is an important point. Various Government Committees have drawn special attention to the question of banking facilities after the war, and it is very desirable that all possible steps should be taken to adapt the banking interest to the new position which will then arise. The point, however, with regard to the size of banks is one of degree only, and it is a question whether the continued practice on the part of exceptionally large firms of resorting to two, or more banks, instead of one, for advances would not suffice to meet all their needs, and whether the existing large banks are not in fact large enough to meet the requirements of the immediate future, at any rate, if supplemented as far as may be necessary, by combinations for special purposes on the lines of German 'Konsortiums' or otherwise. We have received no conclusive evidence on this point. But the following table (on page 321) shows, at any rate, that the resources of our leading banks were very substantial even before the recent amalgamations.

The above argument with regard to postwar trade can of course only be used with some caution as regards foreign trade, in view of the special dependence of English banks on deposits withdrawable at call or on short notice. This is especially the case as regards long term advances for such trade, to which special reference is sometimes made. The following figures, taken from *The Economist*, show how comparatively small are the capital and reserves of English joint stock banks:—

TABLE II – PAID-UP CAPITAL, RESERVE AND DEPOSITS of the
following banks as shown in their BALANCE SHEETS of
31st December 1913 and 31st December 1917

	31st December 1913	31st December 1917
	£	£
London City and Midland	101,882,230	230,083,434
London County & Westminster Parr's	143,000,000	228,000,000
National Provincial Union of London & Smith's	118,864,590	185,223,173
Lloyds	98,720,663	183,076,718
Barclays	June 1914 66,940,267	135,675,971
London Joint Stock	31st December 1913 41,678,237	62,274,280

TABLE III

	Paid-up Capital and Reserves Million £	Deposits Million £	Ratio Per cent
1890	68	369	18
1895	69	456	15
1900	79	587	13
1905	82	628	13
1910	81	721	11
1915	82	993	8
1917	84	1,365	6

x

7. We have endeavoured to review impartially the arguments which have been put forward as justifying the necessity in the public interest—quite apart from questions of profit to shareholders—of bringing about the new type of bank amalgamation. There is undoubtedly much weight in these arguments as far as they go. And even if the absolute *necessity* of large new amalgamations is not clearly proved, yet the absence of proof of the public necessity for business re-organisations is not, in itself, any reason for objecting to them, and it is a serious step at any time to interfere with the natural developments of trade. Before, therefore, considering any restrictive proposals, we endeavoured to ascertain what is the real basis of the fears—often vaguely felt, and vaguely expressed—which have undoubtedly been aroused by recent amalgamation schemes. The main grounds for objecting to further amalgamations appear to be as follows:—

(a) *Writing down of Bank Capital*　The proportion of capital to deposits is now so small in the case of English joint stock banks, even excluding the temporary war increase in the amount of deposits, that any further shrinkage of bank capital is clearly undesirable, in the interest of depositors, if it can be avoided. Attention has been drawn to the fact that amalgamation schemes usually mean a reduction in the total paid-up capital and uncalled liability of the two pre-amalgamation units. This has frequently been the case in the past, and it has also been a feature of recent amalgamations and proposed amalgamations. The amalgamation of the National Provincial Bank of England, Ltd., with the Union of London and Smith's Bank Ltd., resulted in a reduction of over £1,000,000, or 16 per cent, in the total paid-up capital, and of over £9,000,000, or over 48 per cent, in the uncalled liability of the Union shareholders. The amalgamation of Parr's Bank Ltd., with the London County and Westminster Bank, Ltd., while it resulted in an addition of £243,000 to the total paid-up capital, brought about a reduction of nearly £1,770,000, or 17 per cent, in the uncalled liability of Parr's shareholders. The proposed amalgamation of the London City and Midland Bank, Ltd., with the London Joint Stock Bank Ltd., would effect a reduction of nearly £1,000,000 in the total paid-up capital, and of over £9,000,000, or over 50 per cent, in the uncalled liability of the Joint Stock Bank shareholders. In each of these three cases, therefore, substantial benefits to shareholders are purchased at the expense of some of the security of the depositors. But the reduction of capital (as opposed to the reduction of uncalled liability) resulting in two of the cases appears to be only nominal, the sum written off, or some sum approximating to it, being added to the inner reserves, at any rate at present.

(b) *Dangers of Reduced Competition* Although, in the past, we believe that amalgamations have not, in most instances, led to a reduction of bank competition, yet, as we have pointed out in paragraph 6 (a) above, in London (and possibly before long in certain large towns) amalgamations between large joint stock banks must now usually mean a net reduction in the number of competing banks. It is true that this reduction is only slight in each case, and that there still remain at present a fair number of competing banks. But we have received representations from certain municipal corporations to the effect that banks vary very much in their willingness to allow reasonable overdraft facilities to corporations, and that sufficient money, and cheap enough money, has only been obtained hitherto by resorting to different banks, the number of which is now falling steadily. On this ground a number of resolutions have been forwarded to us by corporations protesting against further amalgamations, and suggesting that it is not in the national interest that large funds belonging to the public should be in the hands of a few companies.

Strong representations have, on similar grounds, been made to us on behalf of the Stock Exchange and the Money Market. It is claimed that the world-wide fame of the London Market before the war was due to the freedom with which London bills could be negotiated, owing to the ease with which Discount Houses obtained ample funds from a wide number of banks, and that the fewer the lending constituents in the Discount Market, the less flexible is the market and the less fine the rates. It is added that the number of members, or any greatly preponderant power on the part of particular members, might impair confidence in its smooth working and raise apprehensions in the market. Moreover, it is pointed out that a reduction in the number of important Banks must mean, and has already meant a reduction in the number of first-class acceptors of bills, and that if this reduction proceeded very far, it would become a question whether the Bank of England would not have to place a limit on the amount of acceptances which they would take from any particular bank doing a large acceptance business, and whether Continental buyers would not limit the number of bills taken by them.

(c) *The Danger of Monopoly* It has been represented to us that there is a real danger lest one bank, by the gradual extension of its connections, may obtain such a position that it can attract an altogether preponderant amount of banking business; or alternatively, lest two banks may approach such a position independently and then achieve it by amalgamation.

Any approach to a banking combine or Money Trust, by this or any other means, would undoubtedly cause great apprehension to all classes of the community and give rise to a demand for nationalising the banking trade. Such a combine would mean that the financial safety of the country, and the interest of individual depositors and traders, would be placed in the hands of a few individuals, who would naturally operate mainly in the interests of the shareholders. Moreover, the position of the Bank of England—which would, it may be assumed, stand outside any such Trust—would be seriously undermined by so overwhelming a combination, and the Bank might find it extremely difficult to carry out its very important duties as supporter and regulator of the Money Market. Any such result, would, in our opinion, be a grave menace to the public interest.

Further it has been represented to us that the Government

of the day might not find it easy to adopt a course of which the combine, for its own reasons, disapproved.

While we believe that there is at present no idea of a Money Trust, it appears to us not altogether impossible that circumstances might produce something approaching to it at a comparatively early date. Experience shows that, in order to preserve an approximate equality of resources and of competitive power, the larger English banks consider it necessary to meet each important amalgamation, sooner or later, by another. If, therefore, the argument from size, referred to in paragraph 6 (b) above, is to prevail, it can only lead, and fairly rapidly, to the creation of a very few preponderant combinations; and if those combinations amalgamated, or entered into a joint agreement as to rates and policy, etc. the Money Trust would immediately spring to birth. *Report of the Treasury Committee on Bank Amalgamations* (1918), Cd 9052, 3–6

48 J. W. Birch, B. W. Currie   The Extension of Banking in the 1880s

During the 1880s J. W. Birch served as Governor of the Bank of England and as the President of the newly formed Institute of Bankers. Bertram W. Currie (1827–96) was a partner in the London private bank of Glyn, Mills, Currie & Co which had been formed by amalgamation in 1864. The Currie banking house had been founded in 1773 and B. W. Currie had entered the bank in 1847. Between 1866 and 1896 Currie was the dominant partner in the enlarged bank; he was an orthodox banker and the instigator in 1895 of the Gold Standard Defence Association.

A good many questions have come up in the course of examination of other witnesses on which, as an ex-Governor of the Bank of England, you can give us information; and the first question I should like to ask you relates to the economy of the precious metals through an extension of banking facilities.

Could you tell us anything either in addition to or as qualifying evidence given by Mr. Giffen on that subject, with regard to the extension of banking facilities?—A return which I produce shows a great extension of banks within the last 20 years. This extension has chiefly been in the direction of branches and sub-branches in districts not formerly occupied. In 1865 the total number of branch offices in England, Scotland, Ireland and the Channel Islands was 2,417; in 1885 it was 3,886 showing an increase of 1,469; and banking facilities have thus been brought to persons of moderate means, small shopkeepers, farmers, and others whose transactions were formerly carried out in cash. Thus, small cheques take the place of coin in numerous instances. I notice that where my own bailiff formerly paid in money for sheep or produce, he now brings a good many small cheques. The system of country clearing amongst bankers facilitates the use of cheques for the transmission of small amounts. Where the recipients keep banking accounts these return quickly, but where they do not, the cheque is often paid away again, and may be used instead of coin in more than one transaction. Probably the use of postal orders, in itself a species of banking, to some extent also economises the use of coin. These notes have now attained an issue of about 100,000 a day. Some time ago the Bank of England obtained a very large economy of notes by the establishment of a cotton clearing in Liverpool. The economy in notes was something like £150,000 a week.

I suppose that some of these branch banks supply banking facilities in towns where banking facilities already existed adequate to the needs of the inhabitants; in other words, that it is a competition which may affect the profits of banks, but which does not affect any saving in currency?—It saves to this extent, that formerly in country shops they kept a certain amount in their tills, but now they pay it at once into the bank if there is one. In some places they have a bank open once, twice or three times a week, and in others they have established a regular branch. The money in the neighbourhood is thus drawn in, and then it is transmitted to the head establishment in London, and goes immediately into employment.

But let us suppose that in some country town there is already established a branch of the London and Westminster Bank, and that the London and County Bank subsequently put a branch of their own there; that may affect the profits of the two banks respectively but it does not add materially to the banking facilities of the community in that town?—No; therefore I am referring more especially to small places where there were formerly no banks at all. Now you have these sub-branches opening everywhere, all over the country.

But this increase of 1,469 banks is not solely in places where there were no banking facilities before?—Certainly not.

Some of them are in places where banks were previously established?—Yes; and in such places the effect would to a certain extent be, as you said, to draw business from one to the other, stimulate opposition, and at the same time encourage the development of banking.

Are you of the opinion that the limit has now been reached, or nearly reached, of the extension of banking facilities?—I never like to prophesy. I think it is impossible to say. Various means are cropping up for economising money, and a great deal is economised by simple transfer; you cannot tell to what extent. Evidence of J. W. Birch. *First Report of the Royal Commission Appointed to Inquire into the Recent Changes in the Relative Values of the Precious Metals* (1887), C-5099, 1336–41

And I gather you do not thing that there is that intimate and direct connexion between an increase or decrease in the production of the precious metals which is the standard and the prices of commodities which is suggested by some?—I altogether fail to believe in it. I believe, on the contrary, that it is not gold alone which has an effect upon prices, but all the different media of exchange—book credits, cheques, etc.—and I am prepared to show that they have increased in a marvellous manner. If it would interest the Commission, I have prepared a table to show, first of all, the remarkable increase of postal orders, which are exactly those instruments which would displace gold, because they are issued for small sums; secondly, the increase in the number of suburban banks which evidently apply to a class of customers who would formerly have held gold in their tills, they have developed themselves in an exceptional way; in fact I do not believe that there is a possibility of inconvenience arising from a scarcity of gold, for which I think mankind would immediately set to work to find substitutes, and it most certainly can be proved that these substitutions for gold have largely increased within a recent period. If you will allow me, I will just draw attention to the table. Take the postal orders, which were only established in 1881–82. The postal orders in 1881–82 were in number four-and-a-half millions, and in amount £2,000,000 sterling, in 1885–86 they were in number twenty-five and three-quarter millions, and in amount £10,750,000 sterling. During the same period, postal money orders, which to a certain extent may be said to compete with them, remained nearly stationary, that is to say, the amount in the first period was £23,250,000 and in the second period £22,000,000. Therefore it could not be said that the postal orders had displaced the money orders. Well, then, I have taken the following from our experience: at Glyn's bank, 2,000 postal orders are dealt with daily now as against 500 postal orders six years ago. Then I come to suburban cheques, which I maintain are especially used as an economy of gold, of coin. In 1880 Glyn's dealt with 620 suburban cheques daily, of which 93 were under £10 and over £5, and 215 were under £5. In 1887 they dealt with 1,258 daily, of which 245 are under £10 and over £5, and 505 are under £5.

Would you say what you mean by suburban?—I mean by suburban banks, banks within a radius of seven or eight miles, or possibly nine miles of London; for instance the region with which I am most familiar is about Fulham, Walham Green, and such places. Anybody going down those roads will find they abound with small shops which furnish the inhabitants of those districts, and till those people had banking facilities they were obliged to keep a certain amount of gold in their shop, but I think the suburban banks liberate those stores, in fact they act upon that class exactly as banks of larger description act upon the richer classes.

Would these sums that you think were deposited and drawn upon in these suburban banks be to some extent a substitute for sums that were previously deposited and drawn upon in a central bank, a bank in Lombard Street for instance?—No. I think that these banks have created a new demand altogether, that these traders are so small that previously they had no banking account and were therefore obliged to keep whatever money they had in a till. They now deposit it in the bank and in that way less coin is required, because the bank does not keep any more than it can help.

Is that shown; can you tell by the increase in the total amount of deposits in the London and suburban banks taken together? —I have not with me the actual return of the deposits but this I can tell you that the joint stock banks of England and Wales in 1873 numbered 121 banks with 1,100 branches, and in 1886 there were 119 banks, fewer banks, with 1,755 branches. Therefore there was an increase of 655 branches between 1873 and 1886. I should also like to state something with regard to country cheques, and to compare three days in 1880 with three days in 1887. In 1880 the total number of cheques drawn on country banks for which Glyns acted as agents was in three selected days, 19,950, and the number of them under £1 was 462 or 2¼ per cent of the whole. In 1887 the total number of cheques in the three corresponding days was 35,090 against 19,950 and 1,481 of these were under £1, 4 per cent of the whole so that in these seven years the percentage of cheques under £1 has increased from 2¼ per cent to 4 per cent and the total has increased from 19,950 to 35,090. Then over £1 and under £5 in the first period, 1880, there were 5,299 cheques in three days, or 26 per cent of the whole; and in the second period, 1887, there were 11,682 or 32 per cent, so that the ratio of increase is largest in the small denomination, and that I think is a strong argument in favour of what I have said, that if there was any scarcity of gold, substitutes would be found which would remove any inconvenience, or would obviate the evil of any such scarcity.

Is a larger proportion of your business done by cheques than was formerly done, that is to say, out of the whole business is less done by payment of money over the counter and more done by cheques?—More cheques, I think, certainly . . . Evidence of B. W. Currie. *Second Report of the Royal Commission Appointed to Inquire into the Recent Changes in the Relative Values of the Precious Metals* (1888), C-5248, 6648–52

_____

49 'The Economist' London Joint Stock Banks and International Acceptances

Acceptance business by English banks developed during the second half of the 1860s; in London as a result of the growth of the City's international transactions and also through competitive pressure from branches of Scottish banks in England. Many bankers frowned upon this practice considering such business to be the realm of the merchant houses and the overseas banks.

_____

In the following table (C), on the opposite page, a statement is given of *Acceptances*.

(C) LONDON JOINT STOCK BANKS—Acceptances—1867–8

Banks	Acceptances at				
	1868		1867		1866
	31 Dec.	30 June	31 Dec.	30 June	31 Dec.
	£	£	£	£	£
London & Westminster	1,074,000	970,000	902,000	784,000	901,000
London Joint Stock	n.r.	n.r.	2,784,000	3,869,000	—
Union	6,250,000	7,308,000	5,298,000	7,342,000	8,732,000
City	2,721,000	2,161,000	1,418,000	1,777,000	—
Imperial, Limited	127,000	93,000	134,000	90,000	n.r.
Alliance, Limited	248,000	217,000	98,000	222,000	n.r.
Consolidated Limited	237,000	200,000	102,000	n.r.	n.r.
East London Limited	—	—	—	—	—
Metropolitan Limited	16,000	5,000	n.r.	n.r.	n.r.
London & S.W. Limited	n.r.	18,000	n.r.	n.r.	n.r.
London and County	—	1,676,000	1,790,000	1,397,000	n.r.

A tendency to the *increase* of Acceptances is shown by this table—most notably in the case of the *City Bank*, which considers it prudent to commit itself to an amount of Acceptances a quarter of a million sterling in excess of the whole of its Cash Deposits. The Acceptances of the *Alliance* and *Consolidated* Banks are both larger. The Acceptances of the *Union* are a million less than at 30 June last, and a million more than at 31 Dec. 1867.

Respecting the small increase in the amount of the Acceptances of the *London and Westminster Bank*, Mr. Cattley, the Chairman of the annual meeting of the Bank, held on the 20th inst., gave the following detailed explanation:—

'With respect to *Acceptances*, let me say that it is a matter about which you have heard a great deal from time to time. Observations have often been made about the profit of acceptances, their danger, and so on. It is not necessary that I should go very fully into that question, although I am quite prepared to do so; but it may be interesting to you to know what the £1,074,000, mentioned in the report, really means, that being the amount for which you as partners in this bank are liable. This amount is made up of engagements which have very little to do with each other. They are lumped together, and I will explain them to you. In the first place, there is the sum of £285,000, which represents country drafts drawn for periods of from seven to twenty-one days by country bankers upon the London and Westminster Bank as their agent. Those drafts represent, in fact, a part of the currency of the country. They are drawn for very short periods, and in giving our acceptances for them we are invariably covered, not only by the guarantee of the country bank, but by special securities lodged for the purpose. I think that at the present time it would be difficult to carry on the trade of the country without these facilities; but whether that view be correct or not, I believe that those who most disapprove of the bank's giving its acceptances would not consider this particular class of acceptances open to criticism.

There is another amount £544,000, which represents acceptances given at the instance of our country bankers, in favour of local customers. You can easily understand that a trade or manufacturer living in Dundee, and desiring to buy jute or hemp in Riga or St. Petersburg, may be perfectly solvent and in good credit at Dundee, and yet not be known at those ports. Now in order to carry on his trade, he asks his country banker to get him a London credit, and we give him that credit, being ourselves covered by good commercial bills. These acceptances are usually accompanied by shipping documents. With the value of those documents we have nothing to do; we are not merchants. We send them to the bank which requires the credit from us, and we obtain bills the value of which we are well acquainted with, and we have, in addition, the security of the country banker.

Again, there is the small sum of £98,000, which is given in acceptances under somewhat different circumstances to several respectable country bankers, and this amount is also covered by securities. The whole of the acceptances for which we are liable in London amount to £139,000. That represents the amount which it is possible to control; that is what we are responsible for, and when you hear about bankers damaging themselves by acceptances, I think you must feel that I have offered to you a full and satisfactory explanation. This £139,000 is for acceptances on account of a very few respectable London firms, keeping heavy current accounts with us, and entitled to very great consideration. These acceptances are, I may remark, in every instance secured, not only by shipping documents, but also by bills, and Indian or other securities'.

Mr. Cattley is right in being thus explicit regarding even the comparatively small amount of £1,000,000 of Acceptances appearing in the accounts of the *London and Westminster Bank*. The commercial public view with great and justifiable anxiety the growth of the new system under which London Bankers undertake, for a commission large or small, engagements which properly belong to a merchant. Credit cannot be used twice. It cannot be made the basis of a large business in Cash Deposits and also of a large business in Acceptances at extended dates circulating all over the country.

The following table (D) brings into comparison the Cash Deposits and Acceptances of the *Union Bank* and *City Bank*:—

(D) ACCEPTANCES AND CASH DEPOSITS – UNION BANK AND CITY BANK – 1867–8

Half-year	Union Bank			City Bank		
	Cash Deposits	Acceptances	Per cent	Cash Deposits	Acceptances	Per cent
	£	£		£	£	
'68–31 Dec.	10,840,000	6,250,000	57	2,450,000	2,720,000	111
„ 30 June	10,070,000	7,310,000	73	2,510,000	2,160,000	86
'67–31 Dec.	12,970,000	5,300,000	40	2,230,000	1,420,000	63
„ 30 June	10,610,000	7,340,000	70	2,280,000	1,780,000	80

These figures indicate that the Acceptances of the *Union Bank* have fallen from 73 per cent to 57 per cent of its Cash

Deposits,—and that the Acceptances of the *City Bank* have risen from 86 per cent of its Deposits at 30 June last to an amount which at present *exceeds* the total Deposits by 11 per cent. The Acceptances of the *London and Westminster Bank* are 5 per cent of its Deposits. *The Economist* (1869), 116

———

Suggestions
for Further Reading

THERE are several works of importance which are concerned
with the monetary controversies of the late seventeenth and
early eighteenth centuries and the role of financial institutions.
J. Keith Horsefield's *British Monetary Experiments, 1650–1710*
(1960)* is an invaluable piece of meticulous scholarship which,
despite the complexity of its subject provides a clear account for
the reader. The foundation and early history of the Bank o
England has attracted many historians but a student need not
go further than the official history of the Bank, Sir J. H.
Clapham. *The Bank of England: A History* (Cambridge 1944),
two volumes, and a third volume by Professor R. S. Sayers is in
progress. For details of the internal functioning of the Bank
there is W. Marston Acres. *The Bank of England from Within*
(1931), two volumes, and also R. D. Richards. 'The First Fifty
Years of the Bank of England', in J. G. van Dillen (Ed). *History
of the Principal Public Banks* (The Hague 1934). Recent research
suggests that the Bank of England acted as a lender of last
resort almost from its inception, so that this was the first central
banking function to emerge. Clapham's data for the Bank's
income from discounts show a sharp rise during, and immediately
following, all the major crisis years of the eighteenth century
(Vol I, Appendix E). This aspect of the Bank's activities is more
fully analysed in M. C. Lovell. 'The Role of the Bank of England
as Lender of Last Resort in the Crises of the Eighteenth

* The place of publication of books cited is London, unless otherwise
stated.

Century', *Explorations in Entrepreneurial History*, X (1957). The following articles by J. K. Horsefield deal with different aspects of the Bank's operations during the late eighteenth century and the Restriction period: 'The Duties of a Banker. The eighteenth-century view'. *Economica* (1941), and 'The Duties of a Banker. The effects of inconvertibility', *Economica* (1944): both of which have been reprinted in T. S. Ashton and R. S. Sayers (Eds). *Papers in English Monetary History* (Oxford 1953; reprinted 1954, 1964).

The history of economic thought has a literature of its own and there are a number of general accounts which pay attention to eighteenth century developments in the theory of money of which the most authoritative is still J. A. Schumpeter. *History of Economic Analysis* (New York 1954). More closely concerned with the mercantilists' monetary views is A. E. Monroe. *Monetary Theory before Adam Smith* (Cambridge, Mass 1923) which has now been largely superseded by D. Vickers. *Studies in the Theory of Money 1690–1776* (1959). Also useful is C. Rist. *History of Monetary and Credit Theory from John Law to the Present Day* (English translation, 1940), though the author's tendency to moralise is particularly unfortunate for John Law. There are a number of important relevant background articles which should be read more widely; these are W. G. Grampp. 'The Liberal Elements in English Mercantilism', *Quarterly Journal of Economics*, LXVI (1952); M. Blaug. 'Economic Theory and Economic History in Great Britain, 1650–1776', *Past and Present*, No 28 (1964); T. E. Gregory. 'The Economics of Employment in England, 1660–1713', *Economica*, I (1921); and D. C. Coleman. 'Labour in the English Economy of the Seventeenth Century', *Economic History Review*, 2nd Series, VIII (1956).

Those wishing to read more widely on the particular writers quoted in Part Two will find the following books and articles helpful. Save for his 'glimpse' Hodges was a minor figure and there appears to be little more than the reference to him and his work in Horsefield, cited above, 44–5. Petty is still well served by C. Hull's edition of his collected works, *The Economic*

Writings of Sir William Petty (1899) but two more recent studies are also useful, E. A. J. Johnson. *Predecessors of Adam Smith* (1937) and E. Strauss. *Sir William Petty: Portrait of a Genius* (1954). For the intellectual framework to Locke's economic contributions there is C. B. Macpherson. *The Political Theory of Possessive Individualism: Hobbes to Locke* (Oxford 1962). Both Locke's essays of 1691 and 1696 were reprinted in J. R. McCulloch. *Principles of Political Economy* (1870 edition), 220–360. The most searching discussion of Locke's place in the development of the quantity theory of money can be found in H. Hegeland, *The Quantity Theory of Money* (Goteborg 1951). The Standard work on the economics of Hume is E. Rotweain (Ed). *David Hume: Writings on Economics* (Edinburgh 1955). Hume's monetary theory is developed in the three essays 'Of Money', 'Of Interest', and 'Of the Balance of Trade', all in the 'Political Discourses'. The best short account of his specie-flow mechanism is in J. Viner. *Studies in the Theory of International Trade* (1937), while a more recent discussion of the importance of Hume is M. Arkin. 'The Economic Writings of David Hume: A Reassessment', in J. J. Spengler and W. P. Allen (Eds). *Essays in Economic Theory* (New York 1960). An excellent discussion of Barbon's thought will be found in both Schumpeter, cited above, and Vickers, cited above, however most histories fail to mention him, much less give him the attention he deserves. Barbon's *Discourse of Trade* (1690) has been republished as part of J. H. Hollander, Reprints of Economic Classics series, University of Baltimore Press (Baltimore, 1905). The best accessible analysis of Law is again in Vickers, cited above; in addition there is a study by A. W. Wiston-Glynn. *John Law of Lauriston* (Edinburgh 1906). But the last word has yet to be written on this man who combined a blend of financial genius with entrepreneurial action. It used to be fashionable, following the classical economists, to write Sir James Steuart out of the mainstream of economic thought but in recent years his importance has been rediscovered through the fine edition of his work by A. S. Skinner. *Sir James Steuart: An Inquiry into the Principles of*

Y

Political Economy (1966). This followed an earlier technical reappraisal by S. R. Sen. *The Economics of Sir James Steuart* (1957). The standard works of reference on the growth of the money market are W. R. Bisschop. *the Rise of the London Money Market, 1640–1826* (English translation, 1910; reprinted 1968) which is dated but still very useful, E. T. Powell. *The Evolution of the Money Market, 1385–1915* (1915; reprinted 1967), and W. T. C. King. *History of the London Discount Market* (1936) especially the nineteenth century. On early banking development there is R. D. Richards. *The Early History of Banking in England* (1929) and W. R. Scott. *The Constitution and Finance of English, Scottish and Irish Joint Stock Companies to 1720* (Cambridge 1910–12), three volumes. On provincial banking in the eighteenth century, an altogether later and slower development, L. S. Pressnell. *Country Banking in the Industrial Revolution* (Oxford 1956) is compulsory reading, after which the student is well equipped to tackle some of the large number of the histories of individual banks. These exist for a considerable number of banks and cover the main regions of the English economy but too many consist of a mixture of anecdote and biography to be really useful. Among the older histories which are still useful, there are the following; L. H. Grindon. *Manchester Banks and Banking* (Manchester 1877); J. B. Martin. *The 'Grasshopper' in Lombard Street* (1892); M. Phillips. *A History of Banks, Bankers and Banking in Northumberland, Durham and North Yorkshire* (1894); C. H. Cave. *A History of Banking in Bristol* (Bristol 1899); W. Bidwell. *Annals of an East Anglican Bank, Gurney & Co* (Norwich 1900). W. Howarth's *Barclay and Company Ltd* (1901) has been largely superseded by W. P. Matthews and A. W. Tuke. *Histoy for Barclay Bank* (1928). H. T. Easton. *History of a Banking House* (1903), which is concerned with Smith, Payne and Smith of Nottingham, has also now been replaced by J. S. L. Leighton-Boyce. *Smiths' The Bankers 1658–1958* (1958). There is also P. T. Saunder's history of that remarkable private bank in the West Country, *Stuckey's Bank* (Taunton 1928). Finally on the growth of banking and the money market in London there is the important article by D. M. Joslin. 'London Private Bankers, 1720–1785', *Economic History Review* (1954) and S. R. Cope. 'The Goldsmids and the Development of the London Money Market during the Napoleonic Wars', *Economica* (1942).

On currency and credit instruments there is Sir John Craig. *The Mint: A History of the London Mint from A.D. 287 to 1948* (Cambridge 1953), a mine of detailed information; also important is Sir A. Feavearyear. *The Pound Sterling: A History of English Money* (Oxford 1963 2nd Ed, revised by E. V. Morgan) and T. S. Ashton. 'The Bill of Exchange and Private Banks in Lancashire, 1790–1830', *Economic History Review*, XV (1945), reprinted in Ashton and Sayers, cited above.

The early history of joint stock banking is thoroughly dealt with by S. E. Thomas. *The Rise and Growth of Joint Stock Banking*, Vol I: *Britain's to 1860* (1934), a work that was never completed and there are no subsequent volumes. The 'Introduction' by Sir T. E. Gregory to his *Select Statutes, Documents and Reports Relating to British Banking, 1832–1928* (1929; reprinted 1964), two volumes, is of note as is a recent interpretative essay R. Cameron. 'England, 1750–1844', in R. Cameron *et al. Banking in the Early Stages of Industrialization* (1967) which also contains a chapter by Cameron on Scottish developments. Students should also refer to the relevant chapters in Sir J. H. Clapham. *An Economic History of Mordern Britain* (Cambridge 1929, 1932, 1938; and subsequent editions and reprintings), three volumes. All of the 'big five' clearing banks of the 1950s have had their histories written of which the most informative are: W. F. Crick and J. E. Wadsworth. *A Hundred Years of Joint Stock Banking* (1936) which is the centennial history of the Midland Bank; T. E. Gregory. *The Westminster Bank through a Century* (1936), two volumes; and R. S. Sayers. *Lloyds Bank in the History of English Banking* (Oxford 1957). These histories include accounts of the development of the banks' private country bank forerunners while A. M. Taylor. *Gilletts, Bankers at Banbury and Oxford* (Oxford 1964) shows the development of one particular country bank in the nineteenth century. The various bank house journals often contain historical articles, in particular *The Three Banks Review* and the *National Westminster Bank Quarterly Review*. The development of the national joint stock banks is covered amply by J. Sykes. *The Amalgamation Movement in English Banking, 1825–1924* (1926) and details of particular groupings can be found in the banking histories cited above. A recent study of the 1844 Joint Stock Bank Act is K. S. Toft. 'A Mid-Nineteenth Century Attempt at Banking Control', *Revue Internationale d'Histoire de la Banque*, III (Geneva 1970) while this journal will provide a future international forum for banking history. The effect of the growth of bank deposits is discussed by Cameron in the essay cited above, by D. K. Adie in 'English Bank Deposits before 1844', *Economic History Review*, 2nd series, XXIII (1970) and R. P. Higonnet. 'Bank Deposits in the U.K., 1870–1914', *Quarterly Journal of Economics*, LXXI (1957). A short account of the history of banks' liability and asset structures is to be found in J. E. Wadsworth. 'Banking Ratios Past and Present', in C. R. Whittlesey and J. S. C. Wilson (Eds). *Essays in Money and Banking in Honour of R. S. Sayers* (Oxford 1968). A study of the role of the London joint stock banks at the close of the nineteenth century is C. A. E. Goodhart. *The Business of Banking* (1972).

Acknowledgements

WE wish to acknowledge the generous assistance given us by the librarians and staff of the following institutions: the libraries of the University of Liverpool, particularly the Harold Cohen Library; the Goldsmiths' Library of the University of London; and, not least, the Library of the Institute of Bankers, London. We are grateful to the editors of *The Economist*, *The Bankers' Magazine*, and the *Journal of the Institute of Bankers* for permitting us to use here material that has appeared in their journals. Our colleagues and kindred spirits, Mr W. A. Thomas and Mr G. Fletcher, have given freely their advice and comments. For typing the manuscript we owe a real debt to Miss V. Dodd and Mrs E. Harris of our department's secretarial staff, and to Miss L. Wood and Mrs W. Greer. For our wives, whose good humour emerged marvellously unscathed, we reserve a special thanks.

B.L.A.
P.L.C.

Index

acceptances, 308–9, 311, 324, 330–4
Acts of Parliament (in chronological
    order)
  Million Acts (1693 and 1694), 14,
    27
  Tunnage Act and Bill (1694), 40,
    85
  Bank of England Act (1697), 40
  Bank of England Act (1708), 157
  Banking Co-partnerships Act
    (1826) (7 Geo IV, c 46), 11,
    214, 241, 242, 244, 245, 270,
    272, 298–9; text, 250–67
  Bank Charter Act (1833) (3 & 4
    Will IV, c 98), 281; text, 280–1
  1838 (1 & 2 Vict, c 96), 246
  1840 (3 & 4 Vict, c 111), 246
  1841 (4 & 5 Vict, c 14), 246
  Bank Charter Act (1844) (7 & 8
    Vict, c 32), 89, 246
  Joint Stock Bank Act (1844) (7 &
    8 Vict, c 113), 11, 246–7, 248,
    282, 299, 304
  (1846) (9 & 10 Vict, c 75), 247
  Joint Stock Bank Amendment Act
    (1857) (20 & 21 Vict, c 49), 11,
    248, 304
  Joint Stock Bank Limited Lia-
    bility Act (1858) (21 & 22
    Vict, c 91), 248, 304
  Companies Act (1862) (25 & 26
    Vict, c 89), 248; text, 304–7
  Companies Act (1879) (42 & 43
    Vict, c 76), 249; text, 312–16
advances, 288, 293, 297, 301, 311,
    320
  as a proportion of deposits, 237–8
Althorp, Lord, 242–3
Anne, Queen, 68

annuities, 14, 36, 41
anti-metallists (cartalists), 89, 92–5,
    129ff
Asgill, John, 16, 129
Association of Joint Stock Banks,
    270, 271

Bagehot, Walter, 214
balance of trade, 91, 114–16, 125,
    135
  favourable, 93
  unfavourable, 169–70, 198
bankers' drafts, 152
banking
  defined by Petty, 109
  Joplin, on the role of, 224, 228
Banking School, 93–4
Bank of England
  'Bank of London', 18
  bankers' Bank, 19
  Bank rate, 248, 282, 301, 301–3,
    303–4
  business defined, 50
  central banking functions, 158,
    190–5
  charter, 40–52, 187
    Bank Charter Act (1833), 280–1
    Bank Charter Act (1844), 246
    renewal in 1833, 243
    Select Committee on the
      Charter (1831–2), 237–40,
      242
  constitution (1694), 45–52
  control of credit, 153
  deposits, 67
  Defoe, on the Bank of England,
    74–85
  described by M. Godfrey, first
    deputy Governor, 61–7

Bank of England—*cont.*
　described by Sir S. T. Janssen, a
　　director, 70–4
　discounting, 10, 96, 156, 191–2,
　　193, 197, 204, 208
　discount policy, 154, 208
　establishment of branches, 261
　at Antwerp, 61
　foundation, 9–10, 13–18, 40–52,
　　53
　hostility to joint stock banks of
　　issue, 285–6
　and the government, 10, 18–19
　loan to the government, 18, 41,
　　61, 73, 157, 204
　internal drain of gold, 191–2
　lender of last resort, 104, 197, 198
　and the money market, 151
　monopoly of joint stock banking,
　　40, 151, 157, 232, 241, 243, 251
　note issue, 15, 19, 152, 157, 185,
　　187, 188–9, 191, 192, 194, 200,
　　204, 215, 217, 220, 223, 246
　opposition to joint stock banks, 11,
　　242, 243
　opposition to land banks, 16–17
　opposition to London joint stock
　　banks, 244
　proposed by W. Paterson, 53–60
　relationship with London private
　　banks, 237
　resumption of cash payments, 219
　'Royal' Bank of England, 34, 35
　transfer of stock, 51
Bank of Ireland, 231–2
Bank of Manchester, 249
'Bank on the Tickets of the Million
　Adventure', 14
Bank rate, 248, 282, 301, 301–3,
　303–4
Banque Générale, 134
Banque Royale, 134
Barbon, Nicholas, 16, 92, 129;
　Discourse of Trade, 129–34
Baring, Sir Francis, 194; *Observa-
　tions on . . . the Bank of England*,
　194–9

Bill broker, 155, 158, 205–14, 245,
　285, 285–6
bills of exchange, 50, 71, 81, 95, 148,
　152, 154, 155, 161, 165ff, 175,
　178, 188, 201, 206, 220, 224,
　225, 237, 242, 243, 252–4
　282, 312
　acceptance, 170
　accommodation bills, 212, 213
　indorsement, 171
　in Lancashire, 152, 186, 220
　in Worcestershire, 220
　a means of circulation, 185–6,
　　220–1
　protesting, 170–1
　'real bills' doctrine, 95–6
　usuance, 156, 168
　foreign bills of Exchange, 20, 23,
　　66, 69, 150, 167, 172, 250
　West India bills, 212
　Inland bills of Exchange, 66, 150,
　　167ff
Birch, J. W., 325; evidence to the
　Royal Commission on Gold and
　Silver, 325–6
bonds, 20–1, 23, 24, 26
　India bonds, 187, 193
　personal bonds, 178
Briscoe, John, 16, 27, 129
British Linen Company, 279
bullion, 23, 26, 50
　export of, 64, 65, 238
　external drain of, 95, 198
Bullion Committee, 185
　evidence of T. Richardson, 205–
　　14
　Report of, 89

cash, 23
　resumption of cash payments, 218,
　　221–2, 226; Secret Committee
　　on the Resumption of Cash
　　Payments (1819); evidence of
　　V. Stuckey, 214–23
　suspension of cash payments, 153,
　　211, 214–23

INDEX 345

217
Chamberlen, Dr Hugh, 16, 23, 33;
on land banks, 33–40
Chancellor of the Exchequer, 15,
47, 48, 174, 242
Charles I, 19
Charles II, 17, 19, 33
cheques, 10, 158, 216, 247, 250, 278,
326, 327–30
Circular to Bankers, 242; extract from
(1836), 294–7
City of Glasgow Bank, 249, 308–12
Clay, William, 245, 247, 298
clipper, 23, 97, 101, 102
coinage, 97, 163
coinage controversy of the 1690s,
10
coiner, 23, 97
coins, 10, 185
debasement of, 21, 23, 24, 64, 96,
102, 106, 161
gold and silver, 23
guineas, 33, 98, 186
milled, 97–8, 100, 102
recoinage of 1696–9, 17, 85
small, 107
commercial banking system, 10,
151, 154
commercial expansion, 150, 185
Committee of Country Bankers, 294
competition, 323
company law, 247, 248
Company of the Mine Adventurers,
40
confidence, 17
consumption, 22, 26, 92, 94, 140,
142
convertibility, 96, 153
Conway, R., London private
banker, 267; *A treatise on . . . a
Loan Banking Establishment*, 267–9
correspondent bank, 152, 216, 218
correspondent system, 10, 216
country banks, 10, 19, 150–1, 152,
205ff, 214ff

business described by Joplin, 231
cash ratios, 152, 154, 156, 195,
217, 220
Committee of Country Bankers,
294
constitution, 204
in the crisis of 1793, 196, 197
deposits, 190, 195, 216–17, 218
with a London bank, 218
failures, 155, 196, 220, 225–6,
230, 233
formation, 194, 195
functions, 152
interest paid on deposits, 195, 217
London agent, 152, 216, 218
bill broker as London agent,
205ff
management, 232
note issue, 153, 179, 185, 189, 190,
191, 192, 194, 195, 196, 200ff,
205–6, 220ff, 246; during the
suspension period, 214–16
opposition to joint stock banks,
242, 294
Stuckey's bank, 214–23
credit, 23, 24, 58, 91, 131ff, 141,
188ff
bank credit, 95
commercial credit, 173–85
in Scotland, 177ff
on commodities, 13
for the crown, 21, 25
internal flow of credit, 206–7, 245
on land, 34ff
mechanism of, 18
state credit, 19
credit expansion, 93, 150, 153
and trade, 16, 33, 95–6
Cromwell, Oliver, 161
currency, *see also* coins, money, notes
crisis (1690s), 17, 85, 88, 96, 110
crisis (1793), 174
managed, 93
supply of, 15
Currency School, 89
Currie, B. W., 325
evidence to the Royal Commis-

Curie—*cont.*
   sion on Gold and Silver, 327–30
Customs and Excise duties, 65, 79, 150

deflation, 18
Defoe, Daniel, 18, 74
   Of Banks, 74–85
deposit banking, 157, 158, 241, 243, 247
deposits, 15, 75
   with country banks, 190, 195, 203, 216–17, 218
   with goldsmiths, 159, 160ff
   with joint stock banks, 297, 300, 301–3, 303–4, 318
   with London joint stock banks, 11, 67, 247, 248, 282–5, 301–3, 321
   with London private banks, 152, 195
   with Scottish joint stock banks, 228, 230
depositors, 16, 249, 282, 300–1
devaluation, 96
discount, 169
discounting, 10, 161, 178, 179, 206, 207, 210, 216, 235–6, 285, 285–6, 288, 290, 293, 297
Douglas, W. R., 243
Downe & Co, London private bank, 157, 185

employment, level of, 89, 91, 92, 94, 135
Equitable Loan Banking Company, 269
Everett, Walker & Co, London private bank, 271
Exchequer, The, 22, 24, 41, 74
   'Stop' of the Exchequer (1692), 14, 163
Exchequer bills, 14, 17, 18, 85–7, 187, 193, 204, 210, 290
   issue of (1793), 175, 181–4, 209
Exchequer Orders, 14, 17
Exchequer Tallies, 14, 22, 30, 32, 62, 81, 162

farmers, 216–17, 326
financial crises, 11
   of 1772, 194, 227
   of 1793, 155, 173–85, 194–5, 196, 211
   of 1825, 11, 158, 241, 312
   of 1857, 248, 299, 301–3, 309
   of 1866, 205
   of 1878, 249, 308–12
Forbes, William, 165; *Methodical Treatise*, 165–73
foreign exchanges, 89, 109, 114, 125, 130, 153
   with the continent (1793), 197, 198
   with Holland, 202
   with Lisbon (1697), 80
   transactions, 70, 71, 159

Gilbart, J. W., 242, 271, 285–6; *Practical Treatise on Banking*, 272–6
Glyn, Mills, Currie & Co, London private bank, 325, 328–30
Glyn, G. Carr, 237
   evidence to the Select Committee on the Charter of the Bank of England, 237–40
Godfrey, Michael, 15, 53, 60–1, 71
gold (*see also* bullion), 22, 23, 24, 26, 50, 54, 60, 91, 92, 328
goldsmiths, 10, 64, 66, 67, 74, 75, 79, 87, 96, 97, 100, 118, 132, 150, 156, 159–65
   deposits, 159, 160ff
   notes, 33, 35, 132
Gurney, Samuel, 205

Harris, Joseph, 92
hoarding, 15, 105, 131, 198
Hodge, Sir William, 90, 96
Holland, 26, 29, 60, 115, 134
Hume, David, 91, 95, 116; *Of Money*, 116–29

industrial banking, 250, 301
industrial growth, 150, 185

inflation, 18, 89, 90, 94, 95, 118, 134, 153

Innes, Gilbert, 177

Janssen, Sir S. T., 18, 68
description of the Bank of England, 70–4
joint stock banks (see also London joint stock banks)
advantages of, according to Joplin, 233–5, 241
Association of Joint Stock Banks, 270, 271
amalgamations of, 11, 249–50, 316–25
branches, 246, 249–50, 275, 276, 287, 289, 293, 294–7, 326, 329
capital, 245, 247, 274, 278, 291–3, 297, 321
cash ratios, 245, 249
characteristics of, in the 1830s, 244
constitution of, under the 1826 Act, 272–3
constitution of, under the 1844 Act, 246
continental, 13, 132, 136, 201
described by Sir S. T. Janssen, 68–70
deposits, 297, 300, 301–3, 303–4, 318
Defoe's proposals for a national network of, 82–5
failures, 11, 245, 247, 249
favoured by the government, 241, 243
formed in the late 1820s, 276
formed in the 1830s, 243, 244, 294–7, 298–9
formed in the 1860s and 1870s, 248–9, 307–8
formed under the 1826 Act, 241–2, 244–5, 294–7, 298–9
hindrances to their development, 242, 275–9
mismanagement, 11, 245, 247, 299–301

note issue, 244, 246, 278, 286, 288, 289, 306
number in the 1870s and 1880s, 329
rate of interest on provincial deposits, 248, 303–4
rediscounting, 297
reserves, 290
in Scotland, 227–9, 236–7, 275, 277–8, 292, 308–12
shareholders, 16, 39, 61, 227, 242, 246, 254, 256–7, 272–4, 276, 291, 310

Joplin, Thomas, 223, 241, 242, 270; Advantages of the Proposed National Bank, 276–9; Essay on . . . Banking, 224–37; Examination of the Report of the Joint Stock Bank Committee, 270–1

Killigrew, Sir William, 14, 19
on State Credit, 19–27

land banks, 15–17, 33–40, 90, 92
'Land Bank United', 16
landowners, 15, 34, 66–7, 74–5, 100
land tax, 17, 30, 32, 62–3, 150, 204
Law, John, 53, 92, 93, 94, 134; Money and Trade, 134–9
letters of credit, 166
limited liability, 241, 242, 245, 247, 248, 249, 271, 274, 292, 304, 307–9
Liverpool, Lord, 241
Locke, John, 91, 94, 110; Considerations, 111–16
lombard banks, 13, 54
Lombard Street, 24, 27, 75, 79
London, 20, 53, 55, 132
London and County Bank, 243, 282, 318, 321, 327, 331
London and Eastern Bank, 247
London and Westminster Bank
acceptances, 331–4
acquisitions, 249, 318, 322
branches, 327

London and Westminster—*cont.*
capital of, in 1917 and 1919, 231
deposit rate, 248
described by Sir D. Salomons,
281–5, 301–3
early development, 244
foundation, 243, 271, 297
and the London Clearing House,
286
London Clearing House, 222, 244
enlargement, 247–8
foundation, 158
and London joint stock banks, 286
London correspondent bank, 152,
157–8, 216, 218
London joint stock banks, 243, 250,
281–5
acceptances of, in the 1860s, 331
branches, 247
and the London Clearing House,
286
deposits, 11, 247, 248, 282–5,
301–3, 321
payment of interest on deposits,
243, 282, 301, 301–3
restrictions on, lifted by the Bank
Charter Act (1844), 246
restrictions on, lifted by the Joint
Stock Bank Act (1844), 246–7
London money market, 151, 245, 323
London private banks (*see also*
goldsmiths), 156–7, 159–65, 230
characteristics, 157
City bankers, 157, 238
deposits of country banks, 218
opposition to joint stock banks,
238–9, 267–9
practice, 195
relationship with Bank of
England, 237
West End bankers, 157, 238
Lottery loan (1694), 14, 22, 27
Lowe, Robert, 247
Lowndes, William, 110, 129

Magens, M. Dorrien, 199; *An
Inquiry into . . . Money*, 199–205

Massie, Joseph, 92
merchants, 15, 27, 29, 34, 38, 78,
100, 103
Mill, J. S., 116
'Million Adventure' (1694), 14, 27
Million lottery, 13, 27–33
metallists, 89, 101–29
money, 19, 22, 23, 24, 26, 29, 32, 33,
38, 88, 100, 116
bank money, 90, 101, 154
and economic growth, 139–49
legal tender, 33
medium of exchange, 91, 116–17,
129, 138
metallic standard, 15, 18, 58, 89,
102, 111, 129, 137
numéraire, 94, 129
paper money, 13, 94–5
exchequer bills as, 17
inflationary effect of, 18
secured on land, 15, 93, 137,
143
standard of value, 89
store of value, 91
money supply, 91, 108, 109, 111,
112, 119ff, 124, 127, 134ff,
139ff, 200–3
defined by Thornton, 185–94
money trust, 316, 324–5
monopoly, 324
Montagu, Charles, 15, 17, 85, 110
'Exchequer bills', 85–7
mortgage market, 150
mortgages, 16, 33, 36, 66, 217, 229,
268
Murray, R., 17

national bank, 13, 18
National Debt, 14, 19–25, 65, 156
payment of dividends, 18, 21,
24
National Land Bank, 16
National Provincial Bank of
England, 224, 244–5, 276–9,
318–19, 321, 322
in the 1830s, 287–94
in the 1870s, 303–4

Neale, Sir Thomas, 14, 17, 27
  raising a million, 27–33
Northern and Central Bank of England, 245, 295
North of England Banking Company, 245
Norwich and Norfolk Banking Company, 245, 276
notes, 10, 152
  convertibility, 221
  fiduciary issue, 17
  issued by the Bank of England, 10, 15, 19, 152, 157, 185, 187, 188–9, 191, 192, 194, 200, 204, 215, 217, 220, 223
  issued by the country banks, 153, 179, 185, 189, 190, 191, 192, 194, 195, 196, 200ff, 205–6, 220ff, 246
    during the suspension of cash payments, 214–15
  issued by the joint stock banks, 244, 246, 278, 286, 288, 289, 306
  legal tender, 17–18
  small notes, 218

Overend, Gurney & Co, 205
Overend, John, bill broker, 205
overdraft, 292
  for municipal corporations, 323

Paterson, William, 14, 53
  and the Bank of England, 15, 53–60
Pease, Edward, 205
Petty, Sir William, 90, 101; *Quantulumcunque concerning Money*, 102–10
plate, 101, 109, 159
Political economy, 94, 101
Porter, G. R., 271
postal orders, 326, 328
Potter, William, 90, 93
price level, 91, 94, 95, 116–17, 122, 127–9, 148–9, 153, 185, 215, 221, 327

private banks, *see* country banks, goldsmiths, London private banks
  absorbed by joint stock banks, 244, 249, 317
  bankruptcy, 11, 195, 196
promissory note, 150, 154, 159, 172–3, 224, 252–4
Provincial Bank of Ireland, 223–4, 270, 271, 275, 277

quakers, 46, 48, 205
quantity theory of money, 91, 95, 110, 116–17, 120ff, 140ff

rate of interest, 15, 16, 20, 21, 22, 23, 24, 26, 27, 28, 30, 32, 34, 35, 36, 37, 53, 55, 58, 60, 62, 64, 65, 66, 77, 90, 91, 92, 96, 101, 109, 133, 156, 161, 162, 182, 187, 195, 210, 218, 228, 248, 268, 300, 301–3
  on bank deposits:
    country banks, 195, 217
    joint stock banks;
    London and Westminster, 248
    provincial deposits, 248, 303–4
    Scottish banks, 228
  Bank rate, 248, 282, 301, 301–3, 303–4
recoinage of 1696–9, 17, 85
rediscounting, 245, 297
rent, 37, 38, 99, 161, 216, 217
reserved liability, 249, 312–16
retailers, 26, 35, 132, 326
Ricardo, David, 95, 116, 221
Richardson, Thomas, bill broker, 156, 205
  evidence to the Bullion Committee, 205–14
Robertson, Daniel, 287
  evidence to the Select Committee on Joint Stock Banks (1837), 287–94
Royal Bank of Scotland, 177
Royal British Bank, 247, 282, 299–301

Royal Exchange, 20, 45
Royal Mint, 27, 98, 152, 159

Salomons, Sir David, 281
    evidence to the Select Committee
        on the Bank Acts (1858), 281–5,
        301–3
scriveners, 26, 67, 74
Secret Committee on the Resump-
    tion of Cash Payments (1819)
    evidence of V. Stuckey, 214–23
Secret/Select Committee on Joint
    Stock Banks (1836–8), 245
    evidence of J. W. Gilbart, 285–6
    evidence of D. Robertson, 287–94
    An Examination . . ., Joplin, 270–1
    First Report, 245, 298–9
Select Committee on the State of
    Commercial Credit (1793)
    Report, 173–85
Select Committee on the High Price
    of Gold Bullion (1810), 185
    evidence of T. Richardson, 205–
    14
    Report, 89
Select Committee on the Bank of
    England Charter (1831–2), 242
    evidence of G. Carr Glyn, 237–40
    Report, 242
Select Committee on Banks of Issue
    (1840–1), 245
Select Committee on the Bank Acts
    (1858)
    evidence of Sir David Salomons,
    281–5, 301–3
Select Committee on Banks of Issue
    (1875)
    evidence of R. B. Wade, 303–4
Sheene, Sir James, 22
silver (see also bullion), 22, 24, 26,
    50, 54, 60, 71, 97
Smith, Adam, 92, 93, 94, 95
South Sea Bubble, 68, 156
South Sea Company, 68
State credit (see also National Debt),
    19–27, 27–33, 54
State revenues (see also Customs and

Excise duties, Land tax, taxes),
    22, 26, 30, 41
    plans to capitalise, 13
Steuart, Sir James, 92, 94, 139;
    Inquiry into the Principles of
    Political Oeconomy, 139–49
Stock Exchange, 156, 323
Stuckey, Vincent, country banker,
    214, 271
    evidence to Secret Committee on
        the Resumption of Cash Pay-
        ments (1819), 214–23
Stuckey's Banking Company, 214,
    242, 276

taxes, 17, 20, 25, 27, 28, 32, 62
    advances on tax revenues, 18, 204
    land tax, 17, 30, 32, 62–3, 150, 204
Thornton, Henry, 95, 96, 176, 185,
    200
    definition of the money supply,
    185–94
Tooke, Thomas, 271
trade, 22–3, 24, 26, 53, 55, 57, 60,
    62, 66, 99, 135, 148, 320–2
    East India trade, 27, 103, 126
    Spanish trade, 96, 126
    Turkish trade, 105
Treasury, 17, 21, 44
Treasury Committee on Bank Amal-
    gamations
    Report, 316–25

unemployment, 89–91, 91
    in Scotland (1793), 178, 180
unlimited liability, 249, 272–3,
    308–12
usurers, 29, 30, 34, 57
usury, 22
usury laws, 40, 110, 143, 156, 198,
    243, 268

velocity of circulation, 90, 91, 101
    of bills of exchange, 154
Vere, Glyn and Halifax, London

Vere—*cont.*
    private bank (*see also* Glyn,
    Mills, Currie & Co), 237

Wade, R. B., 303

    evidence to Select Committee on
    Banks of Issue (1875), 303–4
war, 10, 15, 19, 32, 36, 54, 62, 65,
    67, 69, 74, 77, 150, 155, 196
Wealth of Nations, 94, 227